THE TRINITARIAN THEOLOGY OF DR. SAMUEL CLARKE (1675-1729)

CONTEXT, SOURCES, AND CONTROVERSY

BY

THOMAS C. PFIZENMAIER

BRILL

LEIDEN · NEW YORK · KÖLN

1997

Library of Congress Cataloging-in-Publication Data

Pfizenmaier, Thomas C.
  The Trinitarian theology of Dr. Samuel Clarke (1675–1729) :
context, sources, and controversy / by Thomas C. Pfizenmaier.
      p.   cm. — (Studies in the history of Christian thought, ISSN
0081–8607 ; v. 75)
  Revision of the author's thesis (doctoral)—Fuller Theological
Seminary's Center for Advanced Theological Studies, 1993.
  Includes bibliographical references and index.
  ISBN 9004107193 (cloth : alk. paper)
    1. Clarke, Samuel, 1675–1729.   Scripture doctrine of the Trinity.
2. Trinity—History of doctrines—18th century.   I. Title.
II. Series.
BT110.C52P55   1997
231'.044'092—dc21   96–45397
                                                                  CIP

Die Deutsche Bibliothek - CIP-Einheitsaufnahme

Pfizenmaier, Thomas C.:
The trinitarian theology of Dr. Samuel Clarke (1675 – 1729) :
context, sources, and controversy / by Thomas C. Pfizenmaier. –
Leiden ; New York ; Köln : Brill, 1997
  (Studies in the history of Christian thought ; Vol. 75)
  ISBN 90–04–10719–3
NE: GT

ISSN   0081-8607
ISBN   90 04 10719 3

PRINTED IN THE NETHERLANDS

THE TRINITARIAN THEOLOGY OF
DR. SAMUEL CLARKE (1675-1729)

STUDIES IN THE HISTORY
OF
CHRISTIAN THOUGHT

EDITED BY

HEIKO A. OBERMAN, Tucson, Arizona

IN COOPERATION WITH

HENRY CHADWICK, Cambridge
JAROSLAV PELIKAN, New Haven, Connecticut
BRIAN TIERNEY, Ithaca, New York
ARJO VANDERJAGT, Groningen

VOLUME LXXV

THOMAS C. PFIZENMAIER

THE TRINITARIAN THEOLOGY OF
DR. SAMUEL CLARKE (1675-1729)

TUTA SUB AEGIDE PALLAS · 1683 ·

For Donna

"But now abide faith, hope, love these three;
but the greatest of these, is love."
Apostle Paul, to the Corinthians, 13:13.

CONTENTS

PREFACE

This work is a revision of my doctoral dissertation submitted to the faculty of Fuller Theological Seminary's Center for Advanced Theological Studies in 1993. Like all projects of this nature, one's indebtedness is enormous. I would especially like to thank Richard Muller, who served as my mentor Professor at Fuller, and first introduced me to Samuel Clarke. In addition I wish to express my appreciation to Colin Brown, Nancey Murphy, and Jim Bradley, all of whom read various chapters and gave insightful comments. Likewise, I would like to thank Richard Popkin, who served as the external reader.

This work utilizes a number of microfilm manuscripts, particularly in regard to Isaac Newton's theology. These were made available through the assistance of the King's College Library at Cambridge University, the National Jewish and University Library in Jerusalem, and the Clark Memorial Library (UCLA). In addition, Richard Westfall not only helped me secure other Newton manuscripts, but helped me sharpen and develop my line of approach on Newton's thought.

Other research institutions which supported my work, and to whom I am grateful, are the Huntington Library in San Marino, California, the University of California at Los Angeles and Irvine, Fuller Theological Seminary, the Claremont-McKenna Colleges, the Claremont School of Theology, the California Institute of Technology and the University of Edinburgh. I would also like to thank E. Dorothy Asch, who has allowed me to use her unpublished dissertation on Samuel Clarke as a source for my research.

On a personal level, I wish to express my thanks to members of the Westminster Presbyterian Church in Oklahoma City, who encouraged me from the beginning, particularly Mr. and Mrs. John Frank. Also I would like to thank the Session and members of Arcadia Presbyterian Church, who allowed me to use my study leaves while serving on their staff to work on this monograph.

Finally, I would like to express my gratitude to Professor Heiko A. Oberman, first, for his own scholarship which was of great benefit to me in my doctoral study, and now especially for his generous acceptance of this work into his series, Studies *in the History of Christian Thought*.

Arcadia, California   Thomas C. Pfizenmaier
1996

INTRODUCTION

History remembers Dr. Samuel Clarke (1675–1729) primarily as a philosopher rather than a theologian. In fact he was both. In the former capacity he contended with Leibniz in defending the Newtonian natural philosophy against a modified Cartesianism.[1] Clarke also presented two courses of the Boyle Lectures in 1704 and 1705, attempting to establish a philosophical foundation for Christian faith.[2] The secondary literature on Clarke bears out the fact that his primary importance is in the field of philosophy. J.P. Ferguson has produced a study devoted completely to Clarke's philosophy,[3] and several doctoral dissertations have been written on Clarke's moral philosophy.[4] Clarke's contribution to the natural philosophy debate of the early eighteenth century is noted frequently in the various handbooks which treat the subject.[5] This contribution is usually cited in connection with Isaac Newton.

Although historians have emphasized Clarke's contribution to philosophy, he made his living as a divine in the Church of England, and showed early promise as one of its leading theologians. Clarke

---

[1] Samuel Clarke, *A Collection of Papers which Passed between the Late Learned Mr. Leibnitz, and Dr. Clarke, in the years 1715 and 1716 Relating to Principles of Natural Philosophy and Religion* in *The Works of Samuel Clarke* ed. John Clarke, Vol. IV. (London: John and Paul Knapton, 1738. Reprinted, N.Y. Garland Press, 1978), 581–710.

[2] The 1704 series was entitled *A Demonstration of the Being and Attributes of God, More particularly in Answer to Mr. Hobbes, Spinoza, and their followers.* The 1705 series was entitled, *A Discourse Concerning the Unchangeable Obligations of Natural Religion, and the Truth and Certainty of the Christian Revelation* in Clarke, *Works*, Vol. II, 517–733.

[3] J.P. Ferguson. *The Philosophy of Dr. Samuel Clarke and Its Critics* (New York: Vantage Press, 1974).

[4] Thomas D. Kennedy. "God and the Grounds of Morality: The Eighteenth Century British Debate" (Ph.D. diss., Univ. Of Virginia, 1986); William W. Longsworth. "Religious Beliefs and Moral Judgments: Some Patterns of Relations Derived from an Analysis of Samuel Clarke" (Ph.D. diss., Yale Univ., 1977); Ronald Stein. "A Critical Examination of the Ethical Thought of Samuel Clarke" (Ph.D. diss., S.U.N.Y. at Buffalo, 1972); John Gay. "The Idea of Freedom as the Basis of the Thought of Samuel Clarke" (Ph.D. diss., Columbia Univ., 1958).

[5] For examples see Henning G. Reventlow, *The Authority of the Bible and the Rise of the Modern World* trans. John C. Bowden. (London: SCM Press, 1984); Leslie Stephen, *History of English Thought in the Eighteenth Century* Vol. II. (N.Y.: Harcourt, Brace and World, Inc., 1962. First published 1876); W. Von Leyden, *Seventeenth Century Metaphysics: An Examination of Some Main Concepts and Theories* (London: Gerald Duckworth and Co., 1968); Basil Willey, *The Eighteenth Century Background: Studies on the Idea of Nature in the Thought of the Period* (New York: Columbia Univ. Press, 1940).

was ordained a deacon in the church in 1698, and became a priest before the end of the year.[6] He was befriended by Dr. John Moore, then Bishop of Norwich, and made his chaplain. Moore was instrumental in Clarke's ascendance, and presented him with the living at Drayton near Norwich, probably in 1701. Subsequently the Bishop transferred Clarke to St. Bennet's, Paul's Wharf in 1706. This moved Clarke into London circles, and it was during his three years at St. Bennet's that he was appointed Chaplain-in-Ordinary to Queen Anne.[7] In 1709 Clarke was appointed by Dr. Moore, then Bishop of Ely, to be the Rector of the parish church of St. James, Westminster, one of the most influential situations in London. He held this position until he died twenty years later in 1729.[8]

While Clarke was being elevated by the Bishop, he also experienced success as a theologian. Following his successful Boyle Lectures in 1704 and 1705, which will be discussed below, he was examined for the Doctor of Divinity, Cambridge's highest theological degree. The examiner was Dr. Henry James, Regius Professor of Divinity. Clarke defended two theses for the examination.

1. No Article of the Christian Faith, Delivered in Holy Scripture, is Repugnant to Reason (*Nullum Fidei Christianae Dogma, in S. Scripturis traditum, est Rectae Rationi dissentaneum*).

2. All Religion Supposes the Freedom of Human Action (*Sine actionum humanarum libertate nulla potest religio*).

Clarke performed so brilliantly that James restated the customary dismissal "I will now finish, as I have tested you enough (*Finiem iam faciam, nam te probe exercui*)" as "you have taxed me enough (*Name me probe exercuisti*)." James went on to add that he might well retire and leave the Chair, since one so able to fill it appeared among them.[9]

In 1712 Clarke published his *Scripture-Doctrine of the Trinity*, which embroiled him in controversy until his death. Clarke's heterodox views on this subject, although creating something of a sensation in the theological circles of his time, ensured for him a lasting place in the

---

[6] J.P. Ferguson, *Dr. Samuel Clarke: An Eighteenth Century Heretic.* (Kineton: Roundtree Press, 1976), 8.
[7] Ibid., 35.
[8] Ibid., 40.
[9] Ibid., 40–41.

backwaters of theology. As a consequence, little attention has been paid to Clarke as a theologian. The *Scripture-Doctrine* is mentioned frequently in the various histories of doctrine, but not examined. The nineteenth-century historians of doctrine classified Clarke among those who revived the Arian theology. Hagenbach, in his *Textbook of the History of Doctrine*, writes that Clarke's work represented a revival of the Arian system, and holds the "high Arian view."[10] Fisher, in his *History of Christian Doctrine*, views Clarke in the same way when he refers to the *Scripture-Doctrine* as "a defence of Arianism, to be sure, in its highest form."[11] Shedd is more specific in his two volume *A History of Christian Doctrine*, where he writes, "Clarke's views were, in reality, a reproduction of the Origenistic and High-Arian doctrine of subordination, as distinguished from Athanasius."[12] Sheldon's *History of Christian Doctrine* is more specific still. "[Clarke's] position, as gathered from this work, might be described as a position of indecision between Origen and Arius."[13]

This assessment of Clarke by the nineteenth-century historians has been well received in the twentieth century, and is reflected in various books on the trinity. Hodgson's *The Doctrine of the Trinity* holds a similar perspective to Shedd,[14] as does Payne's *Critical History*.[15] More recently, the *New Catholic Encyclopedia* in its article on Clarke, concludes that Clarke was "severely criticized on account of his Arian and Latitudinarian ideas."[16] However, E. Dorothy Asch, in her doctoral dissertation on Clarke, entitled "Samuel Clarke's *Scripture-doctrine of the Trinity* and the Controversy It Aroused," hints that Clarke was not an Arian in the full sense when she writes, "his position differed from that of Arius in that Clarke believed that there was no time at

[10] K.R. Hagenbach, *A Textbook of the History of Doctrines* (New York: Sheldon & Co., 1862), 213, n. 11.
[11] George Park Fisher, *History of Christian Doctrine*. 2d ed. in the *International Theological Library Series* (Edinburgh: T & T Clark, 1896), 371.
[12] William Shedd, *A History of Christian Doctrine*. 2 Vols., 9th ed. (New York: Charles Scribner's Sons, 1887), Vol. I, 386.
[13] Henry S. Sheldon, *History of Christian Doctrine*. 2 Vols., 2d ed. (New York: Harper and Brothers Publishers, 1895), Vol. II, 99.
[14] Leonard Hodgson, *The Doctrine of the Trinity: The Croall Lectures 1942–43* (London: Nisbet and Co., Ltd., 1943), 222.
[15] Levi L. Payne, *A Critical History of the Evolution of Trinitarianism and Its Outcome in the New Christology* (Boston: Houghton, Mifflin and Co., Cambridge: The Riverside Press, 1900), 100.
[16] *The New Catholic Encyclopedia*, ed. J. McDonald et al. 15 Vols. (N.Y.: McGraw Hill Book Co., 1967), s.v. "Samuel Clarke," Vol. 3, 917.

which the Son and the Holy Spirit had not existed, and Arius held that there was."[17]

In addition to the mention of Clarke's *Scripture-Doctrine* in the general histories there exists only Asch's dissertation, which reviews the contents of Clarke's argument with an eye toward the trinitarian controversy, and Ferguson's biography of Clarke, in which he devotes four chapters to a survey of Clarke's role in the trinitarian controversy. As a result there is a substantial lacuna in Clarke studies particularly in the theological area of his work on the trinity.

This monograph proposes to fill this lacuna by examining Clarke's doctrine of God in three stages. In Part I his doctrine will be clarified through exploring the intellectual context within which Clarke worked. Part II will reevaluate his use of sources in light of contemporary scholarship. Part III will review Clarke's position in the trinitarian controversy. Finally, a conclusion will be offered which will challenge the scholarly consensus reviewed above.

Clarke's *Scripture-Doctrine of the Trinity* was composed of three parts. In Part One, Clarke collected from the entire New Testament every text relating to the doctrine of the trinity with "such references and observations, as may ('tis hoped) be of considerable use towards the understanding of their true meaning."[18] This collection consisted of 1,251 texts. In Part Two, were "collected into methodical propositions the sum of that doctrine which (upon the carefullest consideration of the whole matter) appears to me to be fully contained in the texts cited in the first Part."[19] Clarke illustrated his propositions with passages from the Church Fathers which he believed lent support to his position. There were also occasional references to leading authorities of his own time. In Part Three, Clarke collected "a great number of passages out of the present liturgy of the Church of England."[20] In this collection Clarke differentiated those parts of the liturgy which expressly affirmed his doctrine as expounded in Part II, and those which seemed to differ from it.

This work will concentrate on Part II of Clarke's work since it is here, in his fifty-five Propositions, that Clarke expounds his understanding of the trinity. Nevertheless, I will draw on Parts One and

---

[17] Estelle Dorothy Asch "Samuel Clarke's *Scripture-Doctrine of the Trinity* and the Controversy It Aroused." (Ph.D. diss., University of Edinburgh, 1951), 157.

[18] Clarke, *SD*, Introduction in *Works*, Vol. IV, ix.

[19] Ibid.

[20] Ibid.

Three when necessary to illustrate a point made in the second part. I will also concentrate specifically on Clarke's understanding of the relationship between the first two persons of the trinity. This is clearly where the weight of his argument lay, and the relationship between the Father and the Son was the center of the trinitarian debate. This is not to denigrate the role of the Holy Spirit, but only to recognize, as Clarke did, that what was true concerning his scheme in relation to the Son, could logically be applied to the Spirit also.

The heart of the *Scripture-Doctrine* is in the fifty-five Propositions which line out Clarke's understanding of the trinity. Therefore, it is imperative to list them, as they are the foundation for all that will follow in this work.

I. There is one supreme cause and original of things; one simple, uncompounded, undivided, intelligent agent, or person; who is the alone author of all being, and the fountain of all power.

II. With this first and supreme cause or Father of all things, there has existed from the beginning, a second divine person, which is his Word or Son.

III. With the Father and the Son, there has existed from the beginning a third divine person, which is the Spirit of the Father and of the Son.

IV. What the proper metaphysical nature, essence, or substance of any of these divine persons is, the Scripture has no where at all declared; but describes and distinguishes them always by their personal characters, offices, power and attributes.

V. The Father alone is self-existent, underived, unoriginated, independent. He alone is of none, either by creation, generation, procession, or any other way whatsoever.

VI. The Father is the sole origin of all power and authority, and is the author and principle of whatsoever is done by the Son or by the Spirit.

VII. The Father alone is in the highest, strict, proper, and absolute sense supreme over all.

VIII. The Father alone is, absolutely speaking, the God of the universe; the God of Abraham, Isaac and Jacob; the God of Israel; of Moses, of the Prophets and Apostles; and the God and Father of our Lord Jesus Christ.

IX. The Scripture, when it mentions the one God, or the only God, always means the supreme person of the Father.

X. When the word, God, is mentioned in Scripture, with any high epithet, title, or attribute annex'd to it; it generally (I think, always) means the person of the Father.

XI. The Scripture, when it mentions God, absolutely and by way of eminence, always means the person of the Father.

XII. The Son is not self-existent; but derives his being and all his attributes form the Father, as from the supreme cause.

XIII. In what particular metaphysical manner the Son derives his being from the Father, the Scripture has no where distinctly declared; and therefore men ought not to presume to be able to define.

XIV. They are both therefore worthy of censure; both they who on the one hand presume to affirm, that the Son was made (ἐξ οὐκ ὄντων) out of nothing; and they who, on the other hand, affirm that he is the self-existent substance.

XV. The Scripture, in declaring the Son's derivation from the Father, never makes mention of any limitation of time; but always supposes and affirms him to have existed with the Father from the beginning and before all worlds.

XVI. They therefore have also justly been censured, who taking upon them to be wise above what is written, and intruding into things which they have not seen; have presumed to affirm (ὅτι ἦν ποτὲ οὐκ ἦν) that there was a time when the Son was not.

XVII. The Son (according to the reasoning of the primitive writers) derives his being from the Father, (whatever the particular manner of that derivation be,) not by mere necessity of nature; (which would in reality be self-existence, not filiation;) but by an act of the Father's incomprehensible power and will.

XVIII. The (λόγος, the) Word or Son of the Father, sent into the world to assume our flesh, and to become man, and die for the sins of mankind; was not the (λόγος ἐνδιάθετος, the) internal Reason or Wisdom of God, and attribute or power of the Father; but a real person, the same who from the beginning had been the Word, or revealer of the will, of the Father to the world.

XIX. The Holy Spirit of God does not in Scripture generally signify a mere power or operation of the Father, but more usually a real person.

XX. The Holy Spirit is not self-existent, but derives his being from the Father (by the Son) as from the supreme cause.

XXI. The Scripture, speaking of the Spirit of God, never mentions any limitation of time, when he derived his being from the Father; but supposes him to have existed with the Father from the beginning.

XXII. In what particular metaphysical manner the Holy Spirit derives his being from the Father, the scripture hath no where at all defined; and therefore men ought not to presume to be able to explain.

XXIII. They who are not careful to maintain these personal characters and distinctions, but, while they are solicitous (on the one hand) to avoid the errors of the Arians, affirm (in the contrary extreme) the Son and Holy Spirit to be (individually with the Father) the self-existent being: These, seeming in words to magnify the name of the Son and Holy Spirit, in reality take away their very existence; and so fall unawares into Sabellianism (which is the same with Socinianism).

XXIV. The person of the Son, is, in the New Testament sometimes stiled God.

XXV. The reason why the Son in the New Testament is sometimes stiled God, is not upon account of his metaphysical substance, how divine soever; but of his relative attributes and divine authority (communicated to him from the Father) over us.

XXVI. By the operation of the Son, the Father both made and governs the world.

XXVII. To the Son are ascribed in Scripture other the greatest things and the highest titles; even all communicable divine powers: That is, all powers which include not that independency and supreme authority, by which the God and Father of All is distinguished to be the God and Father of all.

XXVIII. The Holy Spirit is described in the New Testament as the immediate author and worker of all miracles, even of those done by our Lord himself; and as the conducter of Christ in all the actions of his life, during his state of humiliation here upon earth.

XXIX. The Holy Spirit is declared in Scripture to be the inspirer of the Prophets and Apostles, and the great teacher and directer [sic] of the Apostles in the whole work of their ministry.

XXX. The Holy Spirit is represented in the New Testament, as the sanctifier of all hearts, and the supporter and comforter of good Christians under all their difficulties.

XXXI. Concerning the Holy Spirit, there are other greater things spoken in Scripture, and Higher titles ascribed to him, than to any angel, or any other being whatsoever, except the only-begotten Son of God.

XXXII. The person of the Holy Ghost, is no where in Scripture expressly stiled, God, or Lord.

XXXIII. The word, God, in Scripture, never signifies a complex notion of more persons, (or intelligent agents) than one; but always means one person only, viz. either the person of the father singly, or the person of the son singly.

XXXIV. The Son, whatever his metaphysical essence or substance be, and whatever divine greatness and dignity is ascribed to him in Scripture; yet in this he is evidently subordinate to the Father; that He derives his being, attributes, and powers, from the Father; the Father nothing from him.

XXXV. Every action of the Son, both in making the world, and in all other his operations; is only the exercise of the Father's power, communicated to him after a manner to us unknown.

XXXVI. The Son, whatever his metaphysical nature or essence be; yet in this whole dispensation, in the creation and redemption of the world, acts in all things according to the will, and by the mission or authority of the Father.

XXXVII. The Son, how great soever the metaphysical dignity of his nature was, yet in the whole dispensation entirely directed all his actions to the glory of the Father.

XXXVIII. Our saviour Jesus Christ, as, before his incarnation, he was sent forth by the will and good pleasure, and with the authority of the Father; so in the flesh, both before and after his exaltation, He, (not a part of him, but himself, his whole person,) in acknowledgment of the supremacy of the person of the Father, always prayed to him, and returned him thanks, stiling him his God, &c.

XXXIX. The reason why the Scripture, though it stiles the Father God, and also stiles the Son God; yet at the same time always declares there is but one God; is because, there being in the monarchy of the universe but one authority, original in the Father, derivative in the Son; therefore the one God (absolutely speaking) always signifies him in whom the power or authority is original and underived.

XL. The Holy Spirit, whatever his metaphysical nature, essence, or substance be; and whatever divine power or dignity is ascribed to him in Scripture; yet in this he is evidently subordinated to the Father; that he derives his being and powers from the Father, the Father nothing from Him.

XLI. The Holy Spirit, whatever his metaphysical nature, essence, or substance be; and whatever divine power or dignity is ascribed to him in Scripture; yet in the whole dispensation of the Gospel, always acts by the will of the Father, is given and sent by him, intercedes to him, &c.

XLII. The Holy Spirit, as he is subordinate to the Father; so he is also in Scripture represented as subordinate to the Son, both by nature and by the will of the Father; excepting only that he is described as being the conducter and guide of our Lord, during his state of humiliation here upon earth.

XLIII. Upon these grounds, supreme honour or worship is due to the person of the Father singly, as being alone the supreme and original author of all being and power.

XLIV. For the same reason, all prayers and praises ought primarily or ultimately to be directed to the person of the Father, as the original and primary author of all good.

XLV. And upon the same account, whatever honour is paid to the Son who redeemed, or to the Holy Spirit who sanctifies us, must always be understood as tending finally to the honour and glory of the Father, by whose good pleasure the Son redeemed, and the Holy Spirit sanctifies us.

XLVI. For the great oeconomy, or the whole dispensation of God towards mankind in Christ, consists and terminates in this; that as all authority and power is originally in the Father, and from him derived to the Son, and exercised according to the will of the Father by the operation of the Son, and by the influences of the Holy Spirit; and all communications from God to the creature, are conveyed through the intercession of the Son, and by the inspiration and sanctification of the Holy Spirit: So on the contrary, all returns from the creature of prayers and praises, of reconciliation and obedience of honour and duty to God; are made in and by the guidance and assistance of the Holy Spirit, through the mediation of the Son, to the supreme Father and author of all things.

XLVII. The Son, before his incarnation, was with God, was in the form of God, and had glory with the Father.

XLVIII. Yet he had not then distinct worship paid to him in his own person, but appeared only as the (Shecinah, or) habitation of the glory of the Father: in which the name of God was.

XLIX. At his incarnation he freely divested himself (ἐκένωσεν ἑαυτὸν) of that glory, which he had with God before the world was, and by virtue of which he is described as having been in the form of God: And in this state of humiliation he suffered and died for the sins of the world.

L. After, and upon account of, the accomplishment of which dispensation, he is described in Scripture as invested with distinct worship in his own person; his original glory and dignity being at the same time revealed, and his exaltation in the human nature to his mediatorial kingdom declared: Himself sitting upon his Father's throne, at the right hand of the majesty of God; and receiving the adoration and thanksgivings of his Church, as the alone mediator between God and men.

LI. This honour the Scripture directs to be paid to Christ; not upon account of his metaphysical essence or substance, and abstract attributes; but of his actions and attributes relative to us; his condescension in becoming man, who was the Son of God; Redeeming, and interceding for, us; his authority, power, dominion, and sitting upon the throne of God his Father, as our law-giver, our king, our judge, and our God.

LII. The honour paid in this manner to the Son, must (as before) always be understood as redounding ultimately to the glory of God the Father.

LIII. The honour which Christians are bound to pay peculiarly to the person of the Holy Spirit, is expressed in the Texts following &c.

LIV. For putting up prayers and doxologies directly and expressly to the person of the Holy Spirit, it must be acknowledged there is no clear precept or example in Scripture.

LV. The titles given in the New Testament to the three persons of the ever-blessed Trinity, when all mentioned together, are, &c.[21]

---

[21] Clarke, *SD*, Table of Contents, Part II.

PART ONE

CONTEXT

CHAPTER ONE

CLARKE'S INTELLECTUAL MILIEU

It is impossible to assess Clarke's *Scripture-Doctrine of the Trinity* accurately apart from the intellectual context within which it was written. Clarke lived during one of the watershed periods of western intellectual history and his *Scripture-Doctrine* was both a product of, and a contribution to, that history. Clarke's position on the trinity developed in the midst of the shift from external to internal constructs of authority which took place in the late seventeenth and early eighteenth centuries in England. Truth was no longer to be determined by the external authorities of revelation and tradition, but by the internal measure of human reason. This shift in the locus of authority was the result of two phenomena: the rise of modern science, and the legacy of the Protestant Reformation.[1]

The Rise of Modern Science

The rise of modern science is customarily traced to the work of Francis Bacon (1560–1626).[2] Bacon rejected the scholastic dependence upon Aristotle's deductive reasoning. Although Aristotle had formulated the

---

[1] Willey, *Eighteenth Century Background*, 3.

[2] Francis Bacon, *New Organon* and *Of the Advancement of Learning* in *The Philosophical Works of Francis Bacon*, ed. John M. Robertson. Reprinted from the texts and translations, with notes and prefaces of Ellis and Spedding. (London: George Rutleage and Sons, 1905). For the role of Bacon in the development of modern science see Basil Willey, *The Seventeenth Century Background: Studies in the Thought of the Age in Relation to Poetry and Religion* (New York: Columbia University Press, 1958), 24–40. Frederick Copleston, *A History of Philosophy*, Vol. III, *Ockham to Suarez* (New York: Doubleday, 1985), 292–309. A.R. Hall, *The Scientific Revolution 1500–1800: The Formation of the Modern Scientific Attitude* (London: Longmans, Green and Co., 1954), 31–32, 192–93. Herbert Butterfield, *The Origins of Modern Science 1300–1800* (London: G. Bell and Sons Ltd., 1965), 97. Charles Singer, *A Short History of Scientific Ideas to 1900* (Oxford: At the Clarendon Press, 1959), 264–267. Richard F. Jones, *Ancients and Moderns: A Study of the Background of the Battle of the Books* (St. Louis: Washington Univ., 1936), 43–64. Robert Burns has nuanced the relationship of Bacon to the British virtuosi and suggests that their dependence upon him has been overdrawn, R.M. Burns, *The Great Debate on Miracles: From Joseph Glanvill to David Hume* (Lewisburg: Bucknell Univ. Press, 1981), 19–46.

rule that induction was operative in the natural realm (moving from
particulars to universals), while deduction was operative in the logical realm (moving from universals to particulars),[3] by the time of the
scholastics, the deductive method had come to dominate in both.
This caused prior intellectual constructs (universals) to serve as a grid
through which particulars were to be interpreted and resulted in the
stultification of new scientific theories, the most notable being the
heliocentric theory and the circulation of blood.[4] Bacon called for
the abandonment of the deductive approach in science, and its
replacement by strict induction. He seized upon and radicalized one
of the poles of Aristotle's epistemology. Bacon called for the abandonment of innate ideas, like substance, and for the substitution of
experience (sensory data) alone as the guide to scientific truth. In
short, deduction was abandoned in favor of induction.

> For the Rational School of philosophers snatches from experience a
> variety of common instances, neither duly ascertained nor diligently
> examined and weighed, and leaves all the rest to meditation and wit . . .
> The most conspicuous example of the first [Rational] class was Aristotle,
> who corrupted natural philosophy by his logic: fashioning the world
> out of categories . . . and imposing countless other arbitrary restrictions
> on the nature of things; being always more solicitous to provide an
> answer to the question and affirm something positive in words, than
> about the inner truth of things.[5]

It comes as little surprise that Bacon would title his work the *New
Organon* [instrument]. As Aristotle's "organon" had been logic, Bacon's
would be the senses.[6] According to Bacon, there were only two ways
of discovering truth. The first ignored the senses and particulars, and
rested on "general axioms" which it understood to be settled and
immovable. From these general axioms this method proceeded to
"judgment and the discovery of middle axioms." The other method

[3] Aristotle, *De Anima*, 402a, 10–21; *Physica*, 184a–b, cf., *Metaphysica* 981a–981b, 9,
in *The Complete Works of Aristotle* 2 Vols. ed. by Jonathan Barnes, the revised Oxford
translation, in the *Bollingen Series LXXI* (Princeton: Princeton Univ. Press, 1985). See
also Copleston, Vol. I, *Greece and Rome* 275–76, esp. 281–82, and Samuel Stumpf,
Socrates to Sartre: A History of Philosophy. 4th ed. (New York, etc.: McGraw-Hill Book
Company, 1988), 84–85.
[4] S.F. Mason, "Science and Religion in Seventeenth Century England," *Past &
Present* 3 (Feb. 1953): 28–44.
[5] Bacon, *New Organon*, Book I, Aphorisms LXII and LXIII.
[6] On the decline of Aristotelianism see Singer, *Short History*, 218–287; Jones *Ancients and Moderns*, 124–153; and William T. Costello, *The Scholastic Curriculum at Early
Seventeenth-Century Cambridge* (Cambridge MA: Harvard Univ. Press, 1958).

derived axioms from the senses and particulars and moved from these to arrive at the most general axioms last of all. For Bacon, this latter method was the true way, but was yet untried.[7] With his entire approach to knowledge resting on sensory data, Bacon was critical of the ancient concept of "notions," which were logically derived. For him, there was no soundness in our "notions," whether logical or physical. Terms like "substance," "quality," "passion" and "essence" were not sound notions and but were "fantastical and ill defined."[8]

Having criticized the ancient rational approach with its corollary of notions, Bacon went on to outline his own method.

> Now my method, though hard to practice, is easy to explain; and it is this. I propose to establish progressive stages of certainty. The evidence of the sense, helped and guarded by a certain process of correction, I retain. But the mental operation which follows the act of sense I for the most part reject; and instead of it I open and lay out a new and certain path for the mind to proceed in, starting directly from the simple sensuous perceptions.[9]

With Francis Bacon we see the laying of the foundation of modern science by a radical emphasis on the empirical method of deriving data solely from the senses.[10] Bacon utilized induction rather than deduction, where Aristotle had held a place for both. Bacon was aware of the consequences that this method carried for the erosion of tradition and authority in science. In fact, this is precisely what he sought.[11] However, Bacon also knew that in other areas, particularly theology, such an erosion could be dangerous. Seeking to protect the theological disciplines, he utilized the idea of the "two books," the respective learning of which was not to be confused. These were the books of God's word (divinity) and of God's work (natural philosophy), each of which persons were to study assiduously. However, Bacon

---

[7] Bacon, *New Organon*, Book I, Aphorism XIX, 261. This view of rejecting universals in favor of particulars was not new. It had roots in the Nominalism of late medieval philosophy. See Heiko Oberman, *The Dawn of the Reformation: Essays in Late Medieval and Early Reformation Thought* (Edinburgh: T & T Clark, 1986), 28. See also Amos Funkenstein, *Theology and the Scientific Imagination from the Middle Ages to the Seventeenth Century* (Princeton: Princeton Univ. Press, 1986), 138–140.

[8] Bacon, *New Organon*, Book I, Aphorism XV, 260.

[9] Ibid., Book II, Preface, 256.

[10] Copleston, Vol. III, 300–302 cf., Vol. IV, 9–10; Bernhard Pünjer, *History of the Christian Philosophy of Religion from the Reformation to Kant.* trans. W. Hastie (Edinburgh: T & T Clark, 1887), 286.

[11] Pünjer, 286.

cautioned that "they do not unwisely mingle or confound these learn-
ings together."[12]

Bacon distinguished between the glory of God, which was reflected
in the first book, the book of nature; and the will of God, which
could only be determined through divine revelation, and not by nature.
It is important to note that he exempts the "mysteries of the Deity,"
creation, redemption, and the moral law from those things which
can be understood by nature's light. Bacon argued that sacred theology was grounded only upon the word and oracle of God, and not
upon the light of nature.[13] He reasoned that it is written that the
heavens declare the glory of God (*Coeli enarrant gloriam Dei*) but not
that the heavens declare the will of God (*Coeli enarrant voluntatem Dei*).
Matters of truth were to be determined not according to the human
voice (*vox*), but by a "voice beyond the light of nature."[14]

Bacon exempted the articles of faith from the scrutiny of reason
by distinguishing two kinds of human reason in religion. The former
kind of reason was used in "conception of apprehension of the mysteries of God to us revealed." This reason extended to the mysteries
themselves, but by way of illustration, and not by way of argument.
Here God descended to our capacity by expressing his mysteries in
a way which was intelligible to our senses, like a key is formed to fit
a lock. The latter reason consisted of "probation and argument."
This use of reason was secondary and respective, but not original
and absolute. For Bacon, once the articles and principles of religion
were placed, and these exempted from reason, then reason might be
brought to bear upon understanding their signification and application. Here he made a distinction between theology and nature, since
in the latter case, the principles themselves could be analyzed by
induction.[15]

In the affirmation of the "two books," and their apparent separation, some scholars have seen the compartmentalization of Bacon's

---

[12] Bacon, *Of the Advancement of Learning*, 45–46. It should be noted that this idea is
ancient, and already present in Psalm 19. It was used by medieval and Protestant
scholastics alike, and was emphasized by Bacon to encourage the exploration of
nature. For Bacon the issue was the clarity of the natural order. This was later
developed by the Deists (as we shall see) so that the issue became not merely the
clarity of the natural order, but its sufficiency.
[13] Pünjer, *History*, 287–288.
[14] Ibid., 168. See Copleston here, who refers to Bacon as an empiricist (Vol. IV, 25).
[15] Ibid., 169.

epistemology. Manuel makes this assumption, and ascribes the policy of the Royal Society not to publish any works in theology to just such a compartmentalization.[16] Yet Bacon's compartments may not be as separate as appears at first glance. Earlier, in *Of The Advancement of Learning* he had written,

> For our Saviour saith, "You err, not knowing the Scripture nor the power of God"; laying before us two books or volumes to study, if we will be secured from error; first the scriptures revealing the will of God, and then the creatures expressing his power; whereof the latter is a key unto the former; not only opening our understanding to conceive the true sense of the Scriptures, by the general notions of reason and rules of speech; but chiefly opening our belief, in drawing us into due meditation of the omnipotency of God which is chiefly signed and engraven upon his works.[17]

Here we find not only the breakdown between the books, but the principle *in nuce* that reason is the key to understanding revelation.

Therefore, while it appeared to many that Bacon could proceed with his radical inductive empiricism, having safely sequestered theology from his method's iconoclastic consequences, this perception proved to be naive. Once this method was in practice, it was only a matter of time until its scrutiny was turned toward theology. Tulloch has noted the scope of the impact of Bacon's epistemology by demonstrating the effects of his thought on the rising school of liberal divines. Baconism was a powerful element at Cambridge from the middle of the seventeenth-century. This is evidenced by the fact that Isaac Barrow, who received his Bachelor of Arts in 1648 had studied Bacon closely. John Ray, the celebrated naturalist and another representative of the emerging experimental philosophy, was also steeped in Bacon. Men like Barrow and Ray adopted Bacon's method and carried on the scientific research which, half a century later would come to fruition in the labors of Isaac Newton, who was Barrow's successor in the mathematical chair at Cambridge.[18]

While Bacon was establishing the inductive method and his "method of elimination"[19] in natural philosophy, his younger contemporary

---

[16] Frank Manuel, *The Religion of Isaac Newton* (Oxford: Clarendon Press, 1974), 30. For a similar assessment see W. von Leyden, 37. Also Pünjer, 288.

[17] Bacon, *Advancement*, 64.

[18] John Tulloch, *Rational Theology and Christian Philosophy in England in the Seventeenth Century*. Vols. I and II. (Hildesheim: Georg Olms Verlagsbuchhandlung, 1966), Vol. II, 21.

[19] Von Leyden, 37.

Rene Descartes (1596–1650)[20] was working toward the establishment
of Rationalism in metaphysical philosophy. While Descartes had read
Bacon[21] and agreed that the classical foundations for human knowledge were weak, his solution to the problem came from the opposite
direction. Where Bacon had abandoned the deductive approach, Descartes radicalized it. Contrary to the traditional view, Popkin has made
a convincing case, referring to Descartes as the "conqueror of scepticism," that Descartes deployed his skepticism in order to undo the
Pyrrhonists and defeat them by using their own method.[22] Descartes
used radical doubt to establish one indubitable truth, the *cogito ergo
sum* formula, from which all others could logically be deduced.[23] Ironically, this radical skepticism, rather than the certitude of the Rational
method it sought to establish, became Descartes' legacy to philosophy. When applied to God, Descartes believed that this skepticism
led to a truth as compelling as the *cogito* formula. G.R. Cragg has
summarized Descartes' position by saying that for him [Descartes]
the criterion for truth was the clearness and distinctiveness of an
idea.[24] No idea was more clear than the idea of God.[25] Since it could
not be derived from sense experience, nor fashioned simply by our-
selves, it must be an innate idea, planted within us by God himself.
Therefore, for Descartes, to think of God was to imply his existence.[26]

While Descartes maintained an orthodox view of revelation, and

[20] Rene Descartes, *The Philosophical Writings of Descartes*, 2 Vols., trans. John Cotting-
ham, Robert Stoothoff, and Dugald Murdoch (Cambridge: Cambridge Univ. Press,
1984); John Veitch, *The Method, Meditations and Philosophy of Descartes* (New York: Tudor
Publishing, 1901); Richard Popkin, *The History of Scepticism from Erasmus to Descartes*
(N.V. Assen, Netherlands: van Gorcum and Company, 1960). E.M. Curley, *Descartes
Against the Skeptics* (Cambridge, MA: Harvard Univ. Press, 1980). Marjorie Greene,
Descartes Among the Scholastics (Milwaukee: Marquette Univ. Press, 1991).
[21] Von Leyden, 37.
[22] Popkin, *History*, 174–75, 187, cf., Burns, 28.
[23] For the context of the *cogito* and description of Descartes method see his *Dis-
course on the Method* (*Discours de la Methode*), 4.32 and 2.18,19. Richard Popkin, *History*,
179, cf., Colin Brown, *Christianity and Western Thought: A History of Philosophers, Ideas
and Movements*. Vol. 1 *From the Ancient World to the Age of Enlightenment* (Downer's Grove,
Ill.: Intervarsity Press, 1990), 184, cf., Von Leyden, 11 for the same point. On
Descartes' *cogito* and view of truth as clear and distinct see, Martial Gueroult, *Descartes'
Philosophy Interpreted According to the Order of Reasons*, trans. Ariem (Minneapolis: Univ.
of Minn. Press, 1984–85), I, 27–101.
[24] For Descartes' use of the term see *Discourse on the Method*, 2.18,21. G.R. Cragg,
The Church and the Age of Reason (Grand Rapids: Eerdmans, 1962), 38.
[25] Popkin, *History*, 189–90.
[26] Descartes, *Discourse*, 4.34–36. See also Brown, *Christianity and Western Thought*,
184.

supported the existence of God, there were those, like the Jesuit priest Fr. Bourdin, who realized that his method could be used to produce unorthodox conclusions, especially when brought to bear on the issue of revelation itself. Bourdin understood that the truths of faith could not be permanently protected from the broadening quest for demonstration. Only natural reason could establish that a pretended revelation did or did not come from God. Bourdin saw the possible implications for Descartes' method on the doctrine of the trinity. He realized that what previous generations had accepted as truths above reason—that three divine persons are one God—might appear contrary to reason in an era of systematic doubt.[27]

In the seminal works of both Bacon and Descartes then, we find radical methods of inquiry, the former according to the senses through induction, the latter through the rational demonstration of innate ideas through deduction. Both called into question the tradition and the authority of classical learning. While neither directly challenged the truth or authority of divine revelation, each in his own way laid the foundation for that challenge: Bacon by his denial of innate ideas and insistence upon sensory induction as the way to truth, and Descartes by his radical skepticism. Tulloch suggests that both Bacon and Descartes were attempting in their respective ways to ultimately ground both natural philosophy and religion in human reason.

> For it is a mistake to represent Descartes as, no less than Bacon, separating philosophy from religion, and desiring to keep them asunder. He only separated the one as well as the other from tradition in order that he might reunite them in the great centre of reason, and plant them together there on a sure foundation.[28]

This trend was also evident in the work of John Locke (1632–1704)[29] who was likewise concerned to find a solid epistemological foundation for both science and religion. While not an experimental scientist,

---

[27] Richard Westfall, "The Rise of Science and Decline of Orthodox Christianity: A Study of Kepler, Descartes and Newton." in *God and Nature*, eds. D. Lindberg and R. Numbers (Berkeley: University of California Press, 1986), 226.

[28] Tulloch, *Rational Theology*, Vol. II, 18–19.

[29] John Locke, *An Essay Concerning Human Understanding* and *A Treatise on the Conduct of the Understanding: Complete in one volume with the author's last additions and corrections* (Philadelphia: James Kay, Jun. and Brother, 1853); John Locke, *The Reasonableness of Christianity As Delivered in the Scriptures*, ed. and intro. by George Ewing. (Washington, D.C.: Regnery Gateway, 1965. orig. published, 1695), 192. Richard Aaron *John Locke*, 2d ed., (Oxford: At the Clarendon Press, 1955, first edition 1936); R.S.

Locke's contribution to the epistemology of the burgeoning mechanical philosophy helped foster the modern scientific emphasis on the gathering of data and induction begun by Bacon. Locke was a medical doctor, and was an intimate friend of the chemist Robert Boyle.[30] Locke was not only acquainted with Boyle's scientific work, but even helped him with it. Both men were members of a group whose interest and discussions on the emerging experimental philosophy led to the founding of the Royal Society of which Boyle was a founder, and Locke subsequently became a member. Locke's closeness to Boyle not only interested him in the new experimental philosophy, but aided his conviction that the empirical method of careful observation and induction should be applied to philosophy in general, in contrast to the Cartesian Rationalism.[31] Like Bacon before him, and with Boyle's encouragement, Locke held that the concept of "innate" ideas which was produced by the ancients, and in a modified form by Descartes, was invalid. The first book of his *Essay Concerning Human Understanding* was devoted to demolishing the concept.

> It is an established opinion amongst some men that there are in the understanding certain *innate principles*, some primary notions, *koinai ennoiai*, characters, as it were stamped upon the mind of man, which the soul receives in its very first being, and brings into the world with it. It would be sufficient to convince unprejudiced readers of the falseness of this supposition, if I should only show (as I hope I shall in the following parts of this Discourse) how men, barely by the use of their natural faculties, may attain to all the knowledge they have, without the help of any innate impressions, and may arrive at certainty, without any such original notions or principles.[32]

Locke recognized however, that for Descartes, God had been such an innate idea. Therefore he felt compelled to offer a new epistemological foundation for God's existence. Rather than the internal testimony of innate ideas, Locke offered three alternatives: sense, perception, and reason.[33] With the abandonment of innate ideas, the

Woolhouse, *Locke's Philosophy of Science and Knowledge: A Consideration of Some aspects of An Essay Concerning Human Understanding* (New York: Barnes and Noble, 1971); Copleston, Vol. V, *Hobbes to Hume*, 67–142; Willey, *Seventeenth Century*, 264–290. Pünjer, *History*, 315–321.

[30] Copleston, Vol. V, 67.
[31] Locke, *An Essay Concerning Human Understanding*, abridged and edited with an introduction by A.C. Woozley. (London: Fontana/Collins, 1964, orig. pub. 1689), Intro., 12. Copleston, Vol. V, 67–78.
[32] Locke, *Essay*, 1, 2, 1.
[33] Ibid., 4, 10, 1.

notion of "substance" or "essence" was also necessarily abandoned as having no epistemological foundation. This abandonment would signal for some a fissure in the metaphysical foundation of the doctrine of the trinity, a concern which will be examined below.

In his discussion on the relationship between faith and reason, Locke distinguished between "original revelation," by which he meant the revelation as God gives it to a given individual, and "traditional revelation," by which he meant revelation which was received from another. While no bounds could be set to the former, the latter was an inferior source of knowledge compared with what could be determined through the senses.[34]

While Locke acknowledged, with medieval scholasticism, that there existed certain matters which were *above* reason, e.g., the fall of the angels, the resurrection etc., which could only be known through revelation, he maintained that anything which was *contrary* to reason must be dismissed. Nothing, even under the guise of revelation, which was contrary to plain reason, could be held to be true. As a result, it was vain to argue any principles of faith which were clearly in contradiction to plain reason.[35]

On the surface, this looks like the medieval construct of the relation between faith and reason. Hefelbower reminds us that Albert had already seen that natural reason had authority in religion. However, that authority was circumscribed by the fact that philosophy had no final answer to certain questions and had to stand "before the antimony of different possibilities." In these cases, revelation decided. "Revelation is above reason, but not contrary to it." Thomas' position was essentially the same—philosophical knowledge, which man may attain unaided, was a lower stage in the realm of grace.[36]

However, closer scrutiny of Locke's thought reveals two fundamental shifts. First was Locke's distinction between "original" and "traditional" revelation which was unknown in scholastic theology. The traditional revelation was to be received by the faithful as original. Secondly, the medieval church had the prerogative of establishing which truths were to be received "according to faith" where reason was an insufficient guide. One example of this was Thomas' insistence

---

[34] Ibid., 4, 18, 4.

[35] Ibid., 4, 18, 5, Copleston, Vol. V, 120–121.

[36] Samuel Hefelbower, *The Relation of John Locke to English Deism* (Chicago: University of Chicago Press, 1918), 47.

that the trinity was a truth which was above reason because it revealed God's nature not *ad extra*, which could be known through
reason, but *in se* which could be contemplated only by faith.[37] Following the Reformation, human reason, rather than church dogma,
gradually became the locus of deciding what was to be considered
contrary to, or above, itself. The role of reason was emphasized, first
with the rejection of Catholic authority, and subsequently through
the splintering of Protestant sects. Epistemologically, the potential now
existed for each person to become his or her own magisterium.

This elevation of the role of reason meant that all the truths previously received on the foundation of revelation alone were now open
to critical examination of reason. In fact, Locke himself struggled
with this consequence of his position and five years after writing his
Essay produced *The Reasonableness of Christianity* which seemed to
strengthen the role of revelation, though not at the expense of reason. Here Locke sought a deeper integration. All of the divine revelation was not necessary for salvation, but those truths "we have seen
by what our Savior and his apostles proposed to, and required in,
those whom they converted to the faith."[38] Soteriologically, Locke
established a canon within the canon. When a person had believed
these truths, nothing more, true as it may be, was required for salvation, other than a general submission to the revelation and will of
God.[39] Thus Locke's epistemology offered two supports to the flow-
ering of the experimental philosophy. The first was the rejection of
innate ideas, with its substitution of the empirical method. The second was the augmentation of the role of reason in the discovery of
truth by altering the traditional understanding of biblical authority.

The great advances in the science of the seventeenth century cul-
minated in the work of Isaac Newton (1642–1727).[40] Newton offered,

---

[37] Thomas Aquinas, *Summa Theologiae*. Vols. 6 and 7, ed. Thomas Gilbey (London:
Blackfriars, Vol. 6, 1965, Vol. 7, 1976), 1. Q.32, a.1.

[38] Locke, *Reasonableness of Christianity*, 192.

[39] Ibid., 192.

[40] Isaac Newton, *The Mathematical Principles of Natural Philosophy*. trans. Andrew Motte.
3 Vols. (London: Printed for H.D. Symonds by Knight and Compton, 1803); idem,
Papers and Letters on Natural Philosophy and Related Documents (Cambridge MA: Harvard
Univ. Press, 1958); David Brewster, *Memoirs of the Life, Writings and Discoveries of Sir
Isaac Newton*. 2 Vols. (Edinburgh: Thomas Constable and Co., MDCCCLV); idem,
The Life of Sir Isaac Newton (New York: Printed and published by J & J Harper,
1831); Gale E. Christianson, *In the Presence of the Creator: Isaac Newton and His Times*
(New York: Free Press, 1984); Louis T. More, *Isaac Newton: A Biography 1642–1727*
(New York and London: Charles Scribner's Sons, 1934); Richard Westfall, *Never at*

through his experimental philosophy and the development of calculus, a new interpretation of the structure of the universe. His method was strictly inductive and, like Bacon, he had little use of hypotheses because they smacked too much of Rationalism.

> For whatever is not deduced from the phaenomena is to be called an hypothesis; and hypotheses, whether metaphysical or physical, whether of occult qualities or mechanical, have no place in experimental philosophy. In this philosophy particular propositions are inferred from the phaenomena, and afterwards rendered general by induction.[41]

Newton's conclusions in the *Principia Mathematica* were in direct conflict with those of Descartes. The Cartesians viewed the universe as an enormous plenum filled by visible and invisible matter. The orbiting of the planets was caused by huge vortices which ordered the circular motions of the heavens. Time and space were relational concepts, and the atomism of the ancients was disapproved. The leading exponent of Cartesian mechanics in Newton's time was the German philosopher and mathematician Leibniz.[42]

In stark contrast to Descartes and Leibniz, Newton postulated a universe which was essentially void, in a vacuum state. He universalized Hooke's law of gravity and made gravitational attraction the governing principle of the ordering of the heavens. Newton also held to a belief in absolute space and time, as well as embracing the ancient teaching of the Greek atomists. Thus the stage was set for a confrontation between the Cartesians and the Newtonians. This confrontation was carried out by Leibniz for the Cartesians and Samuel Clarke for the Newtonians. The Leibniz-Clarke correspondence will be examined in the next chapter. Here we only need to say that it was the Newtonian views which eventually triumphed.

We have seen in the rise of modern science two crucial shifts in the intellectual climate. The first was the abandonment of reliance upon the deductive method; a shift initiated by Francis Bacon and

---

Rest: A Biography of Isaac Newton (Cambridge: Cambridge Univ. Press, 1980). On Newton's scientific method see Singer, *Short History*, 419; Hall, *Scientific Revolution*, 244–74; idem, *The Revolution in Science 1500–1750* (London and New York: Longman, 1983), 179.

[41] Newton, *Principles*, Vol. 2, Book III, 314 (Motte ed.). Note the similarity of Newton's remark to that of Aristotle's understanding of induction noted in Copleston, Vol. I, 281 (cf., Aristotle, *Anal. Post.* I, 2, 72a 1–5).

[42] Derek Gjertsen, *The Newton Handbook* (London: Routledge & Kegan Paul, 1986), 171.

carried forward by John Locke. The second shift was the methodology of doubt, initiated by Descartes. Coupled together, these principles created an environment in which authority and tradition could
no longer be impervious to the faculty of reason. Although Christianity was initially insulated from the consequences of the new
method, the faith eventually came under its scrutiny. Summarizing
the importance of the new science for Christianity, Westfall has stated
that the intellectual challenge to Christianity in the seventeenth century was multi-faceted, but of all these elements, the rise of modern
science was the most important.[43] We turn now to the second reason
for the shift from external to internal constructs of authority; the
legacy of the Protestant reformation.

The Legacy of the Reformation

> The middle of the seventeenth century might seem an unpromising
> date for the beginning of a new era in western thought. Europe had
> been convulsed by strife. Much of it had been devastated by the civil
> wars of Christendom, and its people, in sheer exhaustion, turned back
> to the familiar ways that promised stability and peace. The turbulence
> of recent years confirmed the gloomiest views of man's inherent na-
> ture, and the collapse of morality suggested that anarchy had under-
> mined the spiritual vitality of western Europe.[44]

Such is Cragg's introduction to the developments of our period. The
sentiments he notes developed in a particular context in England
and invited not only the search for a new science, but also for a new
form of Christian religion. The old dogmatism with its propensity
for creating division and intolerance had not produced the kind of
commonwealth it had promised. Rather than producing the society

---

[43] Richard Westfall, "The Rise of Science and the Decline of Orthodox Chris-
tianity," 219; idem, *Science and Religion in Seventeenth-Century England* (New Haven: Yale
Univ. Press, 1958). On the emerging emphasis on the sciences in the university
curricula see Phyllis Allen, "Scientific Studies in the English Universities of the
Seventeenth Century," *Journal of the History of Ideas* 10 (April 1949): 219, 238–39;
R.K. Merton, "Science, Technology and Society in Seventeenth Century England,"
Osiris, IV (1938): 360–624, esp. 388; William T. Costello, *The Scholastic Curriculum at
Early Seventeenth-Century Cambridge* (Cambridge, MA: Harvard Univ. Press, 1958). Also
A.R. Hall *Scientific Revolution*, 187, for the development of science outside the tradi-
tional structures.

[44] Cragg, *The Church and the Age of Reason*, 37. See also idem, *From Puritanism to the
Age of Reason* (Cambridge: Cambridge Univ. Press, 1950).

it seemed to envision, Christianity had created disputes, persecutions and wars. It had split from the Roman See, and was further fragmented into innumerable sects. Locke attributed this failure to two causes: the concealment of biblical truth through the adherence to creeds, and the fact that reason had not been given its proper place in religion.[45] As a result, by the seventeenth century a desire arose to formulate a structure of belief which would be accecptable to all good and reasonable persons.[46] A new way of grounding the Christian faith had to be found. The search for a "reasonable religion" was on.

To establish a religious foundation in reason it was necessary to return to primitive sources. The methods of science and theological study now began to take parallel courses as each set out to lay aside secondary evidences; ideas in the sciences, creeds and theological constructions in theology, and seek primary sources alone; sensory perception in science, and the Bible in theology. As early as 1687 Thomas Spratt, historian of the Royal Society, recognized the parallels.

> Protestantism and science ... both may lay equal claim to the word Reformation: the one having compass'd it in religion, the other purposing it in philosophy. They both have taken a like course to bring this about; each of them passing by the corrupt copies, and referring themselves to the perfect originals for their instruction; the one to the scripture, the other to the large volume of the creatures.[47]

---

[45] Locke, *Reasonableness*, Intro., George Ewing, xii.

[46] Willey, *Eighteenth Century*, 26.

[47] Thomas Spratt, *The History of the Royal Society of London for the Improving of Natural Knowledge* (London: 1687), 345, cited in G.B. Deason, "The Protestant Reformation and the Rise of Modern Science," *The Scottish Journal of Theology* 38 No. 2 (1985): 232–33. Deason argues in this article that the Reformation contributed *indirectly* to the rise of modern science. For an excellent review of the history of scholarship on the relation between science and religion see the Introduction in Lindberg and Numbers, eds., *God and Nature*. For a similar view to Deason see S.F. Mason, "The Scientific Revolution and the Protestant Reformation," *Annals of Science* 9 (1953). But on the contrary see Theodore Rabb, "Religion and the Rise of Modern Science," *Past and Present* 31 (July, 1965): 376–443, who argues that Protestantism cannot be said to have contributed to the *rise* of modern science although it certainly contributed to its promotion. Rabb cites a number of Catholic contributions to the rise of science. For the specific relationship between Puritanism and Modern science see Charles Webster, "Puritanism, Separatism, and Science," *God and Nature: Historical Essays on the Encounter between Christianity and Science*, eds. David C. Lindberg and Ronald L. Numbers (Berkeley: Univ. of California Press, 1986), 192–217, and Robert K. Merton, "Puritanism, Pietism and Science," *Science and Ideas*, eds. A.B. Arons and A.B. Bork (Englewood Cliffs, N.J.: Prentice-Hall, 1964), 232–269. See also John Dillenberger, *Protestant Thought and Natural Science: A Historical Interpretation* (Nashville: Abingdon Press, 1960), 128–132. For background on the Royal Society and similar

As a result, rational religion in England sought to find the lowest common denominator from which to establish the faith. It could not be doctrine, which had been the source of so much conflict. It had to be something all thinking persons shared—the rational process. Hefelbower has defined English religious Rationalism as a way of thinking about religious problems, rather than a doctrinal system. It was the persistent demand that all things believed should be rational. He argues that the striking thing about English Rationalism was that all the religious parties held to a conviction of its importance: churchmen and dissenters, progressive orthodox as well as Arminians, Socinians and Deists.[48]

Although the basic rational method was agreed upon across a wide spectrum of churchmen, its conclusions were debated. The rational approach was widely used, but its products ranged from Orthodoxy to Deism.[49] The Orthodox and the Deists, and those in between, were not concerned so much to justify their rationalism, as they were with the consistent application of its principles. It was this application which yielded the conclusions they so hotly debated.[50]

Along with the search for a common denominator upon which theology could be argued, the Reformation in England bequethed a social and political legacy of intolerance which contributed to the rise of rational religion. During the Restoration with its Act of Uniformity (1660), the Stuart king restored the Anglican Church. There followed a series of legislation, known as the Clarendon Code, which was aimed at the suppression of dissenters. The Act of Uniformity was only one part of the wider program to surpress the Puritans. The Corporation Act (1661) had already debarred them from municipal office; the Five Mile Act (1664) was directed against the minis-

---

institutions see A.R. Hall, *Scientific Revolution*, 186–216; on the Royal Society itself see Jones, *Ancients and Moderns*, 181–187. Burns argues that it is in the thought of the early Latitudinarians; Chillingworth, Tillotson, Wilkins and Glanvill, rather than the Puritans, that we discover the progenitors of the Royal Society's methodology which he terms "moderate empiricism" as over against the epistemological positivism of both Descartes and Bacon, 19–29.

[48] Hefelbower, 79.

[49] On crucial distinctions between Protestant orthodox rationalism and the emerging philosophical rationalism see Richard Muller, *Post-Reformation Reformed Dogmatics: Vol. 1 Prologomena to Theology* (Grand Rapids: Baker Book House, 1987), 92–97. Muller argues that for the Protestant orthodox, reason continued to hold the ancillary position relative to faith, while for philosophical rationalism, reason was dominant. The two had in common, however, their quest for "right method" (96).

[50] Reventlow, 294.

ters, and the Conventicle Acts (1664 and 1670) against those who attended their services.[51] A small space of toleration was provided for about a year by the Declaration of Indulgence (1672) through which dissenting ministers could secure licenses registering their places of worship.[52] Since Charles II had issued this declaration under his own authority a constitutional backlash resulted in which Parliament insisted that the Declaration be rescinded and the Test Act was put in its place. The Test Act safeguarded the state more than the church. It used sacramental tests to exclude Catholics from office. Nonconformists also had to qualify for positions they might hold. Cragg has written that by the Test Act, "a selfishly Anglican parliament prostituted the sacred rite of the church to political ends." He goes on to add that as a result, it raised up hundreds of enemies to the Church of England, and decisively committed the dissenters to political opposition.[53] After a period of Whig leadership under the Earl of Shaftesbury, in which he proposed limiting restrictions on dissent and changing the line of succession by excluding the Duke of York who professed Catholicism, Charles dissolved Parliament and closed ranks with the Tories who in turn persecuted the non-conformists relentlessly.[54]

Under the rule of James II the situation worsened until he committed the fatal error of trying to seize control of the universities and imprison Archbishop Sancroft and six other bishops for not complying with his desire that the Declaration of Indulgence (1688) be read in all the churches. Convinced that this effort revealed James as a threat to the established church, Whigs and Tories joined together to remove him in favor of William of Orange.[55] The Glorious Revolution had important results for English religion. James' rash policy caused Protestants (Anglican and Dissenters) to close ranks. They began to realize that a certain amount of toleration was both essential and inevitable.[56] Here we see that common cause was made between

---

[51] G.R. Cragg, *The Church and the Age of Reason*, 53.
[52] Ibid., 54.
[53] Ibid., 55.
[54] Ibid., 56. It is worth noting that John Locke was the personal physician, private secretary and philosophical advisor to the Earl of Shaftesbury, Anthony Ashley Cooper for sixteen years. (Locke, *Reasonableness*, intro, ix). It is highly probable that in his capacity as philosophical advisor, Locke's toleration directly impacted Shaftesbury's desire to ease the strictures on dissenters.
[55] Ibid., 59.
[56] Ibid.

liberal Anglicanism and the dissenters. In the face of the threat of
a zealous Catholic king, the established church realized the legiti-
macy of dissent in a way in which it had not previously. Out of
this experience the Latitudinarians solidified: liberal Anglicans who
believed that the Toleration Act (1688) should be understood in the
broadest sense. Religious leaders who had survived the vicissitudes
of the late seventeenth century, where political agenda were en-
shrouded in religious rhetoric backed by various dogma, were ready
for a new approach to religion. Their political experience, no less
than their religious, prepared them to search for a rational foundation for belief.

If the Reformation had undermined the authority of the church
by its insistence on returning to the Bible as opposed to tradition, it
also inadvertently raised the question of certainty so that the Bible
could only with difficulty be used as a self-interpreting sole authority.
New developments in textual criticism, linguistic and historical studies opened the doctrine of biblical inspiration to question and the
answers to this questioning were often posed in heterodox formulas.
Commenting on the significance of these studies, Manuel writes,

> The scientific revolution of the seventeenth century is for us so decisive
> that it tends to overshadow the simultaneous upheaval in Christian
> and Jewish scriptural studies. Along with the new reading of the Book
> of Nature, audacious ventures were taking place in the interpretation
> of Scripture at the hands of learned Christian Hebraists like John Selden,
> Vossius father and son, Johannes Buxtorf, John Lightfoot, Edward
> Pocock, John Spencer, . . . Thomas Hobbes, Baruch Spinoza, Richard
> Simon and Jean LeClerc. And to them I would sometimes join the
> unrevealed Newton.[57]

Here too we see the influence of politics on religion. The advent of
biblical criticism in England served not only religious, but political
purposes. The Whigs sought to deprive their opponents, the High
Church Tories, of the support they found in scripture. By denying
its status as the source of revelation and emphasizing the human
elements in its writing, they assaulted the roots of Tory thinking.[58]

We see then, that the Protestant Reformation contributed in three
major ways to establishing an atmosphere where rational religion could
flourish. First, it undermined the concept of external authority ex-

---

[57] Frank Manuel, *The Religion of Isaac Newton*, 29.
[58] Reventlow, 329.

pressed in credal formulations and insisted that faith be built upon the primary source of scripture, which in turn could ultimately be interpreted according to individual conscience. Second, it eventually produced an atmosphere in which doctrinal disputation appeared to be unproductive, creating a consciousness in England which grew weary of doctrinal disputes and sought a new foundation for Christian faith. Third, it promoted the humanist approach to biblical study which sought genuine linguistic and historical foundations for faith. The exploration of these foundations raised questions about doctrines based upon texts now considered unreliable.

These legacies of the Reformation helped to give birth to rational religion in seventeenth and eighteenth-century England. Like most intellectual movements, English rational religion contained a wide array of representatives. For the sake of clarity I will discuss those who embraced the rational religion under three headings. The first were the Deists like Herbert, Blount, Toland, Collins and Tindal. On the other end of the spectrum, and more or less contemporary with the Deists, were the intellectual progenitors of the Latitudinarians, namely the Cambridge Platonists, and Lord Falkland's circle at Great Tew. Finally, there emerged the Latitudinarians themselves, some of whom were orthodox, and some of whom, especially in the early eighteenth century, were heterodox.

English Rational Religion: Deism, Cambridge Platonism and the Great Tew Circle, and Latitudinarianism

As the beginnings of the scientific revolution can be traced in part to the work of Bacon and Descartes, so all three branches of England's rational religion can be traced back to the openness to reason found in Hooker's *Ecclesiastical Politie*. Prior to Hooker, the balance between faith and reason was clearly tipped in favor of faith. Reason was limited and its ability was impaired by the noetic effects of sin. While Hooker still acknowledged the limitations of reason and the reality of sin, he offered a friendlier posture to nature and reason. Hefelbower has written that the catalogue of progressive thinkers in England begins with Hooker, who in his work, appealed to reason, nature and natural law.[59] Hooker opened the door to rational religion's emphasis on

---

[59] Hefelbower, 10.

the natural law by outlining a certain congruence between the natural law and the divine law. The divine law was no longer seen as something radically other, but rather as a restatement of that which had originally been given to the human community. The fog of sin was dissipated with the light of revelation only to reveal what persons should have known all along.

> Neither is it vain that the Scripture aboundeth with so great store of laws in this kind [revealed]. For they are either such as we ourselves could not easily have found out, and then the benefit is not small to have them readily set down to our hands; or if they be so clear and manifest that no man indued with reason can lightly be ignorant of them, yet the Spirit as it were borrowing them from the school of nature as serving to prove things less manifest, and to induce a persuasion of somewhat which were in itself more hard and dark. Unless it should in such sort be cleared, the very applying of them unto cases particular is not without the most singular use and profit many ways for mens' instruction.[60]

Hooker's appraisal of reason had little effect upon his generation or the one that followed.[61] However, his thought was not lost upon the theologians of the late seventeenth and eighteenth centuries to whom we now turn, beginning with the Deists.

Deism

> When we come to the Deists we move in a different atmosphere. Some of them in their teaching differed only a little from the more liberal theologians. Yet the divergence is significant and can be easily detected. Reason becomes something more and revelation something less.[62]

This shift among the Deists is quite pronounced in the father of Deism, Herbert of Cherbury (1582–1648).[63] Lord Herbert served for a time as the English ambassador in Paris. There he became familiar with the skepticism of the new Pyrrhonists and the attempt of the Rationalists to oppose them.[64] Herbert believed God had given each person, by natural means, the ability to know the truths required for

---

[60] Richard Hooker, *Of the Laws of Ecclesiastical Politie* (London: Will. Stansy, 1611), 38.
[61] Tulloch, Vol. II, 82–83.
[62] Hefelbower, 74.
[63] On Herbert see Copleston, Vol. IV, 53–54; Willey, *Seventeenth Century*, 121–132; Punjer, *History*, 292–298.
[64] Brown, *Christianity in Western Thought*, 203–04.

salvation. These "necessary truths" Herbert referred to as *notitae* and he proposed five.

1. There is a Supreme God.
2. The sovereign Deity ought to be worshiped.
3. The connection of Virtue with Piety, defined in this work as the right conformation of the faculties, is and always has been held to be, the most important part of religious practice.
4. The minds of men have always been filled with horror for their wickedness. Their vices and crime have been obvious to them. They must be expiated by repentance.
5. There is a Reward or Punishment after this life.[65]

These five "notions" served as the basis upon which all revelation was to be judged. That which conformed to, and promoted, these five ideas was the truest revelation, and the best religion.[66]

Here we see the shift of balance between revelation and reason. Whereas for Puritan divines the emphasis was clearly on revelation, with the Deists reason was patently definitive. For them, the veracity of the revelation was decided before the tribunal of reason. Moreover, if the revelation was found wanting according to the criteria of the notions, it was to be amended.

> But if carelessness or the passage of time has allowed to creep into a sacred or profane book any passage which maligns God or calls in question those divine attributes which are universally recognized, why should we not agree either to amend the work—and this has been done before—or to charge its interpreters with error, in that they have departed from the writer's meaning and even from the analogy of faith, since they have stated views which conflict with Common Notions?[67]

In Herbert, sacred writing was reduced to the plane of the "profane" and both were to be evaluated by the common notions. This demotion of the previously held position of scripture was made possible by the fact that, for the Deists, scripture was no longer accounted as revelation, which was always immediate, but simply as tradition or history. Herbert believed that revelation could be trusted only under a given set of conditions.[68] The first of these conditions

---

[65] Herbert Edward, Lord of Cherbury, *De Veritate* (Bristol: Published for Univ. of Bristol by J.W. Arrowsmith Ltd., 1937, orig. published, Paris 1624, London, 1633), 289–303. Copleston, Vol. V, 53–54; Pünjer, *History*, 292–299.

[66] Herbert, *De Veritate*, 291.

[67] Ibid., 316.

[68] Pünjer, *History*, 299.

was the pursuit of particular and general providence through prayers, vows, and faith. The second was that revelation must be given directly to some person. Here Herbert stated explicitly that what was received from others as revelation must be accounted not revelation, but as tradition or history. The third condition was that the revelation must recommend a course of action which was good. This was the criterion which determined false revelations from those which were true. The fourth condition was that the breath of the divine spirit must be experienced.[69]

Aside from its radical subjectivity and mystical overtones, we can recognize the likelihood that Herbert's understanding of revelation provided a platform for Locke's. Both held the same distinction between original and traditional revelation. Locke's position was only a minor variation of Herbert's. In both, biblical revelation was reduced to history, and was to be criticized as such. In Herbert of Cherbury then, we see trust placed in the rational faculty in a way far more radical than in the other theologians of the early seventeenth-century. He went beyond the synthesis subsequently sought by those at Cambridge, and placed the Bible in a position relative to other literary works.

The criteria of the *notitae* was subsequently expanded from five to seven by Herbert's follower, Charles Blount.

> Natural religion is the belief we have of an eternal intellectual being, and of the duty which we owe him, manifested to us by our reason, without revelation or positive law: The chief heads whereof seem contained in these few particulars.
>
> 1. That there is one infinite eternal God, Creator of all things.
> 2. That he governs the world by Providence.
> 3. That 'tis our duty to worship and obey him as our Creator and Governor.
> 4. That our worship consists in prayer to him and praise of him.
> 5. That our obedience consists in the rules of right reason, the practice whereof is moral virtue.
> 6. That we are to expect Rewards and Punishments thereafter, according to our actions in this life; which includes the soul's immortality, and is proved by our admitting Providence.
> Seventhly, That when we err from the rules of our duty we ought to repent, and trust in God's mercy for pardon.[70]

---

[69] Ibid., 308.
[70] Charles Blount, *The Oracles of Reason* (London: Printed for R. Bentley and S. Magnes, 1683), 195–96.

In Blount we see a strong assault on traditional belief. His *Oracles* brought together the leading themes in Blount's earlier writings. Here the work of Sprat, Hobbes and Spinoza were used to provide an extenuation of Herbert's natural theology. Blount outlined a cynical view of human nature coupled with a favoring of religious toleration. His aim was to replace the dark clouds of superstition rooted in revelation with the light of natural reason, philosophy and theology.[71] Revelation was merely a shroud for superstition, and Christ was envisioned along the lines of the ancient miracle worker rather than God incarnate.[72] Blount's purpose here was to neutralize one of the Christian proofs of authenticity, the argument from miracles, by showing that Apollonius of Tyana, who lived roughly contemporaneously with Jesus, was also reputed to have performed miracles, and therefore Jesus' performance of them was not unique.[73] Clarke was well aware of this, and his response to Blount will be mentioned in Chapter Two.

While Blount denigrated miracles, reason, in his scheme, approached deification.

> The generality of men are but like so many religious parrots, who are taught to say they believe the scriptures, but why or wherefore they know not, only that Mr. A. the minister of their parish bids them. For my part, neither Socrates, Plato, or Aristotle, shall persuade me, if my judgment be not convinced by reason of what they say; Reason is the only mistress I court, and to her alone will I pay my devotion.[74]

With Blount it was no longer the reliability of reason which was defended, but the rationality of revelation which was attacked. He believed that any rule which was necessary for the happiness of all persons must be universally available. Since revelation was by definition particular, it could not be necessary.[75] Here we notice that the Deists moved to the offensive, and those who had previously defended the role of reason in theology now insisted to know upon what rational grounds those who argued for revelation could stand. One of the standard defenses of those who maintained the authority

---

[71] J.A. Redwood, "Charles Blount (1654–93), Deism, and English Free Thought," *Journal of the History of Ideas* 35 (1974): 490–495.

[72] Cragg, *The Church and the Age of Reason*, 77, with reference to Charles Blount, *The Two First Books of Philostratus Concerning the Life of Apollonius of Tyaneus: Written Originally in Greek, and now published in English: Together with Philological Notes upon Each Chapter* (London: Printed for Nathaniel Thompson, 1680).

[73] Brown, *Christianity in Western Thought*, 204–05.

[74] Blount, *Philostratus*, Lib. 1, Chap. 5, illus. 6.

[75] Blount, *The Oracles of Reason*, 196.

of revelation was the concept of mystery. God had revealed in scripture things which were beyond reason. It was necessary, therefore,
that the Deists dismantle the argument from mystery, which brings
us to the work of John Toland,[76] who inaugurated the period of
Deism's greatest activity and widest influence.[77]

Toland's views over the course of his life encompassed a wide
spectrum including "Deism," Socinianism and Pantheism.[78] As a young
man, Toland wrote *Christianity Not Mysterious* which reflected the rationalists' high estimation of reason.[79] It even echoed Whichcote's formula regarding the two candles. "For Reason is not less from God
than revelation; 'tis the candle, the guide, the judge he has lodged
within every man that cometh into this world."[80] Toland defined
reason as "that faculty of the soul which discovers the certainty of
any thing dubious or obscure, by comparing it with something evidently known."[81] He made an exhaustive inventory of the New Testament texts which used the term "mystery," and concluded that all
of them pointed to the dissolution of mystery with the coming of the
gospel. Christian faith was based not on mystery, but on what had
been revealed in Christ's coming. Possessing Christian faith meant
having been persuaded by the evidences presented to reason. For
Toland, faith was "a most firm persuasion built upon substantial
reasons."[82] In responding to the criticism that his formula reduced
faith to knowledge, Toland offered a distinction in what was meant
by knowledge. If knowledge meant a present and immediate view of
things, Toland held that he never intended that. If, however, knowl-

[76] John Toland, *Christianity Not Mysterious: Or, a Treatise Shewing, That there is nothing in the Gospel Contrary to Reason, Nor Above it: And that no Christian Doctrine can be properly call'd a Mystery* (London, 1696. Garland Reprints, ed. Rene Wellek, N.Y., Garland Publishing, Inc., 1978). Stephen H. Daniel, *John Toland: His Methods, Manners, and Mind* (Kingston and Montreal: McGill-Queen's University Press, 1984); Robert E. Sullivan, *John Toland and the Deist Controversy: A Study in Adaptations* (Cambridge MA: Harvard Univ. Press, 1982).
[77] Cragg, *The Church and the Age of Reason*, 77–78.
[78] Copleston, Vol. V, 163–64. For Toland's relationship to Deistic thought in general, and the difficulty of definition of the term, see Sullivan, *John Toland*, 205–234, 274–77; Cragg, *Puritanism*, 136–155. On his pantheism and esoterism see Sullivan, 173–204, and Daniel, *John Toland*, 211–225.
[79] It should be noted here that *Christianity Not Mysterious* was widely regarded by Toland's contemporaries as a Socinian work (Sullivan, *John Toland*, 109).
[80] Toland, *Christianity Not Mysterious*, 146.
[81] Ibid., 12–13.
[82] Ibid., 137–38.

edge meant understanding what was believed then, "I stand by it that faith is knowledge."[83]

Like the other Deists, Toland acknowledged that Scripture must be tried before the bar of reason. Unlike Herbert and others, however, Toland was more confident of how it would fare. He did not scoff at revelation, but insisted that it could not be exempted from the scrutiny of reason. Scripture was discovered to be divine, not on its own assertion, but from the testimony of the things within it when measured by reason. While scripture had the "birthright characters of divinity" it was reason which found them out and examined them by its principles, approving and pronouncing it sufficient. The conviction of reason in turn produced in us the acquiescence of faith.[84]

For Toland, reason was the only foundation of all certitude, and he held that "there is nothing in the Gospel contrary to reason, nor above it; and that no Christian doctrine can be properly be called a mystery."[85] This statement was a calculated abandonment of the earlier theologies, represented by the scholastic doctrine present in Albert and Thomas, which held that while there was nothing in scripture contrary to reason, there were truths above it. In Toland's mind, there were no such truths—no mysteries. In much of this Toland was dependent on Locke, but moved beyond Locke's contention that Christianity was reasonable, to hold that nothing contrary to reason and nothing above it could be part of Christian doctrine.[86] Thus Toland effectively challenged the defense of "mystery" which was purported to shield certain aspects of revelation and doctrines of the church from rational theology. In Toland we see, not so much the elevation of reason to new heights, but rather the practical implications of its previous elevation in thinkers like Herbert and Blount. With Toland, the citadel of mystery in which the Church had protected certain doctrines had been breached.

Another of the prominent Deist voices was that of Anthony Collins (1676–1729). Like Toland, Collins, although a friend of Locke, attacked Locke's distinction (which was derived from Albert and Thomas) between things which were above reason, and those contrary to it. Collins' *Discourse of Free-Thinking Occasion'd by the Rise and Growth of a*

---

[83] Ibid., 145, cf., Pünjer, *History*, 324.
[84] Toland, *Christianity Not Mysterious*, 32.
[85] Ibid., 5–6.
[86] Cragg, *Puritanism*, 140–41.

Sect Call'd Free-Thinkers (1713) asserted that free inquiry was the only avenue to attaining truth, and that this was commanded by scripture itself.[87] Where Blount had attacked the first of the double pillars of Christian authenticity, viz., the argument from miracles, Collins, in his *A Discourse of the Grounds and Reasons of the Christian Religion* (1724), attacked the second pillar, which was prophecy. Using the tools of biblical criticism, Collins maintained that the prophecies of the Old Testament were fulfilled within the immediate history of the prophets, and that any Christian use of them could be only allegorical.[88] Along with his denial of prophecy, Collins had also promised in a subsequent work to treat the topic of miracles, but this was carried out by his disciple Thomas Woolston (1670–1731). Woolston developed a radical critique of miracles in his *Six Discourses on the Miracles of of our Saviour* (1727–29), which served as a platform upon which Hume would later build.[89] As the prophecies had been allegorical for Collins, so were the miracles for Woolston. He denied the resurrection of Jesus, but ironically held that the greatest miracle was belief in it.[90]

The Deist arrangement, which positioned reason as superior to faith, offered a radical epistemology rooted solely in human experience. The Deists produced a line of thought which emerged in the language of a competing religion, measured by a different standard. This standard was reflected in the words of the mature Deist, Tindal, in his *Christianity as Old as Creation*.

> I desire no more than to be allow'd, that there's a religion of nature and reason written in the hearts of every one of us from the first creation; by which all mankind must judge of the truth of any instituted religion whatever; and if it varies from the religion of nature and reason in any one particular, nay, in the minutest circumstance, that alone is an argument, which makes all things else that can be said for its support totally ineffectual.[91]

---

[87] Anthony Collins, *A Discourse of Free Thinking, Occasion'd by the Rise and Growth of a sect Call'd Free Thinkers*. London: MDCCXIII; Punjer, *History*, 330.

[88] Brown, *Christianity and Western Thought*, 206. Brown notes that Collins failed to see an alternative between literal and allegorical interpretation here, in recognizing the possibility of understanding the prophecies typologically.

[89] Colin Brown, *Miracles and the Critical Mind* (Grand Rapids; Exeter, Devon, U.K.: Wm. Eerdmans Publ./Paternoster Press Ltd., 1984), 49–50.

[90] Thomas Woolston, *Six Discourses on the Miracles of our Saviour in view of the Present Controversy between Infidels and Apostates* 5th ed. (London: Printed for the author, 1728; Reprinted by Garland Publishing, 1979), Discourse Six, 12.

[91] Matthew Tindal, *Christianity as old as the Creation: or, the Gospel as a republication of the Religion of Nature*. 2d ed. in octavo. (London: MDCCXXXII), 50–51.

At the same time, there were parallels between the Deists and rational religionists. Their emphasis on reason, the desire for a moral religion grounded in nature, and the emphais on toleration all were part of the landscape of the rational religion. However, they challenged the historic synthesis of faith and reason in a way in which scripture was, at best, subordinated to reason. In this sense, the Deists represented the radical branch of rational religion. The radicalness of Deism was reflected in the fact that for them mystery was totally evacuated, revelation occupied a supplementary and subordinate role, scripture was set on par with profane writings, and supernatural claims were opened to criticism as being incongruous with what was known from nature. For the Deists, reason became the ultimate arbiter of all truth.[92] We have explored one branch of rational religion in England, the Deists, at the other end of the spectrum were the Cambridge Platonists and the circle at Great Tew.

Cambridge Platonism

Platonism experienced a profound revival at Cambridge in the mid-seventeenth century.[93] Brown has written that the term "Platonists" must be qualified when applied to these Cambridge scholars. They drank deeply from the wells of classical learning, and relied on Plato for their understanding of the role of ideas, the nature of the soul, and the place of reason and moral concepts. However, they drew on other sources as well, and quoted Plotinus more than Plato, the former being instructive on the pertinent issues of their day. In all of this, they perceived themselves in the tradition of the Alexandrian Church Fathers.[94] Tulloch has suggested that the arrival of Cambridge Platonism can be dated from the year 1644 when Benjamin Whichcote

---

[92] Cragg, *The Church and the Age of Reason*, 78.

[93] Major figures among the Cambridge Platonists included: Benjamin Whichcote, Ralph Cudworth, Henry More, John Smith, John Hales of Eton, and J. Taylor. Tulloch *Rational Theology* Vol. II, 6–7. On the Cambridge Platonists see Frederick Powicke, *The Cambridge Platonists: A Study* (Westport, Conn: Greenwood Press, 1970, orig. pub. 1926); G.R. Cragg, ed., *The Cambridge Platonists* (New York: Oxford Univ. Press, 1968); Willey, *Seventeenth Century*, 133–169; Tulloch, *Rational Theology*, Vol. II, et passim; G.R. Cragg, *Puritanism*, 37–60; Rosemary Colie, *Light and Enlightenment: A Study of the Cambridge Platonists and the Dutch Arminians* (Cambridge: Cambridge Univ. Press, 1957).

[94] Brown, *Christianity and Western Thought*, 202, cf., Cragg, ed., *Platonists*, 14; Copleston, Vol. V, 54.

was appointed Provost of King's College.[95] Whichcote held sway over the hearts and minds of the young students enough that his old tutor, turned colleague and adversary, Tuckney, could comment that as a result of his influence, "young ones in the university were tainted."[96] However, the Platonic revival had been underway even during Whichcote's student days. Tuckney wrote to Whichcote that the latter had kept the company of young men at Cambridge who had studied the classics more than scripture, and Plato most of all. Tuckney felt Whichcote and his group overemphasized the power of nature in morals and that they had emphasized right reason (*recta ratio*) at the expense of faith. In the same way they emphasized mind and understanding too much, and heart and will not enough. As a result they quarreled over the decrees of God as being incompatible with God's goodness.[97]

Tuckney has been said to represent the "Puritan" position[98] which was shortly to be supplanted by a more liberal strain. He accurately identified the critical point of transition in Whichcote's thought, writing,

> This saying [that reason in man is a "candle of the Lord"] he holds, has no relation to the truths of supernatural or evangelical theology; nor is the Protestant principle of private judgment, while true against the Pope's pretended claims, to be held as superior to the rule of Scripture, but in subordination to it.[99]

Tuckney understood that now not only the dictates of the church, but scripture itself was to be subject to the scrutiny of reason.

Meanwhile, Whichcote attempted to coordinate the "two lights" of reason and revelation so that each would be seen in the service of God's grace.

> And therefore to speak of natural light, of the use of reason in religion, is to do no disservice at all to grace; for God is acknowledged in both: in the former as laying the groundwork of his creation; in the latter, as reviving and restoring it. So that these do agree together, as God doth agree to himself; God laying the religion of conscience, and making man in such a power of judging; and God restoring him to the self same state again, after he had consented to iniquity, whereby he had marred his principles, and disabled himself; so that I say, these two do

---

[95] Tulloch, Vol. II, 52.
[96] Ibid., 83.
[97] Ibid., 67–68.
[98] Ibid., 68.
[99] Ibid., 65.

as well agree together, as God doth agree with himself; for God is the author of nature, and the restorer of it.[100]

We see this same principle at work in Cudworth's defense of the trinity, where he argued that though there was a great mystery to the trinity, yet there was nothing in it in plain contradiction to human reason, as the Atheists would have us believe.[101]

This positive assessment of reason rested on the Platonic doctrine of innate ideas which, as we have seen, was also found in Descartes and criticized by Bacon, Locke and Newton. There existed for the Platonists eternal truths which were to be normative standards for the human community.[102] Thus for the Platonists, the intersection of the natural law and morality was expected: to obey one was to find the highest form of the other. This resulted, as Tuckney had already detected in Whichcote, in an exaltation of man's natural moral sense. To act aright, a person merely needed to look within for the inscription of the natural law on their heart.[103]

The Cambridge Platonists, unlike many theologians of their time, were supportive of the new science. Boyle and More read each other's work. John Worthington was deeply interested in the development of natural history. John Smith believed that theology and science shared certain presuppostions. Cudworth read scientific literature and was interested in microscopes and telescopes. He was acquainted with medical developments and was knowledgable in physiology. For him, the natural sciences provided a vast wealth of information which supported religious truth. In fact, Cudworth made the first attempt in England to coordinate the new science with the older philosophical and religious traditions.[104]

The Cambridge Platonists' concern for morality, coupled with their support of modern science led them into a dilemma. The political

---

[100] Benjamin Whichcote, *The Works* (Aberdeen: Printed by J. Chalmers, for Alexander, MDCCLI. Garland Reprints, N.Y. 1977), Vol. 1, 371–72.

[101] Ralph Cudworth, *The True Intellectual System of the Universe: Wherein all the Reason and Philosophy of Atheism is confuted and its Impossibility Demonstrated.* 2 Vols. (Andover: Published by Gould and Newman New York, 1838), Vol. 1, 737. Note here that Cudworth willingly embraces the concept of "Mystery" which Toland will criticize later. Cudworth's view is in keeping with Thomas' position and that of Protestant scholasticism. He simply takes the pagan vestiges of the doctrine of the trinity and examines them in order to demonstrate the reality of trinitarian awareness even among the pagans.

[102] Hefelbower, 57.

[103] Willey, *Eighteenth Century*, 58.

[104] G.R. Cragg, ed., *Platonists*, 28–29, cf., Tulloch, Vol. II, 24.

philosophy outlined in Thomas Hobbes' *Leviathan*,[105] was constructed
on the foundation of the new natural philosophy and its empiricism,
but its moral conclusions were opposed to those of the Platonists.
Hobbes had taken up Bacon's method and applied it to the study of
society. He developed a new order for society out of what he believed to be the real nature of human beings as socially experienced.
This order was in direct opposition to that envisioned by the Platonists,
who forcefully resisted Hobbes. Thus while Platonism existed prior
to Hobbes, it may be said that its opposton to him is what galva-
nized the movement and gave it its dogmatic direction.[106]

The Cambridge Platonists also altered English religious thought
by dramatically elevating the "light of reason" to a place alongside
that of scripture. Whereas for the Deists, reason was superior to scripture, the Platonists sought a synthesis, balancing faith and reason. In
the Platonist John Hales, reason was to become the infallible guide
to truth.

> An infallibility there must be; but men have marvelously wearied them-
> selves in seeking to find where it is... We see many times a kind of
> ridiculous and jocular forgetfulness of many men, seeking for that which
> they have in their hands; so fares it here with men who seek for infal-
> libility in others which either is, or ought to be, in themselves:... For
> infallibility is not a favor impropriated to any one man: it is a duty
> alike expected at the hands of all—all must have it.[107]

The Platonists did, however, recognize that reason could err. Therefore they created a distinction between schism, which was caused by
flawed reasoning, and heresy, which was an act of the will. Hales
argued that ancient heresies and separations in the church were the
result of persons dogmatizing opinions which were not rooted in either
revelation or reason. He included under the name of schism: Arianism,
Eutychianism, Nestorianism, Photinianism, and Sabellianism. Under
the name of heresy, which he differentiated from schism as a lie
rather than a mistake, he included: Manichaeism, Valentinianism,
Marcionism, and Mahometanism.[108] Here we find the principle of

---

[105] Thomas Hobbes, *Leviathan or the matter Form and Power of a Commonwealth Ecclesiastical and Civil* (London: Printed for Andrew Crooke, 1651).
[106] Tulloch, Vol. II, 25–26.
[107] From Hales sermon, "Of Enquiry and Private Judgment in Religion," in *Golden
Remains of the Ever-Memorable Mr. John Hales of Eton College*, cited by Tulloch, *Rational
Theology*, Vol. I, 244.
[108] From Hales' tract on "Schism" in *The Golden Remains*, cited by Tulloch, Vol. I,
227–28.

toleration at work as Hales tried to redefine the previous categories of theological statements seeking a conciliatory middle ground which was necessary in view of the Platonist esteem for reason.

The Platonists also played a role in attempting to limit theological statements to the language of scripture, thereby avoiding metaphysical disputes. Whichcote had made a comment to this effect in a sermon he preached in the fall of 1651. This comment prompted a letter from Tuckney in which he wrote,

> Your first advice—"That we would be confined to Scripture words and expressions—in which all parties agree—and not press other forms of words which are from fallible men; and this would be for the peace of Christendom"—I look at as more dangerous.[109]

Tuckney's response is reminiscent of what Calvin had inserted in the 1559 edition of his *Institutes* in the context of his trinitarian argument.

> But I have long since and repeatedly been experiencing that all who persistently quarrel over words nurse a secret poison. As a consequence, it is more expedient to challenge them deliberately than to speak more obscurely to please them.[110]

We see, then, several emphases which developed among the Cambridge Platonists. These divines were friendly toward the emerging natural philosophy albeit finding its metaphysical foundations shallow. They exalted reason as an equal partner with scripture in discerning religious truth. As a result of their Idealism, especially in the realm of morals, they stressed a virtuous and moral Christianity. They also favored a broader sense of religious tolerance. Finally, there were among them those who believed that a return to the scriptural pattern of language about the nature of God would have a conciliatory effect. All of these ideas would be found in the Latitudinarian generation of clergy which followed them.[111] Alongside the Cambridge group, formed a circle of men who developed a similar set of concerns, who, in turn, also served as a theological tributary to the stream of Latitudinarianism. This was Lord Falkland's circle at Great Tew.

---

[109] Tulloch, Vol. II, 60.

[110] John Calvin, *The Institutes of the Christian Religion.* 2 Vols., ed. John T. McNeil, trans. Ford Lewis Battles. (Philadelphia: Westminster Press, 1960), I, XIII, 6.

[111] Reventlow, 223.

The Great Tew Circle

This second group, which existed alongside the Platonists at Cambridge, and also served as an intellectual tributary of the Latitudinarians was the *"convivium theologicum"* of Lucius Cary, second Viscount Falkland. They met at Cary's spacious estate at Great Tew in Oxfordshire, about twenty miles from the university.[112] This group was composed of faculty members at Oxford and some who lived in London. They came and stayed at Falkland's home making use of his extensive library and conversing with one another on a variety of topics, especially theology. Among the circle were Sheldon, Morley, Hammond, Earles and Chillingworth.[113] In describing them Griffin writes,

> The characteristic thought of his circle was consciously and directly in the tradition of sixteenth century Christian Humanism, with its stress on free will, theological minimalism, charity in inessentials, and a concern for morality above credal speculation.[114]

Here we see some of the same agenda expressed in the thought of the Platonists. The circle at Great Tew had connections with some of the Dutch Remonstrants, and for them Grotius was the leading light. Falkland referred to him as "our age's wonder,"[115] and Grotius' *De Veritate religionis Christianae* (1622) was the immediate inspiration of Chillingworth's *Religion of the Protestants*.[116] As Whichcote, Cudworth and More had provided the intellectual leadership for the Cambridge Platonists, Chillingworth did so for the circle at Great Tew.

William Chillingworth,[117] was raised an Anglican and his acting godfather was Laud.[118] In his search for a firm foundation for belief he began to doubt the Anglican position on eccleisiastical order and authority. He questioned the authenticity of Protestantism, and its

---

[112] Martin Griffin, *Latitudinarianism in the Seventeenth-Century Church of England.* Annotated by Richard Popkin. Edited by Lila Freedman. Volume 32 in Brill Studies in Intellectual History Series (Leiden: E.J. Brill, 1992), 89.

[113] Ibid.

[114] Ibid.

[115] Ibid., 90.

[116] Ibid., 92.

[117] William Chillingworth, *The Religion of the Protestants, A Safe Way to Salvation* in *Works* (Philadelphia: Hooker and Agnew, 1841). On Chillingworth's thought see J.D. Hyman, *William Chillingworth and the Theory of Religious Toleration* (Cambridge, MA: Harvard Univ. Press, 1931); Robert Orr, *Reason and Authority: The Thought of William Chillingworth* (Oxford: Clarendon Press, 1967).

[118] Orr, *Chillingworth*, 1.

ability to unite the Church. Consequently he was converted to Catholicism and was induced by the Jesuits to study at Douay in 1630.[119] There they asked him to write out his reasons for his conversion. As he did, Chillingworth began to have second thoughts and became a "doubting Papist." He returned to Oxford and declared himself a Protestant again in 1634. For Chillingworth, neither the dogmatism of Rome, nor the various dogma of the Protestant churches provided the foundation for faith he sought. Finally, he produced his *The Religion of the Protestants* in 1628. This work was neither an attack on Catholicism nor a defense of Anglicanism, but promoted the right of free inquiry and personal conviction.[120] Chillingworth's work served as something of a Magna Carta for the role of reason in religion. His work saw a renaissance following the Restoration, and became dominant following the Revolution. It marked an epochal shift in English theology from dogmatic system to a greater emphasis on the role of reason and the defense of rational theology.[121]

Chillingworth, building on Grotius' discussion on the various kinds of evidence, posited one of the cornerstone ideas of the Great Tew circle; the epistemology of moral certainty for the proof of faith. This development subsequently served as a centerpiece in Latitudinarian thought.[122] The argument for the distinction in kinds of evidence was nothing new and was part of the stock of basic apologetics, deriving ultimately from Aristotle's *Ethics*.[123] Chillingworth's contribution came at the point of admitting that faith was built on an inferior kind of certainty, as opposed to physical, mathematical, or metaphysical certainty. Nonetheless, even though the certainty of faith was inferior to that of knowledge, faith had a foundation in the evidence of testimony, which, albeit inferior, was nevertheless, evidence. This kind of moral certainty, built upon the evidence of testimony, was, for Chillingworth, and ultimatly the Latitudinarians, the essence of faith.[124]

---

[119] The site of Douay is probable but not certain. See Orr, *Chillingworth*, 38–39.

[120] "Chillingworth, William," by M. Creighton, in Leslie Stephen, ed., *Dictionary of National Biography* (London: Smith, Elder & Co., 1886), Vol. X, 254–55.

[121] Ibid., 256–57.

[122] Griffin, 94–95. See also W.M. Spellman, *The Latitudinarians and the Church of England, 1160–1700*. (Athens, GA, and London: The University of Georgia Press, 1993), 21.

[123] Griffin, 95.

[124] Ibid. Griffin points out that on the question of certainty, the Latitudinarians followed Chillingworth and Great Tew, rather than the Cambridge Platonists, who argued, in accordance with Thomas, that faith was a higher and surer way of knowing, because it came from God, than any other form of knowing. (96f.)

In this regard the Latitudinarians were heirs of Chillingworth and Great Tew, rather than the Platonists. Griffin has summed up the matter succinctly in writing regarding the relationship between Cambridge Platonism and Latitudinarianism concerning the roles of faith and reason,

> Thus it is pellucidly clear that the similarities between Cambridge Platonism and Latitudinariansim were merely superficial: it is true that for both groups "reason" and "faith" were inextricably interconnected concepts; but the difference was that while the Cambridge Platonists divinized reason, the Latitudinarians rationalized divinity.[125]

This "rationalization of divinity" found its source in Chillingworth and the circle at Great Tew. Thus after Chillingworth, for those who chose to follow him, Christian epistemology was secularized and could no longer beat a hasty retreat into fideism. For this reason the theology of the Latitudinarians was often criticised as being overly rational. The benefit, however, was that now the epistemic playing field for apologetics was level, and the Christian could share the evidences for faith freely with the unbeliever, fully acknowledging that moral certainty was not as unimpeachable as physical or mathematical certainty, but that it possessed a level of certainty worthy of attention and trust nonetheless.[126] Out of these two streams of thought; Cambridge Platonism and the circle at Great Tew, flowed the thought of the Latitudinarians.

The Latitudinarians

The term "Latitudinarian" was first used perjoratively to caricature certain Cambridge Platonists, but ultimately became a term of respect.[127] Soon the term was applied to a wider circle of theologians and clerics who embraced the liberal theological agenda which was emerging in the last half of the seventeenth-century.[128] Cragg has pointed out that the term itself was vague, and that Bishop Fowler's comment that Latitudinarians were "men of wide swallow" could be

---

[125] Griffin, 101.

[126] The current work of Pannenberg in his *Theology and the Philosophy of Science* seems to reflect a similar tendency.

[127] Griffin, 4. Griffin and Spellman provide the best discussions on the term relative to theology; see the first chapter of each work. Also, Cragg, *Puritanism*, 61.

[128] Ibid., 62.

said of the term itself.[129] Griffin has helped clarify the modern use of
the term by differentiating the Latitudinarians from both the Cambridge Platonists and the circle at Great Tew. He assigns the term to
the group around Archbishiop Tillotson, and includes within it
Edward Stillingfleet, Bishop of Worcester, Simon Patrick, Bishop of
Ely, Thomas Tenison, successor to Tillotson as Archbishop of Canterbury and William Lloyd, who served as bishop in several loca-
tions.[130] Others like Jeremy Taylor and Thomas Sherlock were also
Latitudinarians as well.

While Donald Greene, in his article on Latitudinarianism,[131] reminds
us that it did not represent a coherent theological perspective, it is
nonetheless true that their were certain characteristic convictions held
among its representatives. Spellman has written,

> Acceptance of the Thirty-nine Articles, "and all other points of Doc-
> trine contained either in the Liturgy or book of Homilies," placed the
> Latitude-men firmly within a tradition which viewed the depth of human
> sinfulness as a lasting bar to salvation through works and ethical be-
> havior. The unmerited grace of God, offered to mankind through the
> life and death of Christ, together with the faith of the believer who
> understood the sin of pride involved in works righteousness, provided
> the intellectual framework for the Latitudinarian picture of Reformed
> Christianity.[132]

While on the one hand, the Latitudinarians were heirs of an Augus-
tinian and Reformed understanding of the human fall, they were
also recipients of the Thomistic insistence on the viability of the mind
in knowing God.[133] Theologically then, Latitudinarianism can be described as an attempt to find a path which incorporated an Augus-
tinian seriousness regarding the implications of the fall, coupled with
Thomas' optimism regarding the human ability to know God. Much
of the misunderstanding associated with the positive remarks by
Latitudinarians concerning our ability to know God, derives from a
failure to distinguish in their comments as to whether they were
speaking about a prelapsarian, postlapsarian, or idealized state.

In addition to this general theological matrix, we also find in the

---

[129] Ibid., 63. For more on the relationship between the Platonists and Latitudinarians see Cragg, *Puritanism*, 63f.
[130] Griffin, 45.
[131] Donald Greene, "Latitudinariansism and Sensibility: The Geneology of the
'Man of Feeling' Reconsidered," *Modern Philology* 75 (1977): 159–183.
[132] Spellman, 31.
[133] Ibid., 63–65.

Latitudinarians an emphasis on the importance of the role of reason, a preference for moral rather than speculative theology, a positive disposition toward natural philosophy, a distrust of the deductive method, a desire for religious toleration and a desire to use biblical language in constructing doctrine.[134] In all of this they were indebted, as we have seen, both to the Cambridge Platonists and Lord Falkland's circle at Great Tew.

Two branches of Latitudinarian thought derived from Cambridge Platonism and the circle at Great Tew. The first I will call the orthodox Latitudinarians, represented by those already mentioned. The second group were the heterodox Latitudinarians.

The influence of Cambridge Platonism and the circle at Great Tew can be seen through a survey of a few of the orthodox Latitudinarians of the subsequent generation. In his *Discourse on the Liberty of Prophesying* the Latitudinarian Jeremy Taylor expressed his support for the principle of toleration by writing that persons could extend their own creeds, should they choose. They could even make deductions in their own belief system. However, they may not insist that others follow them in these as articles of faith.[135] Like the Cambridge Platonists, Locke, and the Deists, Taylor sought a common set of biblical truths which would provide the common foundation of Christian faith.

> the great Gospel verities . . . such as are—Jesus Christ the Son of the living God, the crucifixion and resurrection of Jesus, forgiveness of sins by His blood, resurrection of the dead and life eternal. Salvation is promised to the explicit belief of those articles, and therefore those only are necessary, and those are sufficient.[136]

The scientific interest of the Platonists was likewise carried over into the orthodox Latitudinarian theology. Here we see the emergence of the "physico-theological" systems which so dramatically illustrated the desire of the age to integrate scientific and theological truth. As many as fifty such systems had developed by 1774.[137] Richard Bentley, in the first course of Boyle Lectures in 1692, tried to link science and theology through a two stage version of the teleological argu-

---

[134] Griffin, 38–43, esp. 43.
[135] J. Taylor, *Discourse on the Liberty of Prophesying*. Section 1:10, in Tulloch Vol. I, p. 383.
[136] Ibid., Section 1.5, Tulloch, Vol. I, 381.
[137] Reventlow, 339.

ment, proved by the double demonstrations of the miraculous construction of the human body and the origin and ordering of the cosmos. John Ray in his *Three Physico-Theological Discourses* (1693) developed Bentley's first proof. Samuel Clarke's first series of Boyle lectures *A Demonstration of the Being and Attributes of God* can also be classified with this genre.[138]

We see also the influence of the Platonist agenda in Stillingfleet's proposal for toleration,[139] *Irenicum: A Weapon Salve for the Church's Wound; or, the Divine Right of Particular Forms of Church Government, discussed and examined according to the principles of the Law of nature, the positive Law of God, the practice of the Apostles and the primitive Church, and the judgment of Reformed Divines. Whereby a foundation is laid for the Church's peace, and the accommodation of our present differences.* The full title is instructive in that it hints at major areas of concern which Stillingfleet had inherited from the Platonists and the circle at Great Tew: toleration, the law of nature, and the relationship of the natural law to revelation.

Stillingfleet also reflected a sensitive synthesis of reason and revelation. He affirmed the divine origin of revelation, while recognizing the role of human reason in understanding that revelation. In his invented conversation between a Papist and a Protestant concerning the trinity and transubstantiation he wrote,

> P. I begin with Scripture. And the whole dispute as to both, depends on this: Whether the Scripture is to be understood literally or figuratively. If literally, then Transubstantiation stands upon equal terms with the Trinity; if figuratively, then the Trinity can no more be proved from Scripture, than Transubstantiation.
>
> Pr. As though there might not be reason for a figurative sense in one place, and a literal in another.
>
> P. It seems you resolve it into reason.
>
> Pr. And I pray, into what would you resolve it? Into no reason?
>
> P. No: there may be reason for that authority, but not for the thing which I believe upon it.

---

[138] Reventlow, 338–39. Other noted physico-theologies include, W. Derham, *Physico-Theology: or a demonstration of the Being and Attributes of God, from his works of creation*, Boyle Lectures of 1711/12 publ. 1715, and John Craig's *Theologiae Christianae Principia mathematica*, 1699.

[139] While the desire for toleration did not originate with the Platonists, they crystalized it in such a way that the Latitudinarians were able to build on their foundation.

Pr. Then you believe the doctrine of the Trinity, merely because the
Church tells you it is the literal sense of Scripture which you are to
follow. But suppose a man sees no reason for this authority of your
Church; (as for my part, I do not;) have you no reason to convince
such a one that he ought to believe the Trinity?

P. Not I. For I think men are bound to believe as the Church teaches
them, and for that reason.[140]

Here we notice Stillingfleet's acceptance of revelation, but also the
role of reason in discerning its meaning. For Stillingfleet, reason
operated *within* the parameters of revelation. It did not criticize the
revelation as God's word, but was given full reign in determining its
meaning. When two different senses of scripture were offered, reason
was to choose the most preferable.[141] This positioning of the "two
lights" allowed Stillingfleet to utilize reason within the context of
scripture. It should be noted however, that he gave a significant place
to the tradition of the church in matters of interpretation, and this
was one of the things which separated the orthodox Latitudinarians
from the Deists and heterodox Latitudinarians. As to which sense of
scripture was most preferable, Stillingfleet stated that it was the sense
the church had generally received as authoritative. His rationale was
that the early church had been greatly concerned about doctrine,
and because of their proximity to the events, they were in a better
position to accurately assess the mind of the apostles. In this he also
showed a certain suspicion of what he termed "modern inventions,
or criticisms, or pretenses to revelation."[142]

A second element in which Stillingfleet represented the orthodox
Latitudinarians was his retention of a role for mystery. Although the
Deist Toland challenged the validity of mystery, and the heterodox
Latitudinarians followed his inclination, Stillingfleet and the ortho-
dox Latitudinarians retained it.

We are certain the word mystery is used for things far less difficult and
abstruse; and why may it not then be fitly applied to such matters,
which are founded on divine revelation, but yet are too deep for us to
go to the bottom of them? Are there not mysteries in arts, mysteries in

---

[140] Edward Stillingfleet, "Second Dialogue on the Doctrine of the Trinity and
Transubstantiation Compared," in John Randoph's *Enchiridion Theologicum, or a Manual
for the Use of Students in Divinity* (Oxford: Clarendon Press, MDCCCXII), Vol. 1,
405–06.
[141] Stillingfleet, "Discourse on Scripture Mysteries," in John Randolph, *Enchiridion
Theologicum* (Oxford: Clarendon Press, MDCCCXII), 382.
[142] Ibid., 382–83.

nature, mysteries, which in some measure are known, but in much greater unknown to us? Although therefore in the language of Scripture it be granted, that the word mystery is most frequently applied to things before hidden, but now revealed, yet there is no incongruity in calling that a mystery, which being revealed, hath yet something in it which our understandings cannot reach to.[143]

In his discourse on 2 Cor. 5:10–11, discussing the doctrine of the resurrection, Thomas Sherlock, another orthodox Latitudinarian, addressed several of the crucial issues involved for those who followed the Cambridge Platonists. For instance, the doctrine of the resurrection touched upon the relation of revelation and reason, of morality, and of natural law. Regarding the first he wrote that the expectation of life beyond death was possible to reason alone, and was even found in the heathen philosophies. In fact, Sherlock argued, the hope of life after death dictated by natural reason and revelation were the same. However, the manner in which this would occur was supplied by revelation. To the natural desire for eternal life the gospel added the specifics: that it would be achieved through the resurrection of the body, that Christ was the judge of the world, and that there would be reward and punishment in proportion to our earthly conduct.[144]

Secondly, Sherlock extracted a moral teaching from the resurrection. That event was the proof that persons would be held accountable for their deeds. Natural religion, which carried with it an emphasis on morality, had no way to determine whether or not human beings were actually held morally culpable for their life on earth. This deficiency was remedied by revelation's account of the judgment following the resurrection from the dead. The doctrine of a reunited body and soul overcame natural religion's speculation as to how an eternal soul might suffer the consequences of sins committed in the body. Thus the gospel teaching of the resurrection was essential to the maintenance of natural religion.[145]

Thirdly, Sherlock tried to answer the question of how the resurrection could be understood in relation to the natural law. He argued that some persons held that a resurrection was naturally impossible, because it seemed so to the human perspective. For Sherlock, this limited God to the horizon of human possibilities. While it was true

---

[143] Ibid., 387.
[144] Thomas Sherlock, Discourse XLIX in *The Works of Bishop Sherlock*. 4 Vols. (London: A.J. Valpy, 1830), Vol. 2, 432.
[145] Ibid., 433–34.

that our powers were bounded by nature, it did not follow that the same was true of God, who authored the laws of nature and could have authored others had he so chosen. Sherlock wrote, "what can induce us to suppose that he cannot give life to a body a second time, who we certainly know gave life to it at first?"[146] In Sherlock we see that revelation itself was not enough, it must be coordinated with reason, made to serve moral purposes, and found to relate in a meaningful way to the laws of nature. The issue is not whether Sherlock argued his points well, but simply that he felt compelled to argue them at all. The contours of his argument are further evidence of the Cambridge Platonists' and circle of Great Tew's influence on the orthodox Latitudinarians who followed them. We have examined one of the branches of Latitudinarianism which stemmed from the Platonists, and Great Tew; the orthodox Latitudinarians. We now turn to the heterodox Latitudinarians.

The heterodox Latitudinarians are differentiated from the Deists, on the one hand, by their restraint in methodology, in which they resemble the Platonists and the orthodox Latitudinarians already mentioned. On the other hand they differ both from the Platonists, and the orthodox Latitudinarians in the conclusions they reached. A major distinction was their understanding of the trinity.

We see a foreshadowing of trinitarian heterodoxy in the theology of Chillingworth at Great Tew. It should be remembered that the circle had been impacted by the Remonstrants, who after 1660, admitted Polish Socinian refugees to their worship and sacraments.[147] We catch a glimpse of Chillingworth's doubts concerning the traditional understanding of the trinity in a letter to Dr. Sheldon (1635) explaining that he could not accept a preferment from the Lord Keeper of the Great Seal, Sir Thomas Coventry, because he would have to subscribe to the Thirty-Nine Articles. He could not because he did not affirm the anathemas of the Athanasian Creed.[148] In another letter we discover that more than the damning sentences may have stood in Chillingworth's way. A friend, now unknown, had asked him what he thought about Arianism in light of the witness of Antiquity. He responded in a letter, after citing Patristic sources,

---

[146] Ibid., 434–35.
[147] Herbert McClachlan, *The Religious Opinions of Milton, Locke and Newton* (Manchester: Manchester University Press, 1941), 72.
[148] Chillingworth, *Works*, xiii.

In the first [document] you shall find that the eighty fathers, which condemned Samosatenus, affirmed expressly, that the Son is not of the same essence of the Father; which is to contradict formally the Council of Nice, which decreed the Son co-essential with the Father . . . In a word, whosoever shall freely and impartially consider of this thing, and how on the other side the ancient fathers' weapons against the arians are in a manner only places of scripture (and those now for the most part discarded as impertinent and unconcluding), and how in the argument drawn from the authority of the ancient fathers, they are almost always defendants, and scarce ever opponents; he shall not choose but confess, or at least be very inclinable to believe, that the doctrine of Arius is either a truth, or at least no damnable heresy.[149]

The legacy of Chillingworth can be found in one of the members of the heterodox Latitudinarians; Benjamin Hoadly, Bishop of Winchester. In his account of Clarke's life and work we encounter a display of Latitudinarian themes. In commenting on Clarke's production of the *Scripture-Doctrine*, he wrote that Clarke understood the outcome to be based on scripture and not on metaphysics. Clarke had used the inductive method of searching through all the available texts, rather than starting with dogma or tradition. He had used the best rules of grammar, criticism and linguistics and had laid his results before the public. These results had not been met with toleration, as Hoadley believed they should have been.[150] On so many Latitudinarian themes then, we see Hoadley in alignment: the rejection of hypothesis (which we found in Bacon and Newton), the suspicion of metaphysical approaches to the trinity and the validity of exclusively biblical sources, the affirmation of the desire for toleration toward divergent views, and the approbation of the humanist advances in biblical criticism. In addition to standard Latitudinarian convictions we find, as we did in Chillingworth, a tolerance for diverse views on the trinity. Here Hoadly was politic. He never denied the Athanasian perspective outright, but his silence was deafening. Instead of affirming the traditional doctrine at the perfect opportunity he declined to render his opinion on "so difficult a question."[151] Beyond this we see his avid support of two men who held heterodox views; Rev. Emlin and Wm. Whiston. In his satirical *Dedication to Pope Clement XI* Hoadley described

---

[149] Ibid., xi.
[150] Benjamin Hoadly, "An Account of the Life, Writings and Character of Dr. S. Clarke" in *The Works*, Vols. I–IV (London: W. Bowyer and J. Nichols, MDCCLXXIII), Vol. III, 461–62.
[151] Ibid., 461–62.

the situation of intolerance in England. For some, it was preferable to blaspheme God rather than to denigrate the Virgin Mary. Indeed many commended bringing down the Father to the level of the Son, but to place the Son below the Father in any real degree of perfection was "an unpardonable error."[152] Hoadly was clearly sympathetic to the heterodox views held by these two men. It is not merely a sympathy derived from a sense of toleration, but a sympathy of thought. The language of "bringing down" the Father to the level of the Son, and placing the Son "below" his Father, reveals Hoadly's subordinationism. Moreover, if this were not enough, we have Whiston's remark in his memoirs of Clarke, of having written in his *Historical Preface*, after having become convinced that the early church Fathers did not hold the traditional trinitarian view, that he met with certain divines to check his conclusions. In that work, he says,

> I did not name the persons meant; but I name them now. They were Dr. Bradford, Mr. Benjamin Hoadly, Mr. Clarke and Mr. Sydal. And at their recommendation it was, that I took that great pain of transcribing the testimonies themselves at large, which I there give an account of.[153]

Hoadly was a heterodox Latitudinarian. He approved of the major agenda of the Latitudinarians and was supportive, although in a covert manner, of those who questioned the standard teaching of the Church on the trinity.

Those who were influential among these heterodox Latitudinarians were not all churchman. William Whiston succeeded Isaac Newton in the Lucasian chair at Cambridge but was eventually removed for his denial of the trinity. Unlike Hoadly, Whiston was outspoken in his views. He too embraced the heterodox Latitudinarian views and published his opinions on the teaching of the early church on the trinity under the title *An Account of the Primitive Faith Concerning the Trinity and Incarnation* in 1708. He offered a brief summary of his views in his *Defense*.

> I was once, as the world will see by the occasion of the latter *Errata* in the common opinion, that the father, Son and Holy Ghost, the three divine powers (persons) were truly in some sense one God, or the One God of the Christian Religion. That is, before I particularly examin'd

---

[152] Benjamin Hoadly, "Dedication to Pope Clement XI," in *The Works*, Vol. I, 537.

[153] William Whiston, *Historical Memoirs of the Life of Dr. Samuel Clarke* (London: Fletcher Gyles, J. Roberts, 1730), 15–16.

that matter in the scriptures, and the most primitive writers: but since I have thorough inquired into it, I am so fully satisfied that the Father alone is the one God of the Christian religion, that I must now own, that when once I deny or doubt of that doctrine, I must deny or doubt of our common Christianity: there being no one Article more plain, or more universally acknowledg'd in all of the first ages of the church than that was: . . .

3. That the Son is inferior as well as subordinate to the father.
4. That the Son was begotten or created by the father, only before the world, whatever secret eternity he had before his generation or creation.
5. Jesus Christ, the word and Son of God, is a divine being, a (or) person far inferior to his Father in nature, attributes and perfections.
6. That the Holy Ghost is inferior as well as subordinate to both the Father and Son.[154]

Another heterodox Latitudinarian who was not a clergyman, but exhibited profound influence, was the already mentioned John Locke. We have seen Locke's influence upon the epistemological developments of our period. He helped to complete the demolition of the Cartesian emphasis on innate ideas, and fostered the empirical method. Locke was also deeply influenced by Chillingworth,[155] and belonged with the Latitudinarians for several reasons. Aside from his general religious views, he also shared the Latitudinarian conception of the relationship of church and state, of natural law and revelation, and of the key phrase "true religion," which for him meant confessing Christ. Like other Latitudinarians, he was indifferent to a number of the externals of religion, like liturgical forms, and he generally followed the liberal Anglican position.[156]

Locke's ideas on the trinity are less publicized, but, for our purposes, very significant. We discovered earlier that Locke had abandoned the concept of "substance" or "essence" as a meaningless innate idea. Locke's disregard for the notion of essence alarmed Stillingfleet, who saw in this position the undermining of the doctrine of the trinity, which presupposed substance and subsistence as realities for its explanation. In his *Essay*, Locke had criticized substance as

---

[154] William Whiston, *Mr. Whiston's Defense of Himself, from the Articles Objected to Him by Dr. Pelling before the Court of Delegates, in a Cause of Heresy. To which is Prefix'd the Articles Themselves.* (London: Printed for J. Roberts, 1715), 4, 5. Extracts taken from his *An Historical Preface to Primitive Christianity Revived* and *A Reply to Dr. Allix's Remarks.*
[155] McClachlan, 75.
[156] Reventlow, 245.

> a Substratum, a supposition of we know not what support of such qualities as are capable of producing simple Ideas in us, an obscure and relative idea: That without knowing what it is, it is that which supports accidents; so that of Substance we have no idea of what it is, but only a confused, obscure one of what it does.[157]

He responded to Stillingfleet's reproach by saying,

> I must confess this, and the like, I have said of our Idea of Substance; and should be very glad to be convinced by your Lordship, or any body else, that I have spoken too meanly of it.[158]

Further Locke added, "in my whole Essay, I think there is not to be found any thing like an objection against the trinity:"[159] However, in controversy with the Bishop of Gloucester in 1698, we find that Locke had biblical reservations. Locke wrote that the Bishop had said that the scripture offered Locke a proposition to be believed concerning the trinitarian formulation of three persons in one nature, but that Locke had doubted it. Locke retorted, that his Bible must be faulty for he never remembered reading in it the precise words "there are three persons in one nature."[160]

Locke was pronounced a Socinian by the Puritan orthodox John Edwards in his *Some Thoughts Concerning the Several Causes and Occasions of Atheism,* 1695. Locke responded in his *A Vindication of the Reasonableness of Christianity*. He received support from S. Bolde and from an anonymous author who wrote *The Exceptions of Mr. Edwards in his "Causes of Atheism" against "The Reasonableness of Christianity as Delivered in the Scriptures."* Edwards retorted in *Socinianism Unmasked* and *The Socinian Creed*, that Locke's desire for a minimum confession that Jesus is the Christ was a guise for Socinianism.[161]

Locke reached his conclusions not only through biblical reflection and empirical reasoning. When the Monmouth rebellion failed and his patron, the Earl of Shaftesbury was forced into exile, Locke likewise left England. His time abroad and the circle of friends he developed were crucial in the development of his trinitarian thought. While in Holland he met the Remonstrants, particularly Philip van Limborch, professor of theology at Amsterdam (1674–1712), who

---

[157] Locke, *Essay*, 2.13.2.
[158] Locke, *The Works*, 3d ed. (London: Printed for Arthur Bettesworth etc., Paternoster Row, MDCCXXVII), Vol. I, 345.
[159] Ibid., I, 343.
[160] McClachlan, 89.
[161] Reventlow, 547, n. 146.

became his intimate friend.[162] This friendship was to prove to have a formative influence on Locke's religious opinions. We have already seen that the Remonstrants welcomed Polish Socinian refugees to their worship and sacraments after they had been driven from Poland in 1660.[163] Locke was abroad for six years (1683–89), during which time he continued working on the *Essay*. While he finalized his position on the rejection of innate ideas, including "substance" he was being exposed to the ideas of toleration found in the Remonstrants, and in their circle to Socinian views on the trinity, all of this during the most fecund period of his intellectual life. The evidence from his correspondence with the Bishop, his rejection of innate ideas, and his connections in Holland point in the direction of one who held heterodox views on the trinity. His connection with Isaac Newton, to whom we now turn, also leads to this conclusion.

We have already seen how Newton, like Locke, helped destroy the Cartesian natural philosophy. While Locke worked from its epistemological assumptions, Newton shattered its mechanics in the *Principia*. Newton constantly sought to understand the relationship of the Creator to the creation. His was not the mechanistic Deism of those who followed. Rather, Newton's theology could be summarized by the word "Dominion."[164] This understanding of how God related to the universe was worked out in Newton's central contribution regarding the universal law of gravity. Newton distinguished here between the creation of gravity and its ongoing work.

> The original creation of gravity demonstrates God's general providence but its continuous operation since that point reveals His special providence. God's sustained preservation of the order of nature and natural laws demonstrates divine special providence because of the very nature of gravitational attraction.[165]

Matter itself contained no animating principle. For Newton all of the animation of creation was provided by the immediate, active presence

---

[162] Maurice Cranston, *John Locke: A Biography* (Oxford: Oxford University Press, 1985), 233.

[163] McClachlan, 72.

[164] Edward Davis, "Newton's Rejection of the 'Newtonian World View': The Role of Divine Will in Newton's Natural Philosophy," *Fides et Historia* XXII, 2 (Summer 1990): et passim.

[165] Newton cited in James Force, "Hume and the Relation of Science to Religion Among Certain Members of the Royal Society," *Journal of the History of Ideas* 45 No. 4 (1984): 523.

of the Creator. He reflected the Calvinist distinction[166] between
general and special providence noted above, and applied it to the
whole arena of creation. As Newton wrestled with the explanation of
gravity, he came to see not only gravity, but all of the general forces
of nature as a manifestation of God's active presence in the world.
Although he hesitated to ascribe gravity directly to God's activity
publicly, privately he held the view that God caused gravitational
attraction by his omnipresent activity which could be traced according to the principles Newton had established, which he called "active
principles" or "laws of motion." Working according to these principles, God brought dead matter to life.[167]

In attempting to examine Newton's theological opinions, we encounter something of a dilemma. Newton wrote over one million
words on theological subjects, but the vast majority remain unpublished.[168] Like so many great thinkers, he had more than one intellectual passion. Theology was one of his abiding intellectual pursuits
from the time he turned to it seriously in the early 1670's, when he
was about thirty, until his death fifty-five years later.[169]

Newton was highly regarded in his time as a learned critic of
scripture,[170] particularly in the area of prophecy in which he developed an expertise. Like Bishop Ussher and others, he was fascinated
by Old Testament chronology. Twenty-seven percent of his library

---

[166] Calvin, *Institutes*, I, XVI, 1.
[167] Deason, "The Protestant Reformation and the Rise of Modern Science," 239.
[168] Frank Manuel, *The Religion of Isaac Newton*, 8–10. The bulk of Newton's non-
scientific manuscripts were sold at an auction by Sotheby's in 1936. The Portsmouth collection was divided into three main groups: the Yahuda collection is in
the Jewish National and University Library in Jerusalem, the Keynes collection is in
the King's College Library, Cambridge Univ., and the Babson Collection, formerly
held at Babson College, but now held by the Dibner Institute of M.I.T. (Reventlow,
589, n. 4, cf., Christianson, 251). Several of the more important documents for
determining Newton's trinitarian views include: "Argumenta and Twelve Points on
Arian Christology"—some extracts to be found in L.T. More, *Isaac Newton*, 642, and
Richard Westfall, *Never at Rest*, 315–16. Published works on the subject include: Isaac
Newton, *Two Letters of Isaac Newton to Mr. LeClerc* (London: Printed for J. Payne,
MDCCLIV; more easily found in Isaac Newton, *The Correspondence of Isaac Newton*,
ed. by Alfred R. Hall and Laura Tilling. (Cambridge: Cambridge U. Press for the
Royal Society of London, 1976), III, 83–144 as "An Historical Account of Two
Notable Corruptions."
[169] Westfall, "Isaac Newton's *Theologiae Gentilis Origines Philosophicae* in *The Secular
Mind: Transformations of Faith in Modern Europe*," ed. W. Wagar (New York: Holmes
and Meier, 1982), 16.
[170] John D. North, *Isaac Newton*, in the Clarendon Biography Series No. 12 (London: Oxford U. Press, 1967), 58.

were titles in Bible and Theology.[171] His niece's husband, Conduitt, stated in his intended life of Newton, that Archbishop Tenison had offered the Mastership of Trinity College to Newton at the time it was given to Montague, and encouraged Newton to take a preferment in the Church, saying, "Why will you not? You know more divinity than all of us put together."[172]

Like other Latitudinarians, Newton had roots in Cambridge Platonism's interest in nature. While rejecting Platonism's metaphysical grounding in innate ideas, Newton nevertheless followed in the Cambridge tradition in seeking a common foundation for natural philosophy and revelation. For Newton, as for the Platonists, and especially Henry More, who influenced him deeply, if one were to know the Creator, one must study his workmanship in the original ordering of matter and the laws which govern its composition and motion.[173]

Newton's relationship to Deism has been debated. Westfall concludes, based on Newton's *Theologiae Gentilis Origines Philosophicae*, that Newton was a Deist. Newton asserted in this work that the necessary truths of religion were known in the times of Noah, and that Christianity offered merely a restitution of these, and not something new.[174] Westfall finds a number of points of comparison between Newton and the Deists.

> It is instructive to compare Newton with deists like Toland and Tindal. He shared their hatred of superstition and mystery and their conviction that evil men had introduced false doctrines into religion to promote their selfish interests. He shared their concept of an immutable God who would not conceal necessary truths through thousands of years in order arbitrarily reveal them later to a small minority of mankind. Newton's religion of Noah was identical to Tindal's Christianity as Old as the Creation.[175]

While Westfall's position is attractive for these reasons, it is an inaccurate perception of Newton. Force convincingly argues against Westfall's conclusions in writing, concerning the Deist rejection of Scripture,

---

[171] John Harrison, *The Library of Isaac Newton* (Cambridge: Cambridge U. Press, 1978), 59.

[172] L.T. More, *Isaac Newton*, 608.

[173] Gale Christianson, *In the Presence*, 248. For the influence of Henry More on Newton see Derek Gjertsen, *The Newton Handbook*, 369.

[174] Richard Westfall, "Isaac Newton's *Theologiae Gentilis Origines Philosophicae*," 30.

[175] Ibid., 29.

And this negative deism is in no way shared by Newton who, in the fashion later made public by Whiston, utilizes the books of nature, scripture, and pagan antiquity to get to the truth about God. It is the case that the scriptures become one source among three for comparison. One might argue that his method may possibly make Newton's theology heterodox. But, precisely because the scriptures, especially the prophecies, retain a role in Newton's theology, Newton is no deist.[176]

Albeit Newton did see the mission of Christ primarily as recalling people to the religion of Noah, Christ's role here was indispensable, and this also separated Newton from the Deists. The conception of Christ's mission as one of restoration, was consistent with heterodox Christian theism, although inconsistent with the classical Christian emphasis on soteriology. However, this emphasis on restoration was even more inconsistent with the "scoffing dismissal of the 'fables of Jesus Christ' by the deistic natural theologians."[177] Nor can Newton be called, in the strict sense like the Deists, a religious rationalist. He believed that while true religion was indeed reasonable, that it was "contrary to God's purposes that the truth of his religion should be as obvious and perspicuous to all men as a mathematical demonstration."[178] Newton belongs with those of Latitudinarian sympathy for several reasons. First, like them, he believed in toleration, and in seeking a common ground upon which all Christians could agree. He wrote,

The fundamental requisites to communion in the Church of England [are] . . .
To renounce the Devil and all his works . . . and the carnall desires of the flesh.
To confess the faith conteined in the . . . Apostles Creed. And the profession of faith in the primitive church the Apostle [Paul] calls faith toward God and the resurrection of the dead and eternall judgment.
To keep God's commandments; that is the ten commandments as is explained in the church catechism. These and baptism and laying on of hands are all the fundamentals requisite to communion in the Church of England.[179]

---

[176] James E. Force, "The Newtonians and Deism," in *Essays on the Context, Nature, and Influence of Isaac Newton's Theology* (Dordrecht: Kluwer Academic Publishers, 1990), 43–76. Force argues in this article that the Newtonians: Whiston, Clarke and Newton offer a "third way" between the Deists and Orthodox.
[177] Ibid., 69.
[178] Davis, 10; cited from Yahuda MS. 1, folio 19r.
[179] Keynes MS. 3, p. 14, in Christianson, 254.

We have seen this tendency to seek a common Christian denominator in Locke and Taylor. It is worth noting how much more biblical and historical is Newton's approach to the common ground than Herbert's or Blount's.

Like other Latitudinarians, as an inheritance from the Cambridge Platonists, Newton was known for his high moral standards. He lived a celibate and strict moral life.[180] He was also dedicated to critical reason as contrasted with speculative reason. His denouncement of hypothesis in the "General Scholium" of his *Principia* carried over into his theological work where he eschewed anything that was not directly evident from scripture. In this regard he was suspicious of "mystery" as a rationale for faith, and could not abide it when contrary to reason,[181] but was not as radical in this regard as Toland. Newton's views on the trinity will be treated in detail in Chapter Four, where the question of whether they provided one of the sources of Clarke's thought will be considered. Here it must simply be noted that Newton belongs among the heterodox Latitudinarians for the reasons mentioned above.

In summary then, we have seen in this chapter that in the late seventeenth and early eighteenth centuries there was a shift from external to internal sources of authority; from revelation and tradition, to reason. We have proposed that this shift was facilitated by the rise of modern science and the legacy of the Protestant Reformation. In the shift away from innate ideas to empirical means of verification we have seen the insistence of the modern age upon evidence, an insistence ignited by Francis Bacon. Although Empiricism ultimately triumphed over Cartesian Rationalism, we find the indelible imprint of Descartes' radical doubt assumed into the methodology of the age. Both this empiricism and this methodological doubt combined to offer an epistemological foundation upon which venerated truths could be not only questioned, but denied.

Alongside the shift in science was the legacy of the Reformation which provided a theological foundation for the challenge to Church authority in which the individual's capacity for understanding the faith was brought to the fore. The Reformation also bequeathed a turbulent political history which led to a disenchantment with dogma and a desire for religious toleration. This desire to move away from

---

[180] Ibid, 258.
[181] Ibid., 261–62.

the dogmatic divergences was reflected in the search for a religion with a common denominator in human reason. These factors combined to produce a theological spectrum of Rational religion which included the Deists, Cambridge Platonists and Lord Falkland's circle at Great Tew, and the Latitudinarians: orthodox and heterodox, who descended from them. Each coped with the essential problem of the relationship between faith and reason; revelation and natural law, in their own way. This is the world of thought in which Samuel Clarke lived and wrote, and it is within this intellectual matrix that his work must be understood. Our task now is to examine Clarke's thought within the context of this intellectual milieu.

CHAPTER TWO

CLARKE WITHIN HIS CONTEXT

Having outlined Clarke's intellectual context in chapter one, the task of situating him among his peers in the school of English rational religion can now be undertaken. The things will be done. First, I will compare and contrast Clarke's thought with that of other exponents of English rational religion. Second, I will examine the impact of Newtonian natural philosophy on Clarke's epistemology and his understanding of the Godhead. Finally, I will locate Clarke's position among his peers.

Clarke among the English Rationalists

In the previous chapter, we encountered a spectrum of English rational religion which contained three basic groups: Deists, Cambridge Platonists and the circle at Great Tew, and the Latitudinarians; orthodox and heterodox, who descended primarily from these last two. Among the first group were figures like Herbert, Blount, Toland, Collins and Tindal. Among the Cambridge Platonists and Great Tew circle were Whichcote, Cudworth, More and Chillingworth. Two branches developed from the Platonists and Great Tew in the thinking of the orthodox and heterodox Latitudinarians. The orthodox group included Sherlock, Stillingfleet and Taylor. Locke, Hoadly, Whiston and Newton were among those Latitudinarians who reached heterodox conclusions. Five topics of concern emerged from the total spectrum of these thinkers, and it is Clarke's treatment of these foci which enables us to locate him on the spectrum. The five foci were:

1. The relationship of revelation and natural religion, or faith and reason.
2. The importance of moral virtue in religion.
3. Religious toleration.
4. Suspicion of the use of "mystery" in validating doctrinal formulation.
5. The role of the Christian tradition in doctrinal formulation.

Faith and Reason

Seeking the point of integration for the concepts of faith and reason
was a central theological preoccupation of Clarke's period. The issue
was posed in the most radical terms by the Deistic controversy. As
we have seen, the Deists established the poles of natural and revealed religion. They were supporters of a radical establishment of
natural religion only. Others, like the English mystic William Law,
favored revealed religion as the only sure guide to God. In between,
were a variety of positions which attempted to synthesize the two
epistemologies. Here the Latitudinarians, including Clarke, were
found.[1]

In Clarke's second course of Boyle Lectures, the *Discourse Concerning the Unchangeable Obligations of Natural Religion and the Truth and Certainty of the Christian Revelation*, he outlined four types of Deists. The
first were those who believe in the existence of a God, whom, having made the world, was not concerned with its governance. The
second type were those who believe in God *and* God's providence in
natural things, but that God made no moral distinctions. The third
were those who believed that God existed, and who had a right
understanding of God's nature and attributes. They believed that God
was also providential and had moral perfection, but they believed
persons perish at death, because they did not believe in the immortality of the soul. The fourth type believed in God, had a right
understanding of God's nature and attributes, knew God's providence,
that God possessed moral perfection and they believed in an after-
life. But all of this was known by the light of nature *only*—not by
revelation. For Clarke, this last group were the only Deists worth
answering.[2]

Clarke asserted that the natural religion of Deism had been eclipsed
by the gospel. It was not that natural religion was defective in and
of itself, but rather by its extent, i.e., it needed the completion of
divine revelation.

> The sum is this. There is now no such thing, as a consistent state of
> Deism. That which alone was once such, namely the scheme of the
> best Heathen Philosophers; ceases now to be so, after the appearance
> of revelation: Because (as I have already shown, and shall more largely

---

[1] James Force, "The Newtonians and Deism," 46.
[2] Clarke, *A Discourse Concerning the Unchangeable Obligations of Natural Religion and the
Truth and Certainty of the Christian Revelation* in *Works*, II, 600–01.

prove in the sequel of this discourse,) it directly conducts men to the belief of Christianity.[3]

Here Clarke opposed the teaching of the Deists to that of the ancient philosophers. The Deists thought that the light of nature alone was sufficient. Yet even the ancients understood that they lacked a clear communication from God, and anticipated it with eagerness.

> The philosophers themselves, the best and wisest, and the least superstitious of them, that ever lived; were not ashamed to confess openly, their sense of the want of a divine revelation; and to declare their judgment, that it was most natural and truly agreeable to right and sound reason, to hope for something of that nature.[4]

The light of nature alone was no longer sufficient to pierce the darkness of the human mind. Clarke took the effects of sin as more damaging than did his Deistic opponents. Human society lacked a divine revelation which it needed to overcome corruption and degeneracy. Without this kind of assistance, the necessary reform of humankind would have been impossible. Natural religion alone was insufficient to the task. Human beings stood in need of the specific teaching and instruction available only in scripture.[5]

For Clarke, revelation was not merely reason made clear. It provided additional information concerning salvation which was essential for human beings. Through revelation we discovered how God was to be worshiped and the kind of expiation God would accept for sin. In addition, revelation communicated the assurance of the future state of rewards and punishments beyond death. Finally, Clarke asserted that revelation was necessary to provide the "extraordinary assistances" which enabled us to overcome our corrupted natures.[6]

Not only did Clarke challenge the Deistic assertion that revelation was superfluous, but he specifically refuted the assertion by Blount in his *Oracles of Reason* that since revelation was not universal, it could

---

[3] Ibid., 607.
[4] Ibid., 668. Clarke cites [pseudo] Plato, *Alcibiades*, 2. It should be noted that the are two Alcibiades. Some have suggested the first was probably an immediate follower of Plato, while W.R.M. Lamb in his introduction to the first Alcibiades in the *Loeb* series believes it was written by Plato himself and was one of his earliest sketches. (Loeb, *Plato, Vol. 8, 97*). The second Alcibiades is late, probably from the third or second centuries B.C. and therefore not by Plato. It is from the second *Alcibiades* that Clarke is quoting. For the text see *Loeb* Series, *Plato*, Vol. 8, 271.
[5] Ibid., 666–67.
[6] Ibid., 667.

not be necessary. In fact, Clarke argued, natural religion faced the same dilemma since it was not universally acknowledged either. Not all persons had the same natural capacity to comprehend the truth of the natural religion, and therefore it was not available to all. This being the case, Clarke asserted that his opponents must assume that since those ignorant of the natural religion were quite able to cope with the basic exigencies of life, through the simple inclinations of the senses, and since some were not endowed with the intellectual faculties capable of perceiving the moral imperatives of the natural religion, that those imperatives must not be necessary. For Clarke, the logical conclusion of the Deist's reasonings was nothing less than atheism.[7]

While revelation was an essential addition to reason, it could in no way be contradictory to it. In Clarke's thought the congruity of reason and revelation was the foundation of rational religion.

> If these things be the ordinances of One, who came to contradict the dictates of right reason, and not to perfect the law of nature, but to destroy it; then let all wise men forsake the assemblies of Christians, and profess themselves again disciples of the philosophers. But if these things be perfectly agreeable to nature and right reason, and tend exceedingly to the supplying the deficiencies thereof; then let none under pretense of maintaining natural religion, revile and blaspheme the Christian; least they be found liars unto God.[8]

This rational conviction underlaid Clarke's rejection of the classical interpretation of the doctrine of the trinity formulated at Nicaea. Not only did he maintain that the doctrine was unbiblical and unsupported by the primitive church, but it was inherently illogical. In speaking concerning the substance of God in the first course of Boyle Lectures in 1704, Clarke wrote,

> Nevertheless, 'tis very necessary to observe here by the way, that it does not at all from hence follow, that there can possibly be in the unknown substance or essence of God, any thing contrary to our clear ideas. For as a blind-man, though he has no idea of light and colours, yet knows certainly and infallibly that there cannot possibly be any kind of light which is not light, nor any kind of colour which is not a colour.[9]

---

[7] Clarke, *Discourse* in *Works*, II, 672.

[8] Ibid., 679.

[9] Clarke, *A Demonstration of the Being and Attributes of God. More Particularly in Answer to Mr. Hobbes, Spinoza, and their Followers.* In *Works*, II, 538.

While Clarke did not believe that natural religion was sufficient without revelation, he did recognize its importance and authority. Clarke agreed with the five *notitae* of Cherbury[10] and with the two added by Blount.[11] He disagreed, however, that these could be known "without revelation or positive law."[12] Nevertheless, the natural law had a positive role to play. Revelation was not made over and against natural law, but intended to clarify and supplement it. In fact, for Clarke, the natural law was ultimately rooted in the nature of God.

> This is the law of nature, which (as Cicero excellently expresses it) 'tis of universal extent, and everlasting duration; which can neither be wholly abrogated, nor repealed in any part of it, nor have any law made contrary to it, nor be dispensed with by any authority . . . but its obligation was from eternity, and the force of it reaches throughout the universe which being, founded in the nature and reason of things, did not begin to be a law, when it was first written and enacted by men; but is of the same original with the eternal reasons or proportions of things, and the perfections and attributes of God himself.[13]

Moreover, we see that for Clarke, God's will is constrained by God's attributes to act in accordance with the natural law. The divine will must always and necessarily determine itself to do the best thing, to act according to the "eternal rules of infinite goodness, justice and truth."[14] The goodness and rightness of natural religion were not derived from the will or commandment of God, but from God's nature, and as such were prior to the positive law.

> Further yet: As this law of nature is infinitely superior to all authority of men, and independent upon it; so its obligation, primarily and

---

[10] Herbert, *De Veritate*, 291–303.
[11] Blount, *The Oracles of Reason*, 195–96.
[12] Ibid., 195–96.
[13] Clarke, *Discourse*, in *Works*, II, 625.
[14] Ibid., 612. Clarke's evidence upon the "constraint" of God by the "laws" of nature was in keeping with the pervasive influence in the seventeenth century of the late medieval distinction between God's *potentia absoluta* and God's *potentia ordinata*. Just as God had bound himself to save humankind through his covenant (*pactum*, *foedus*), so he had "bound" himself in the ordering of the universe to operate within certain regular patterns (laws of nature). While it was certainly possible for God to abandon these laws *potentia absoluta*, in fact he did not. By this understanding of God's power, God was understood to be both perfectly free, and perfectly dependable. This distinction within the powers of God served as the assumptive basis for the work not only of Clarke, but of Bacon, Descartes, Boyle, Newton, and Leibniz. See Oakley, *Omnipotence, Covenant, & Order: An Excursion in the History of Ideas from Abelard to Leibniz* (Ithaca and London: Cornell Univ. Press, 1984), 83–85.

originally is antecedent also even to this consideration, of its being the positive will or command of God himself.[15]

Clarke's positive regard for the role of reason and the natural law, was part of the legacy of the Cambridge Platonists, and of seventeenth-century rational theology in general.[16] These attitudes were shared by his both his Latitudinarian contemporaries and the Deists, and were constituent parts of the rational religion of the late seventeenth and early eighteenth centuries. Where Clarke separated himself from the Deists was in the respective weight he placed upon natural religion and revelation. In the tradition of many orthodox Reformed thinkers and of Cambridge Platonists like Whichcote, he attempted to coordinate the "two lights" rather than supplant revelation with natural religion.[17] Clarke clearly belongs with the Latitudinarians in his treatment of the relationship between natural and revealed religion. On this issue there was no appreciable distinction between the orthodox and heterodox Latitudinarians.

The Importance of Moral Virtue in Religion

As Clarke had been influenced by the emphasis on reason found in the Cambridge Platonists and Falkland's circle at Great Tew, he was likewise influenced by their emphasis on moral virtue. Here we see the practical importance of the addition of revelation to natural religion reflected in his *Discourse*. As a result of revelation we could know the positive will of God which directed the actions of human beings. In this sense also, revelation "perfected" natural religion by gathering persons together as a worshiping community. As a result of this revelation, individuals were united into a civil as well as religious community where they were able, under the divine revelation, to offer mutual assistance and improvement. Likewise it was God's revelation which provided for the ordained offices which instructed the unlearned in God's ways, and warned them of the danger of abandoning the divine precepts.[18]

In fact, for Clarke, moral virtue was at the heart of both natural and revealed religion, and was the purpose for which both were given.

---

[15] Clarke, *Discourse* in *Works*, II, 626.
[16] Willey, *Seventeenth Century*, 119–169; Tulloch, et passim; Muller, *PRRD*, Vol. 1, 243–49.
[17] Muller, *PRRD*, Vol. 1, 191.
[18] Clarke, *Discourse* in *Works*, II, 679.

I have been the longer upon this head, because moral virtue is the foundation and the sum, the essence and the life of all true religion: for the security whereof, all positive institution was principally designed: For the restoration whereof, all revealed religion was ultimately intended.[19]

Clarke's intellectualist theology is further revealed in his belief that, like reason, moral virtue was rooted in the nature of God and was therefore antecedent to God's will. Since God was inherently moral, all of God's commandments were expressions of God's moral nature, both clarifying that nature and bringing the creation into conformity with it. While these eternal moral obligations were incumbant upon all rational creatures, even prior to their being the will of God, the fact that they derived both from the perfections of God, as well as his will, and also from the nature of things, pointed to the fact that from every direction, moral goodness was required of all God's rational creatures.

> That is: As these eternal moral obligations are really in perpetual force, merely from their own nature, and the abstract reason of things; so also they are moreover the express and unalterable will, command, and law of God to his creatures, which he cannot but expect should, in obedience to his supreme authority, as well as in compliance with the natural reason of things, be regularly and constantly observed through the whole creation.[20]

Clarke, like the Cambridge Platonists before him, grappled with the moral nature of the universe in an attempt to counter the materialism of Hobbes. In the *Discourse* he refuted Hobbes' thesis that

> there is no such thing as just and unjust, right and wrong originally in the nature of things; that men in their natural state, antecedent to all compacts, are not obliged to universal benevolence, nor to any moral duty whatsoever; but are in a state of war, and have every one a right to do what ever he has power to do; (and that), in civil societies, it depends wholly upon positive laws or the will of governors, to define what shall be just or unjust.[21]

---

[19] Ibid., 637.
[20] Ibid., 637.
[21] Ibid., 631. Clarke cites from both *De Cive* (1642) and the expanded English version, *Leviathan* (1651). The pertinent material can be found in Thomas Hobbes, *Leviathan* ed. Osker Piest with intro. by Herbert W. Schneider. (Indianapolis & N.Y.: Bobbs-Merrill, 1958), Chpts. 13–15.

Clarke marshalled five arguments against Hobbes.[22] His first argument was in response to Hobbes' assertion that every individual had a right to everything, which set persons in a state of natural conflict; a "state of war." Clarke responded that such a notion was illogical by claiming two legitimate rights to the same thing. Instead, Clarke argued, an individual had a right to a *proportion* of the whole of those things which were necessary and useful to life. Clarke's second argument responded to Hobbes' claim that a person had the absolute right to self-preservation according to any and all devices available. Clarke responded by asking what could be more absurd than a war of all against all for the preservation of all? His third argument was that Hobbes did in fact operate with certain *a priori* assumptions of natural law. In the state of nature, Hobbes had argued, individuals had an inherent responsibility to seek peace and get out of the state of war. Clarke asked from where these responsibilities came, if not from an eternal natural law?[23] Clarke's fourth argument was simply that Hobbes had mistaken the state of nature for the fallen state. Finally, Clarke argued against Hobbes' idea that persons must obey God only because of God's power and dominion, and not because of the perfection of God's attributes made manifest in the law. Clarke asked whether we would be obligated to obey the devil if he had total dominion and power.

Underlying Hobbes's thesis and Clarke's arguments was the basic question of who held the proper understanding of the "state of nature." For Hobbes the state of nature was a state of war, and all moral law was a secondary device meant to govern that war. There was no eternal natural law. The binding power of moral legislation was not to be found in an eternal moral order, which was a reflection of God's nature and will, but in compacts made among societies and their members. For Clarke, the state of nature was a perfect expression of the attributes of God. It was an eternal ordering of goodness, justice, beauty etc., and as such was subsequently expressed in the divine commandments, the purpose of which was to restore conformity between the eternal moral order and the human society.

The importance of moral virtue to Clarke is clear. This was an

---

[22] Clarke, *Discourse* in *Works*, II, 631–37.

[23] Hobbes seems to admit this directly in chapter 15 where he writes, "The laws of nature are *immutable and eternal*, for injustice, ingratitude, arrogance, pride, iniquity, acception of persons, and the rest can never be made lawful. For it can never be that war shall preserve life and peace destroy it." (*Leviathan* 131, my emphasis).

emphasis the Latitudinarians inherited from the Cambridge Platonists. Henry More had published his *Enchiridion Ethicum* in 1667 as
an alternative to Hobbes' system.[24] Likewise, Ralph Cudworth's *A
Treatise Concerning Eternal and Immutable Morality* was viewed by its pub-
lisher, Dr. Edward Chandler, Bishop of Durham, to be a repudiation of Hobbes and others.[25] Regarding the real existence of moral
virtue as Ideals, Cudworth wrote that morals could not possibly be
arbitrary things, brought into existence by will without a foundation
in nature, because things are what they are in and of themselves,
not merely by what they were said to be.[26]

Commenting on Cudworth's position, Cragg locates him in the
historical debate. His comments on Cudworth are equally applicable
to Clarke's perspective on morals.

> He confronted two views of the nature of good and evil, both of which
> he was convinced were wrong. It was contended, on the one hand,
> that moral distinctions were determined by the will of God. This view
> was propounded by Duns Scotus and Ockham. It was held, in charac-
> teristic form and with characteristic force, by Calvin. In the seven-
> teenth century, its principal representative was Descartes: God, he said,
> could make a cube a sphere if he so desired, and he could make the
> right to be wrong, just as he had actually determined it to be the
> right. On the other hand, Hobbes declared that good and evil were
> fixed by the will of sovereigns, and that ethics accordingly became a
> branch of politics. Against both of these views Cudworth upheld the
> "essential and eternal distinctions of good and evil." According to his
> belief, the difference between right and wrong had an objective reality,
> and reason could grasp that difference as effectively as it did the rela-
> tions of space or number. Man might be dependent on God for his
> knowledge of these distinctions, but it was divine reason, not the di-
> vine will, to which man owed his awareness of ethical truths. As
> Cudworth said in his sermon at Lincoln's Inn, "Virtue and holiness in
> creatures . . . are not therefore good because God loveth them and will
> have them to be accounted such; but rather God loveth them because
> they are in themselves good."[27]

---

[24] The *Enchiridion Ethicum* had reached four editions by 1711. An English translation appeared in 1690 entitled, *An Account of Virtue: Or, Dr. Henry More's Abridgment of
Morals, Put into English*. Edward Southwell was the translator. It was reproduced in
1930 by the Facsimile Text Society of New York. See Cragg, ed., *The Cambridge
Platonists*, 262, n. 1. See p. 261 on More's system as a response to Hobbes.

[25] Preface to *A Treatise Concerning Eternal and Immutable Morality* in Ralph Cudworth,
The True Intellectual System of the Universe. Vol. 2, 365.

[26] Ibid., 373.

[27] Cragg, *Platonists*, 270–271.

It is clear that Clarke took his lead from the Platonists, in resisting Hobbes' separation of morality from the eternal ordering of nature. Likewise, Clarke followed the Cambridge tradition, which, on this point, had roots in Thomism and in many of the Reformed thinkers of the seventeenth century, in his intellectualist locating of eternal moral truth prior to divine willing.[28] Here Cudworth was more explicit than Clarke, specifically locating the origin of the moral order in the wisdom of the mind of God.[29]

At the other extreme, Clarke took pains in the *Discourse* to separate himself from the Deists on the issue of moral virtue. His first argument was that the Deists refused to admit their indebtedness to Christian revelation for their moral teaching. Deism had its moral reasoning clarified by the Bible. The same was true for its understanding of the future state of rewards and punishments.[30] Secondly, while acknowledging their appeals to morality, he accused them of being insincere.

> The truth, at the bottom, is plainly this. All the great things that modern Deists affect to say of right reason, as to its sufficiency in discovering the obligations and motives of morality; is only a pretence, to be made use of, when they are opposing Christianity. At other times, and in reality, they have no hearty regard for morality, nor for the natural evidences of the certainty of a future state. They are willing enough to believe, that men perish absolutely at death; and so they have no concern to support effectually the cause of virtue, nor care to make out any consistent scheme of things; but unavoidably recur, in truth, to downright Atheism. At least, in the manners of most of them, 'tis too plain and apparent, that absolute Libertinism is the thing they really aim at; And however their creed may pretend to be the creed of Deists, yet almost always their practice is the practice of very Atheists.[31]

Clarke, like the other Latitudinarians, followed the Platonist emphasis on moral virtue and located that virtue in the archetype of the divine mind. Meanwhile, he distinguished himself from the Deists. It becomes apparent then, based upon the importance Clarke gave to moral virtue, that he clearly belongs with the Latitudinarians. They were in agreement on the centrality of this issue, whether orthodox

---

[28] On the Latitudinarian's use of reason see Cragg, *Puritanism*, 65–70. On their relationship to the Cambridge Platonists, ibid., 62–65.
[29] Cudworth, Vol. 2, 382.
[30] Clarke, *Discourse* in *Works*, II, 670.
[31] Ibid., 671.

or heterodox. Likewise, they were in agreement regarding the need for religious toleration.

Toleration

In 1662 a pamphlet appeared in London entitled "A Brief Account of the New Sect of Latitudemen." The author was a certain "S.P."[32] This pamphlet praised the new school of thinking at Cambridge, led by Whichcote, More and Cudworth. With that title, the author pointed to one of the distinguishing features of these thinkers; they believed in religious toleration. Essentially they tried to maintain the middle ground between the positions of Calvin and Laud.[33] Greene has defined the Latitudinarians as

> those Anglican divines who, before 1662, tried to mediate between the Puritan and High Church wings of the Church of England and, after 1662, to bring about the reunion of the Protestant Nonconformists with the church by the (unsuccessful) attempts at comprehension in the 1670s and 1689; who supported the concessions made to the Nonconformists in the Toleration Act, 1689, and later resisted attempts such as those in the Occasional Conformity Act, 1711, and the Schism Act, 1714, to withdraw or restrict those concessions and, still later, supported the repeal, in 1719, of those two acts and efforts to repeal the Test and Corporation Acts.[34]

The historical events which gave rise to Latitudinarianism have been outlined in Chapter One. The central consequence of these events was the search for a Christianity of the lowest common denominator which could serve as a standard for mutual toleration. The consensus among the Latitudinarians was that the fundamental doctrines of scripture expressed in the baptismal vows and represented by the Apostle's Creed were sufficient for membership in the church. In ascertaining the "determinate sense" of those articles of faith found in the Creed, Clarke wrote,

> They are expressed as clearly in the sermons of Christ and in the writings of his apostles, as the Spirit of God thought fit they should be exprest; and the wisdom of man cannot express them more clearly.[35]

---

[32] Simon Patrick ("S.P."), "A Brief Account of the New Sect of Latitudemen (London: 1662), reprinted in *The Phenix*, [sic] v. 2 (1708), 499–518.

[33] Cragg, The *Church and the Age of Reason*, 70.

[34] Donald Greene, "Latitudinarianism and Sensibility," 177.

[35] Clarke, "A Letter to the Rev. Dr. Wells" in *Works*, IV, 244.

The search for a foundation for toleration was exemplified by Stillingfleet's *Irenicum* (1659) and Jeremy Taylor's, *Discourse*. In the same
way, John Hales in his tract on "Schism" had differentiated between
schismatics and heretics in an attempt to promote toleration.[36] In
Clarke's Introduction to his *Scripture-Doctrine of the Trinity* he cited not
only Hales, but aligned himself with the other Latitudinarians in his
support for toleration. He quoted from Stillingfleet's *Irenicum* that the
main source of divisions in the Christian community was the adding
of other conditions of Church communion than Christ himself taught.[37]
He cited Dr. Claget in the same regard. Claget had argued that the
Apostle's Creed had been the sufficient measure of faith by the early
church for those seeking baptism.[38] When accused of being a Latitudinarian by Dr. Wells, Clarke responded,

> Thus Mr. Chillingworth, and Archbishop Tillotson, and some others of
> the ablest and best men that the Protestant and Christian cause was ever
> defended by; when they could not be answered, were called Latitudi-
> narians; only to raise an odium against them among the ignorant people,
> who cannot easily distinguish between hard words and hard arguments
> and are too apt to be prejudiced with hard words whose meaning they
> understand not. I am very sure, that these Latitudinarians, whom both
> you and I have upon this occasion mentioned by name, are men that
> sincerely endeavoured to follow the doctrine of Christ and his Apostles:
> And though you now seemed shamed to be joined with such com-
> pany, yet God grant I may be found with them at the Great Day.[39]

Thus we see Clarke not only making use of the Latitudinarian doctrine of toleration at the outset of his own work, but clearly, even
emphatically, identifying himself with that group. He was at home
with them not only in his understanding of the relationship of reason
and revelation and in regard to the centrality of moral virtue in
religion, but also in his desire for religious toleration.

Suspicion of "Mystery" in Doctrinal Formulation

The Protestants in general, and the rational religionists in particular,
expressed suspicion when the term "mystery" was given as an expla-

[36] John Hales of Eton, tract on "Schism" in *The Golden Remains of the Evermemorable
Mr. John Hales of Eton College*, in Tulloch, Vol. I, 244.
[37] Clarke, *SD* in *Works*, IV, Intro., vi, citing Stillingfleet, Pref. to *Irenicum*.
[38] Ibid., citing Dr. Wm. Claget *Discourse of Church Unity*.
[39] Clarke, "Letter to the Reverend Dr. Wells" in *Works*, IV, 244.

nation for any given doctrine. This was a response to the Roman Catholic appeal to mystery as the ultimate defense of its doctrine of transubstantiation.

However, the rational religionists were not of one mind regarding mystery. The Deists, following the lead of John Toland's *Christianity Not Mysterious*, eschewed the idea that Christianity contained any mystery whatsoever. Toland argued that Christianity was the definitive revelation of all that may have previously been mysterious to the human community. It laid open for all to see the wonders and works of God.[40] The Latitudinarians, on the other hand, were not united on this issue. The orthodox Latitudinarians, like Stillingfleet and Sherlock, tended to accept mystery as a valid explanation for certain theological doctrines which, they believed, were beyond the grasp of reason, for instance the doctrine of the trinity. There continued to be things which, while not contrary to reason, were above it. In this sense they approximated the formula of the scholastics Albert Magnus and Thomas Aquinas. Here the orthodox Latitudinarians followed the Cambridge Platonists, and virtually all Reformed thinkers of the age in general.[41]

Unlike the Deists, Clarke believed that there could be certain truths of scripture validly termed "mysterious." Where he differed from the orthodox Latitudinarians was in his identification of those truths. He did not place the doctrine of the trinity among them. On the contrary, Clarke believed that the trinitarian difficulties were not the result of scripture, but the metaphysical speculations of the human mind. Speaking of the doctrine of the trinity Clarke wrote,

> There are others who have thought that we ought not at all to treat concerning any of these matters, because they are mysterious. By which if they meant, that so far as the words of God are mysterious, we ought to acquiesce in them implicitly, and not presume to be wise beyond what is written; no man could say that herein they judged amiss. But if they mean that the words of men [Humanity, divinity, human nature, divine nature; being nothing but abstract terms or notions-footnote] are mysterious; and that we must not reason concerning them, nor enquire whether or no, and in what sense, they are agreeable to the words of God: What is this but substituting another mystery in the stead of the true one; and paying deference to the mystery of man's making, instead of the mystery of God?"[42]

---

[40] Toland, 46ff.
[41] Muller, *PRRD*, Vol. 1, 235–36, 243–49.
[42] Clarke, *SD*, Intro., xiii.

On the understanding of the role of mystery, then, we see a difference of opinion among Latitudinarians. While united in their views
on the relationship between revealed and natural religion, the importance of moral virtue in religion, and the necessity for toleration, on
this issue the orthodox among them stayed in line with their Cambridge heritage, and the heterodox, like Clarke, while affirming the
Cambridge position in principle, denied its relevance to the trinitarian
doctrine. This fissure and one other; their disagreement about the
authority about the Church's tradition, ultimately led the two groups
to different conclusions regarding the trinity.

The Role of the Christian Tradition in Doctrinal Formulation

For the Deists, the question of the role of the Christian tradition in
doctrinal formulation was a non-issue. Their proposal was that the
religion of nature be the normative paradigm for human faith and
practice. Indeed, it had been doctrinal formulae based on claims to
revelation which had helped cause the obscurity of the natural religion in the first place. Their religious doctrine was found not in
revelation and/or the history of the Church, but in the experience
of human reason. Cherbury's five points in his *De Veritate*, which were
enlarged to seven in Blount's *Oracles of Reason*, are illustrative of their
approach.[43] This leaves us to consider any differences on this point
among the Latitudinarians.

The issue of the role of the tradition regarding doctrinal decisions
in the Church was an emotional one for Protestants. In their rejection of Catholicism they rejected the idea that the Church was the
primary arbiter of doctrine. This position was stated most memora-
bly in England by the erstwhile Catholic and formative mind of the
circle at Great Tew, Wm. Chillingworth.

> By the religion of Protestants I do not understand the doctrine of Luther,
> or Calvin, or Melancthon; nor the Confession of Augusta, or Geneva;
> nor the Catechism of Heidelberg; nor the Articles of the Church of
> England; no, nor the Harmony of Protestant Confessions; but that
> wherein they all agree, and which they all subscribe with a greater
> harmony, as a perfect rule of their faith and actions; that is, the Bible.
> The Bible, I say, the Bible only, is the religion of Protestants. What-
> soever else they believe besides it, and the plain, irrefragable, indubi-

---

[43] Herbert, *De Veritate*, 291–303, and Blount, *The Oracles of Reason*, 195–96.

table consequences of it; well may they hold it as a matter of opinion: But as matter of faith and religion, neither can they, with coherence to their own grounds, believe it themselves; nor require the belief of it of others, without most high and most schismatical presumption.[44]

While the Latitudinarians agreed that all doctrine must be biblical, not all agreed that they should distance themselves from the traditional interpretation of scripture on crucial doctrines like the trinity. The orthodox Latitudinarian Bishop Stillingfleet had argued in his "Second Dialogue on the Doctrine of the Trinity and Transubstantiation Compared" that when there was conflict over biblical interpretation, the opinion of the early church should be sustained.

In contrast, Clarke cited the opinion of Hooker. In his *Ecclesiastical Polity*, Hooker had argued that even if ten thousand councils stood to the contrary, one point of scripture would be sufficient to overturn them.[45] In addition Clarke cited Dr. Wake, Tillotson's successor. In his *Commentary on the Christian Catechism*, Wake wrote, "I chuse rather to regulate my faith by what God hath delivered, than by what man hath defined."[46] Clarke also cited Hales on the weight of traditional authority. Hales affirmed that it was the vain desire to know more about the nature of God than the scripture allowed which had led the Church into disarray. With Tillotson and Wake, he minimized the authority of the tradition.[47]

Clarke pressed on to show that this position was consistent with the Church of England as he cited from the 6th, 20th, and 21st articles of the Thirty-Nine Articles that scripture alone contained all that was necessary to salvation.[48] In the same way, Clarke held, the church must not ordain anything contrary to God's word, nor may

---

[44] Chillingworth, *The Religion of the Protestants*, Chpt. 6, sec. 56.

[45] Clarke, *SD*, Intro., v., in Tillotson's *Rule of Faith*, 2d ed., 18. Here Clarke's position is in keeping with that of Luther, Calvin and the Reformed orthodox, who however, did not have a problem with the councils on the issue of the trinity. Hooker did not disagree with the councilior trinitarian formulation either. Thus Clarke is using a generic statement by Hooker, and applying it in a field where Hooker may well have disagreed with its application.

[46] W. Wake, *Commentary on the Christian Catechism*, 21, in *SD*, Intro., v.

[47] John Hales of Eton, tract on "Schism" in *The Golden Remains of Mr. John Hales of Eton* in Tulloch, Vol. 1, 227–28.

[48] The issue arises here as to whether one had not only to subscribe the Articles themselves, as Clarke was willing to do, or subscribe as well the intended interpretation of their Calvinistic authors. Clarke was willing to subscribe the "letter" of the articles, and resisted the idea that this meant he had subscribed their "spirit." On this issue he disagreed with those like Wm. Whiston.

it expound of one place of scripture what is repugnant to another. Clarke believed,

> That even General Councils,—(forasmuch as they be an assembly of men, whereof all be not governed with the Spirit and Word of God,) may err, and sometimes have erred, even in things pertaining unto God: Wherefore things ordained by them, as necessary to salvation, have neither strength nor authority, unless it may be declared that they be taken out of Holy Scripture.[49]

On the locus of authority Clarke wrote,

> Wherefore in any question of controversy concerning a matter of faith, Protestants are obliged (for the deciding of it) to have recourse to no other authority whatsoever, but to that of Scripture only.[50]

In summary it is evident that Clarke clearly belongs with the heterodox Latitudinarians. Examined in the context of the five topics central to their thought, he clearly was not a Deist because of the strong role revelation played in his thought. He was in general agreement with the Latitudinarians regarding the balance of faith and reason, the important role of moral virtue, and their emphasis on toleration. He aligned himself with the heterodox group on the issues of mystery and the role of tradition, and produced heterodox trinitarian conclusions.

Clarke and Newtonian Natural Philosophy

In his Dedication to the *Clarke-Leibniz Correspondence* (1715–16), addressed to the Princess of Wales, Clarke wrote,

> The occasion of his [Leibnitz] giving your Royal Highness the trouble of his first letter, he declares to be his having entertained some suspicions, that the foundations of natural religion were in danger of being hurt by Sir Isaac Newton's philosophy. It appeared to me, on the contrary, a most certain and evident truth, that from the earliest antiquity to this day, the foundations of natural religion had never been so deeply and so firmly laid, as in the mathematical and experimental philosophy of that great man.[51]

---

[49] Clarke, *SD*, Intro., viii in *Works*, IV.
[50] Ibid., iv.
[51] Clarke, *Leibniz-Clarke Correspondence*, in *Works*, IV, 582.

Clarke was a younger contemporary of Isaac Newton, and a close friend. William Whiston, in his memoirs, described Clarke as a "bosom friend" of Newton's.[52] Whiston's opinion was likely derived from the variety of connections between Clarke and Newton. Newton's correspondence demonstrates that Clarke socialized with scientific luminaries like Edmond Halley and Newton.[53] From his early days as a student Clarke was reading and espousing Newtonian philosophy. "About 1694, the celebrated Dr. Samuel Clarke, while an undergraduate, defended, in the public schools, a question taken from the Newtonian philosophy."[54] When Newton needed a fine Latinist to translate his *Optics* for reading on the continent, he turned to Clarke, and paid him the handsome price of five hundred pounds—one hundred for each of his five children.[55] Newton served on the vestry of Clarke's church, St. James, and was a Governor of King Street Chapel in Clarke's parish. Upon Newton's death, it was Clarke who was offered his position as Master of the Mint. When a new Latin translation of Rohault's *Traite de physique* was needed, Clarke supplied one. Rohault was a Cartesian and his book was a standard university text on natural philosophy. In his translation, Clarke took the liberty of adding annotations from Newtonian natural philosophy which functioned as a running critique of Rohault's Cartesianism. The new Latin translation was issued in 1697 and was followed by four subsequent ones. Over the course of the editions, Clarke's endnotes grew into copious footnotes which contained an extensive amount of Newtonian commentary. By the time the 1723 english edition was published, the full title read, *Rohault's System of Natural Philosophy Illustrated with Dr. Samuel Clarke's Notes taken mostly out of Sir Isaac Newton's Philosophy.*[56] The result was the conversion of a generation of university students from the natural philosophy of Descartes to that of Newton.

If Newton's vocation was natural philosophy, and his avocation

---

[52] William Whiston, *Memoirs of the Life and Writings of William Whiston, M.A.* (London: 1753) Vol. 1, 256. See Ferguson *Heretic*, 215 cf., 251 n. 23.

[53] For example see the invitation by Littleton Powys to have Newton, Halley and Clarke dine with him at Serjeants Inn. Isaac Newton, *The Correspondence of Isaac Newton*, eds. Alfred Hall and Laura Tilling (Cambridge: Cambridge Univ. Press for the Royal Society of London, 1976), VII, 180.

[54] Sir David Brewster, *Memoirs of the Life, Writings and Discoveries of Sir Isaac Newton* 2 Vols. (Edinburgh: Thomas Constable & Co., MDCCCLV), Vol. 1, 336.

[55] Ferguson, *Heretic*, 35.

[56] Gjertsen, 531.

was theological studies, the converse was true for Clarke. Both men, from their respective vocations sought to link the two, thereby creating an apologetic which could withstand the onslaught of Atheism and Deism. The instrument for such an apologetic was supplied in the will of Robert Boyle, the renowned chemist. Boyle, like Newton and Clarke, was interested in natural philosophy and theology. Boyle's stated intent in his will was that a series of annual lectures be designed "to prove the truth of the Christian religion against infidels, without descending to any controversies among Christians, and to answer new difficulties, scruples, etc."[57] Boyle died in 1691, and the first series of Boyle Lectures was given by Richard Bentley in 1692 entitled, *A Confutation of Atheism*. It is quite likely that Newton was at least indirectly involved in the formulation of the lectures. In what is known as the "Gregory Memorandum" of December 28, 1691, the scientist David Gregory related Newton's role in the formulation of the Lectures.

> In Mr. Newton's opinion a good design of a public speech (and which may serve well as an Act) may be to shew that the most simple laws of nature are observed in the structure of a great part of the universe, that the philosophy out ther [sic] to begin; and that cosmical qualities are as much easier as they are more universal than particular ones, and the general contrivance simpler than that of animals plants etc.[58]

In 1704 Clarke was invited to deliver a series of the Boyle Lectures, which he entitled *A Demonstration of the Being and Attributes of God.* This series was intended to confute Atheism. The structure of Clarke's argument has led some scholars to the conclusion that Clarke was a Cartesian. He is understood by both Stephen and Asch as an exponent of the *a priori* method. Stephen writes that Clarke was "the great representative of the *a priori* method of constructing a system of theology" with the apparent ambition of producing what would be to Christianity the equivalent of what the *Principia* was to astronomy. For Stephen, Clarke clothed his arguments, more than any other English writer, with the "quasi-mathematical phraseology which was common to most of the followers of Descartes."[59] Surprisingly, Asch agrees with Stephen and writes that Clarke was a representative of the *a priori* method in both philosophy and theology.[60]

---

[57] Ferguson, *Heretic*, 23.
[58] Newton, *Correspondence*, Vol. 3, 191.
[59] Stephen, 100–101.
[60] Asch, 51–52.

It should be noted in response to Stephen that Clarke never produced a "system of theology" at all. Secondly, Clarke, like Locke and Newton, rejected the Cartesian doctrine of innate ideas, and emphasized that his proof of God's existence was not from innate ideas, but from arguments demonstrable both negatively and positively.[61] There are, however, reasons for the conclusion reached by Stephen and Asch. In the Preface to the *Demonstration* Clarke wrote concerning his method,

> For which reason I have also confined my self to one only method or continued thread of arguing; which I have endeavoured should be as near to mathematical, as the nature of such a discourse would allow.[62]

Clarke began by offering modifications of the deductive cosmological and ontological arguments to which he added an argument based on the nature of space and time. But when he moved in his eighth proposition, which he identified as his main point, to demonstrate that the self-existent Being was intelligent, he consciously shifted to arguments *a posteriori*.

> VIII. The self-existent and original cause of all things, must be an intelligent being. In this proposition lies the main question between us and the atheists.

> Now that the Self-existent being is not such a blind and unintelligent necessity, but in the most proper sense an understanding and really active Being; does not indeed so obviously and directly appear to us by considerations *a priori*; because (through the imperfections of our faculties) we know not wherein intelligence consists . . . But *a posteriori* almost everything in the world demonstrates to us this great truth; and affords undeniable arguments, to prove that the world, and all things therein, are the effects of an intelligent and knowing cause.[63]

Clarke was, in fact, using mixed proofs in the *Demonstration*, and was well aware of it. Concerning the *Demonstration* he wrote,

> I endeavoured, in my former discourse [the *Demonstration*] to strengthen and confirm the arguments which prove to us the being and attributes of God, partly by metaphysical reasoning, and partly from the discoveries (principally those that have been lately made) in natural philosophy.[64]

---

[61] Clarke, *Demonstration* in *Works*, II, 529–30.
[62] Clarke, *Demonstration* in *Works*, II, 517.
[63] Ibid., 543.
[64] Clarke, Preface to *Discourse* in *Works*, II, 581.

In the subsequent *Discourse* he stated plainly that his method would be empirical rather than deductive.

> The same demonstrative force of reasoning, and even mathematical certainty, which in the main argument was there [in the *Demonstration*] easy to be obtained, ought not here to be expected; but that such moral evidence or mixt proofs from circumstances and testimony, as most matters of fact are only capable of, and wise and honest men are always satisfied with, ought to be accounted sufficient in the present case.[65]

Here, in his utilization of "moral evidence" and mixed proofs we see Clarke's indebtedness to Chillingworth and Great Tew as opposed to the Cambridge Platonists. Regarding Clarke's claim to have used the *a priori* method in the *Demonstration* Ferguson writes,

> When the earlier and later parts of Clarke's *Discourse*[66] have thus been shown to follow an *a posteriori* course, not a great deal is left that can be considered purely *a priori*, and Clarke's earlier assertion that he would confine himself to one method begins to appear overconfident.[67]

In fact Clarke was probably mixing the method of proofs because this was the customary procedure in arguing the existence of God. For example, Descartes also used mixed proofs. Copleston writes,

> It does not seem to me that Descartes' different ways of speaking can be rendered perfectly consistent. At the same time a general line of harmonization can be found if we bear in mind his distinction between the *ordo inveniendi* the order of discovery or the order in which a philosopher investigates his subject analytically, and the *ordo docendi*, the order of teaching or systematic exposition of truths already discovered. In the order of discovery, as far as explicit knowledge is concerned, we know our own imperfection before the divine perfection. Hence the order of discovery seems to demand an *a posteriori* proof of God's existence; and this is given in the third Meditation.[68]

Leibniz also used both methods of proof by including an *a posteriori* argument from the pre-established harmony of things to God's existence.[69] It seems that Clarke was simply following the established

---

[65] Ibid., 600.

[66] Ferguson is here referring to the *Demonstration*. When the two lectures were published in 1706 they were under the single title *A Discourse concerning the Unchangeable Obligations of Natural Religion, and the Truth and Certainty of the Christian Revelation.* He is using this title.

[67] Ferguson, *The Philosophy of Dr. Samuel Clarke and Its Critics*, 12.

[68] Copleston, Vol. IV, 114.

[69] Ibid., 325.

philosophical method of employing both *a priori* and *a posteriori* arguments to prove the existence of God. By relying on an *a posteriori* approach on his crucial point in the *Demonstration*, and almost completely on *a posteriori* support in the *Discourse*, we can see that he favored the *a posteriori* method, and can hardly be called a Cartesian. Moreover, where Clarke used the *a posteriori* method in arguing for God's existence, he relied on evidence from the "lately made" discoveries in natural philosophy, that is to say, Newtonian discoveries. Thus while the method of using both types of proofs was standard, it was the evidence presented in the *a posteriori* proofs which was new. The old arguments could now be buttressed by the new science. Therefore Clarke was not a Cartesian, but one who employed the usual methods of arguing for God's existence, with the twist of showing himself a committed Newtonian in the evidence he supplied in his *a posteriori* proofs.

Further evidence of the influence of Newtonian philosophy on Clarke is found in his correspondence with the celebrated Leibniz.[70] The correspondence was precipitated by a letter from Leibniz to the Princess of Wales in which he castigated the Newtonians for their idea that the creation needed occasional repair. The Princess showed the letter to Clarke. She was interested that the relationship between Newton and Leibniz might be mended following the accusations made during the priority dispute over the invention of Calculus. Brewster's account of the events is slightly different; he credits the initiation of the correspondance to the King, but the result was the same. Newton was entrusted with the mathematical part of the controversy, and Clarke with the defense of the English philosophy.[71] The precise extent of Newton's contribution to Clarke's responses is uncertain. What seems certain is that the project enjoyed their collaboration. Brewster tell us that Newton had helped Clarke on some of the astronomical points. This is supported by the fact that in some of

---

[70] Gottfried Wilhelm Leibniz, *Philosophical Papers and Letters*, ed. with an intro. by Leroy E. Loemker. 2 vols. (Chicago: Univ. of Chicago Press, 1956); Leroy Loemker, *Struggle for Synthesis: The Seventeenth Century Background of Leibniz's Synthesis of Order and Freedom* (Cambridge, MA: Harvard Univ. Press, 1972); Nicholas Rescher, *The Philosophy of Leibniz* (Englewood Cliffs, N.J.: Prentice Hall, 1967); Bertrand Russell, *A Critical Exposition of the Philosophy of Leibniz*, 2d ed. (London: George Allen & Unwin, 1937); Copleston, Vol. IV, 264–332.

[71] Brewster, *Memoirs*, Vol. 2, 285–86.

Newton's papers there are manuscripts containing the same views as Clarke produced in the correspondence.[72]

In his first paper Leibniz had written,

> Sir Isaac Newton and his followers, have also a very odd opinion concerning the work of God. According to their doctrine, God Almighty wants to wind up his watch from time to time: otherwise it would cease to move. He had not, it seems, sufficient foresight to make it a perpetual motion. Nay, the machine of God's making, is so imperfect, according to these gentlemen; that he is obliged to clean it now and them by an extraordinary concourse, and even to mend it, as a clockmaker mends his work.[73]

Clarke responded,

> The reason why, among men, an artificer is justly esteemed so much the more skilful, as the machine of his composing will continue longer to move regularly without any farther interposition of the workman; is because the skill of all human artificers consists only in composing, adjusting, or putting together certain movements, the principles of whose motion are altogether independent upon the artificer: such as are weights and springs, and the like; whose forces are not made, but only adjusted, by the workman. But with regard to God, the case is quite different; because He not only composes or puts things together, but is himself the author and continual preserver of their original forces or moving powers: and consequently 'tis not a diminution, but the true glory of his workmanship, that nothing is done without his continual government and inspection. The notion of the world's being a great machine, going on without the interposition of God, as a clock continues to go without the assistance of a clockmaker; is the notion of materialism and fate, and tends, (under pretense of making God a supramundane intelligence,) to exclude providence and God's Government in reality out of the world.[74]

At issue was the true structure of the universe, and how God, as Creator, related to that structure. Leibniz and the Cartesians held that the universe was a vast plenum consisting of visible and invisible matter which God had set in motion foreseeing all conditions with His wisdom and investing that creation with sufficient energy to sustain it. The rotation of the planets was explained through the concept of vast vortices in the plenum. The Newtonians, including Clarke, be-

[72] Ibid., 287. The material in parentheses is from Brewster's n. 4.
[73] Leibniz' first letter in Clarke, *Works*, IV, 587.
[74] Ibid., Clarke's First Reply, 590.

lieved that the universe was a vacuum sprinkled with matter.[75] For
them, the motion of the planets was explained by the universal law
of gravity which served as a sign of God's constant providence. Leibniz
did not deny God's providence, but described it as the prescinding
wisdom of God at the creation.[76] The Newtonians understood it as
God's perpetual ontological support for the order of creation.

Here Clarke and Newton shared the same notion of divine providence as it related to the creation. Force describes Newton's understanding.

> The original creation of gravity demonstrates God's general providence
> but its continuous operation since that point reveals His special provi-
> dence. God's sustained preservation of the order of nature and natural
> laws demonstrates divine special providence because of the very nature
> of gravitational attraction.[77]

Clarke's understanding was identical.

> And not only so; but that most universal principle of gravitation itself,
> the spring of almost all the great and regular inanimate motions in the
> world, answering (as I hinted in my former Discourse,) not at all to the
> surfaces of bodies, (by which alone they can act one upon another,)
> but entirely to their solid content; cannot possibly be the result of any
> motion originally impressed on matter, but must of necessity be caused
> (either immediately or mediately) by something which penetrates the
> very solid substance of all bodies, and continually puts forth in them a
> force or power entirely different from that by which matter acts on
> matter. Which is, by the way, and evident demonstration, not only of
> the world's being made originally by a supreme intelligent cause; but
> moreover that it depends every moment on some superior Being, for
> the preservation of its frame; and that all the great motions in it, are
> caused by some immaterial power, not having originally impressed a
> certain quantity of motion upon matter, but perpetually and actually
> exerting itself every moment in every part of the world.[78]

---

[75] Edwin Burtt, *The Metaphysical Foundations of Modern Science*, Vol. 3 in *The Rise of
Modern Science* series (Atlantic Highlands, N.J.: Humanities Press, 1952; repr., 1980),
111–12, 244–50, 259; Rupert Hall, *From Galileo to Newton* (repr. New York: Dover,
1982), 304–06.

[76] Leibniz's second paper, sects. 7, 8 and 9, in Clarke, *Works*, IV, 592–93. Leibniz's
view here is utterly traditional with the exception of the terms employed, "general/
special." The medieval and Protestant scholastics used the terms concurrence, or
concursus. See Richard Muller, *God, Creation, and Providence in the Thought of Jacob Arminius:
Sources and Directions of Scholastic Protestantism in the Era of Early Orthodoxy* (Grand Rapids: Baker Book House, 1991), 247–57.

[77] Force, "Hume and the Relation of Science," 523.

[78] Clarke, *Discourse* in *Works*, II, 601.

This dynamic concept of providence also influenced the way in which
Clarke and Newton understood miracles. Miracles were not supernatural interruptions of the natural order, but were unusual and un-
expected exhibitions of God's providence upon an order which was
constantly maintained supernaturally. Force comments on Newton's
understanding,

> Newton tends generally to discount the traditional conception of miracles
> held by Boyle, Wildins, and some of the other founders of the Royal
> Society. A miracle is not a transgression of natural law. Rather, the
> sustained operation of natural law is itself a miracle and illustrative of
> divine providence.[79]

In the *Discourse* Clarke wrote,

> Consequently there is no such thing, as what men commonly call the
> course of nature, or the power of nature. The course of nature, truly
> and properly speaking, is nothing else but the will of God producing
> certain effects in a continued, regular, constant and uniform Manner:
> Which course or manner of acting, being in every moment perfectly
> arbitrary, is as easy to be altered at any time, as to be preserved. And
> if, (as seems most probable,) this continual acting upon matter, be
> performed by the subserviency of created intelligences appointed to
> that purpose by the supreme Creator; then 'tis as easy for any of them,
> and as much within their natural power, (by the permission of God,)
> to alter the course of nature at any time, or in any respect, as to
> preserve or continue it.[80]

So we see that Clarke was thoroughly Newtonian in his understanding of natural philosophy. He was involved in arguing Newton's ideas
from an early age, and had a working relationship with Newton on
a number of projects both eccleisiastic and scientific. He was deeply
involved in refuting the Cartesian mechanics, as well as a lecturer in
a series which served as a platform for synthesizing Newton's natural
philosophy and Christianity. It should not surprise us that if Newton
and Clarke shared similar views on so many subjects, that they might
also be alike in their understanding of other areas of mutual interest.
One of these was the trinity, and the relationship of Newton's thought
to Clarke's on that subject will be explored in Chapter Four.

   As Clarke is set within his context we can now see that he was
profoundly influenced by the legacy of the Cambridge Platonists and

---

[79] Force, "Hume and the Relation of Science," 523.
[80] Clarke, *Discourse* in *Works*, II, 697–98.

Falkland's circle at Great Tew, and should be seen as an important figure in the school of Latitudinarians descendant from them. He was sympathetic to the broad Latitudinarian agenda: a balance between revelation and reason, an emphasis on moral virtue, and an insistence on religious toleration. He tilted toward the heterodox Latitudinarians in his disavowal of mystery and in his view of the role of the Church in formulating doctrine. His scientific and philosophic views were state of the art. He was a convinced Newtonian in his mechanics and agreed with Locke's conclusions regarding epistemology. Clarke was not only a product of his age, but contributed to the triumph of its views. His powerful defense of the Newtonian mechanics against Leibniz, and his succesive editions of Rohault's work certainly contributed to the decisive victory of Newton's system. His support of religious toleration also contributed to broader freedom for the dissenters of his period. Clarke, therefore, was both a representative and a formative figure of his age. He was the epitome of an Anglican rational theologian.[81] As a divine, he applied the rational method at which he had arrived in natural philosophy to theology, where he encountered stiff resistance. This was particularly true regarding his explanation of the doctrine of the trinity, to which we now turn.

---

[81] On the Anglican theological mood see Henry McAdoo, *The Structure of Caroline Moral Theology* (London and New York: Longmans, Green, 1949).

PART TWO

SOURCES

CHAPTER THREE

CLARKE AND THE PATRISTIC DOCTRINE OF GOD

Clarke believed his doctrine of God to be firmly supported in scripture, and, in addition, to be consistent with the teaching of the church fathers. He approached the Patristic materials with the Rationalist viewpoint and skills he acquired in his context. Clarke utilized the best textual and linguistic studies available, appealed always to original sources, pleaded for toleration in understanding doctrinal differences, and relied upon reason as a reliable guide in drawing conclusions. In examining Clarke's use of the Fathers, this chapter will be divided into four sections. The first will analyze the trajectories of thought within the Arian controversy, in the light of contemporary scholarship. The second will examine Clarke's use of the Patristic sources and will identify the trajectory of thought in the Patristic debate closest to his. The third section will examine Clarke's use of his contemporaries' understandings of the Patristic sources. The fourth section will consider the conclusions by historians of doctrine, in light of the first three sections.

Trajectories of Thought within the Arian Controversy,
in the Light of Contemporary Scholarship

Classical treatments of the Arian controversy have been written largely from confessional vantage points, and have amounted to a reading of trinitarian orthodoxy back into the events of the fourth century. An excellent example is Bishop Bull's *Defensio Fidei Nicenae.*[1] Hanson writes,

> The accounts of what happened which have come down to us were mostly written by those who belonged to the school of thought which eventually prevailed and have been deeply coloured by that fact. The supporters of this view wanted their readers to think that orthodoxy on the subject under discussion had always existed and that the period

---

[1] George Bull, *Defensio Fidei Nicenae* in *Opera Omnia* (London: Samuel Bridge, 1703).

was simply a story of the defence of that orthodoxy against heresy and error. But it ought to be obvious that this could not possibly have been the case.[2]

The primal figure in any attempt to understand the difficulties of the doctrine of God in the fourth century is Origen, who has been called the father of both orthodoxy and Arianism.[3] The divergent directions which the descendents of Origen took can be explained by the linguistic ambiguity of the terms he used in discussing the nature of God. The primary terms in view are ὑπόστασις and οὐσία. Hanson[4] has argued that in Origen's work these were simply synonyms for the same thing—distinct individual entity. In Origen, οὐσία seldom or never meant essence or substance. In fact, the meaning of οὐσία was much more fluid, and not, as earlier scholarship had supposed, to be understood either as meaning "of the same stuff" or "the very same object." This fluidity also meant that its usage was less controversial in the early period of the church.[5]

Origen's doctrine carried a markedly subordinationist strain. Franks[6] has offered several texts from Origen's *De Principiis* in proof of this, one of which says,

> The God and Father who holds all things together, reaches by his influence each one of the things that are, bestowing being upon each from what is His own. One of these things is the Son who is less than the Father and whose influence reaches to rational beings only, for He is second from the Father. Still inferior is the Holy Spirit, who penetrates only the saints; so that in this way the power of the Father is greater than that of the Son, but that of the Son is more than that of the Holy Spirit.[7]

Likewise, Origen argued in his Commentary on John 2:2, in reference to 1:1, that there is a difference between ὁ θεός and θεός. The former

---

[2] R.P.C. Hanson, *The Search for the Christian Doctrine of God: The Arian Controversy 318–381* (Edinburgh: T & T Clark, 1988), xviii–xix. Other general treatments of the controversy are: Colm Luibheid, *The Council of Nicaea* (Galway: Irish Academic Press, 1982), and Charles Kannengiesser, *Arius and Athanasius: Two Alexandrian Theologians* (Aldershot, Hampshire, Great Britain: Variorum; Brookfield, Vermont, USA: Gower Pub. Co., 1991).

[3] George L. Prestige, *God in Patristic Thought* (London: S.P.C.K., 1952), 131.

[4] Hanson, *The Search*, 66.

[5] Ibid., 170.

[6] Robert S. Franks, *The Doctrine of the Trinity* (London: Gerald Duckworth, 1953), 90–95.

[7] Origen, *De Principiis*. Book I, Chpt. 8. (From Justinian's Fragment). Franks, 93–94.

implied aseity and the later simply divinity. Thus the *logos* was rightly called θεός, but not ὁ θεός.[8] While the forms of subordinationism varied, virtually all Ante-Nicene theologians engaged in some form of it. Hanson writes, "There is no theologian in the Eastern or Western Church before the outbreak of the Arian Controversy, who does not in some sense regard the Son as subordinate to the Father."[9] Prestige states that Eusebius of Caesarea derived his subordinationism from Origen.[10] While this is true, it is clearly a different subordinationism than that of Arius. Eusebius represented a *via media* between the thought of Athanasius and that of Arius. He appropriated Origen along a different trajectory. Lyman[11] has suggested that the key distinction was their notions of the generation of the Son. Origen's doctrine of eternal generation is well known. Here the eternity of the Son as Word and Wisdom was essential to the perfection of the Father (*Prin.* 1.2.2). For Origen, the Son was a product of both the nature and the will of the Father. The Son was a middle principle which allowed the Father to pour out his likeness and life into the creation. While Eusebius adopted a similar Platonic structure, he denied the necessity or eternity of the Son's generation. The Son was begotten before time, herein lay his uniqueness. The Son was in the Father's image, but not of his essence. Here Eusebius was concerned to heighten the voluntary power of the Father and to guard the uniqueness of the Son.[12] This uniqueness had both soteriological and cosmological significance for Eusebius.

> In the theology of Eusebius, the explicit distinction of the Son from the Father is therefore important for the independent activity of the Son in his cosmological and historical activity as well as to affirm the transcendence of the Father. On the other hand, in order to do the work of the Father in redemption, the Son must be divine. For Eusebius this may be defined as a unique status and essence possessed by the Son because of his direct derivation from the Father.[13]

---

[8] Franks, 92–93.
[9] Hanson, *The Search*, 64.
[10] Prestige, 131.
[11] J.R. Lyman, "Substance Language in Origen and Eusebius," in *Arianism: Historical and Theological Reassessments*, ed. Robert C. Gregg. Patristic Monograph Series No. 11 (Philadelphia: The Philadelphia Patristic Foundation, Ltd., 1985).
[12] Ibid., 258–59.
[13] Ibid., 264.

While Eusebius distinguished his position from those who held an identity of substance on the one hand, he distinguished himself from those who held that the Son was a creature, which was one of the tenets of Arianism, on the other. This balance was reflected in the position he took following Nicaea.

> After Nicaea in response to Arians and Marcellus, Eusebius clarified the specific Christological intentions behind his cosmological structures. Against the Arians he defended the uniqueness and the divinity of the Son: The Son is begotten, not created [*Eccl. Theo.* 1.8, 1.9]. He is generated prior to time [*Eccl. Theo.* 1.6]. Yet, especially against Marcellus, Eusebius retained the critical distinctions between the Father and the Son: The Son is not a mere attribute or activity of the Father, but his obedient agent.[14]

While Eusebius insisted on the uniqueness of the Son's generation, he also stipulated that no one could know the manner in which it occurred.[15]

In Theodoret's *Ecclesiastical History*, we have Eusebius' statement that while at the Council of Nicaea he offered a formula of faith for consideration.

> We believe in one God, Father Almighty, maker of all things, visible and invisible; and in one Lord Jesus Christ, the Word of God, God of God, Light of Light, Life of Life, Only-begotten of the Father before all worlds; by Whom all things were made.

> We believe in the being and continual existence of each of these; that the Father is in truth the Father; the Son in truth the Son; the Holy Ghost in truth the Holy Ghost.[16]

Seeberg[17] has suggested that Eusebius' Confession had all the advantages and disadvantages of a compromise formula. Both the [later called] *Homoiousians* and Arians could find their views expressed there. Yet, taken as a whole, it probably expressed the view of the majority. It was the Emperor, Constantine, who suggested the inclusion of the

---

[14] Ibid., 263.
[15] Hanson, *The Search*, 50.
[16] Eusebius' formulary in Theodoret, *Ecclesiastical History*. Book I, Chpt. XI. *NPNF* Vol. 3, 49. See also, Colm Luibheid, *Eusebius of Caesarea and the Arian Crisis* (Dublin: Irish Academic Press, 1981).
[17] Reinhold Seeberg, *Text-Book of the History of Doctrines*. Trans. by Charles E. Hay. 2 Vols. (Grand Rapids: Baker Book House, 1954.), Vol. 1, 216–17.

word ὁμοούσιος[18] Eusebius explained how he interpreted this and was able to accept it.

> When they had set this formulary, [the Nicene Creed] we did not leave without examination that passage in which it is said that the Son is of the substance of the Father, and consubstantial with the Father. Questions and arguments thence arose, and the meaning of the terms was exactly tested. Accordingly they were led to confess that the word consubstantial [ὁμοούσιος] signifies that the Son is of the Father, but not as being a part of the Father. We deemed it right to receive this opinion; for that is sound doctrine which teaches that the Son is of the Father, but not part of His substance. From the love of peace, and lest we should fall from the true belief, we also accept this view, neither do we reject the term "consubstantial." For the same reason we admitted the expression, "begotten, but not made;" for they alleged that the word "made" applies generally to all things which are created by the Son, to which the Son is in no respect similar; and that consequently He is not a created thing, like the things made by Him, but is of a substance superior to all created objects. The Holy Scriptures teach Him to be begotten of the Father, by a mode of generation which is incomprehensible and inexplicable to all created beings. So also the term "of one substance with the Father," [ἐκ τῆς οὐσιός τοῦ πατροῦ] when investigated, was accepted not in accordance with bodily relations or similarity to mortal beings. For it was also shown that it does not either imply division of substance, nor abscission, nor any modification or change or diminution in the power of the Father, all of which are alien from the nature of the unbegotten Father. It was concluded that the expression "being of one substance with the Father," implies that the Son of God does not resemble, in any one respect, the creatures which He has made; but that to the Father alone, who begat Him, He is in all points perfectly like: for He is of the essence and of the substance of none save of the Father. This interpretation having been given of the doctrine, it appeared right to us to assent to it, especially as we were aware that of the ancients some learned and celebrated bishops and writers have used the term "consubstantial" with respect to the divinity of the Father and of the Son.[19]

Eusebius and others at the Council had been hesitant to accept the term ὁμοούσιος. Three successive synods had been held in Antioch between the years 264 and 269, during which Paul of Samosata,

---

[18] Possibly under the influence of Bishop Hosius of Cordova who accompanied Constantine to the Council, was his representative and was one of the only Western Bishops in attendance. But see Hanson, 169–170.

[19] Eusebius' formulary in Theodoret, *Ecclesiastical History*. Book I, Chap. XI. *NPNF* Vol. 3, 50.

who was the Bishop of that See, and therefore the highest ecclesiastic of the East,[20] was deposed for holding the ὁμοούσιος and the term was condemned.[21] The term was associated with the modalistic monarchianism of Sabellius which denied the reality of individuation in the Godhead, and understood the persons as merely "modes" of the only God. The reason the Bishops had condemned the term was that it had been used by Paul as a foil for his adoptionism. He had argued that if the Son were truly of the same essence with the Father, as his opponents argued, yet was truly distinct from the Father, as all orthodox believed, then there must exist an antecedent essence in which both the Father and the Son participated, and from whom they derived their essence, and that therefore neither of them could be God.[22] It was ὁμοούσιος, understood in this material sense, and derived from Stoic philosophy,[23] which was repudiated by the Bishops. As a result, only when the Bishops at Nicaea were convinced that the ὁμοούσιος was to be understood in a non-material sense, were they persuaded to accept it. The centrality of this concern was evident in Eusebius' letter explaining the action of the Council and the interpretation of the Emperor.

> He explained that this term [consubstantial] implied no bodily condition or change, for that the Son did not derive His existence from the Father either by means of division or of abscission, since an immaterial, intellectual, and incorporeal nature could not be subject to any bodily condition or change.[24]

The choice before the bishops was whether the dangers of a Sabellian interpretation of ὁμοούσιος outweighed the benefits of the term's use as a bullwark against Arianism. Since the Arian threat was foremost in their minds, they agreed to adopt the term.

It became clear following the Council at Nicaea that the agreement to the term was fragile. On the surface it appeared that an overwhelming majority of the "318"[25] Bishops attending were in agree-

---

[20] Charles J. Hefele, *A History of the Christian Councils, from the Original Documents, to the Close of the Council of Nicaea, A.D. 325.* Translated and edited by William R. Clark. Second edition (Edinburgh: T & T Clark, 1894), 118.
[21] Prestige, 202.
[22] Ibid., 202.
[23] Hanson, *The Search*, 67.
[24] Epistle of Eusebius in Theodoret, *Ecc. Hist.* Book I, Chap. XI. *NPNF*, Vol. 3, 49.
[25] The number of Bishops present at Nicaea is uncertain. The numbers range from "more than 250" to 318. The probable number is between 250–300. (Hanson, *The Search*, 155–56).

ment with the formulation. Of those present only five refused to sign it.[26] Historians, on the other hand, have suggested political motivations for doing so.

> This insertion in the Creed [of the phrase ὁμοόυσιον τῷ πάτρι] was made by the majority against the remonstrances of Eusebius of Caesarea, and the great body of bishops of Syria and Palestine; and was only accepted by them with their own explanations, which did not altogether satisfy the Alexandrians and the Westerns . . . Unfortunately the Creed was forced upon the East by imperial authority, and the Eastern conscience rebelled. Subsequently the imperial authority vacillated taking now one side and then another, thus promoting confusion.[27]

Franks suggests that the Nicene Creed was not the product of a majority at all, but rather of a minority of Eastern Bishops, who, with the allegiance of those from the West and the weight of the Emperor, were able to force the Creed on the majority.[28] While the political factor was very real, it is hard to imagine that the theological sensibilities of such a diverse group could be so easily overwhelmed by the presence of the Emperor. Instead, it seems that while the majority of the bishops, like Eusebius of Caesarea, disliked the term ὁμοόυσιος, and worried about its Sabellian overtones, they came to realize that it was the only term strong enough to expose the Arians. This situation at the Council was reflected by Athanasius, who stated that when the party at Nicaea which he regarded as orthodox proposed the *homoian* formula and the Son to be exactly as the Father in all things as well as immutable and always in the Father, the Arians present winked and muttered to one another that they could accept these terms because they could find them used in scripture of creatures.[29] For this reason then, although they did not prefer the language of the ὁμοόυσιος, the Bishops accepted it as a necessary safeguard against an Arian interpretation.[30]

Hefele has written that, viewed as a whole, the Nicene Council can be said to have been composed of four parties. On the right

---

[26] The five who did not sign immediately were: Eusebius of Nicomedia, Theognis of Nicaea, Maris of Chalcedon, Theonas of Marmarica, and Secundus of Ptolemais. Eventually all but Theonas and Secundus signed. They, along with Arius and his writings, were anathematized and excommunicated (Hefele, 295).

[27] Charles A. Briggs, *Theological Symbolics in International Theological Library Series* (N.Y.: Charles Scribner's Sons, 1914), 91–92.

[28] Franks, 106.

[29] Athanasius, *De Decretis* Chapter 5, sect. 20, *NPNF*, 163–64. See also Hanson, *The Search*, 162.

[30] Hanson, *The Search*, 162. Also Franks, 106.

were those who held the position later to be called orthodox, identified
with Athanasius. On the left were those of a like mind with Arius.
At the left of center, was the party of Eusebius of Nicomedia, which
leaned toward the Arians. At the right of center were those sympathetic
with Eusebius of Caesarea who finally stood behind the ὁμοούσιος
for the reason stated above.[31] Although the term ὁμοιούσιον did not
occur until the Second Council of Sirmium (357),[32] this last group
anticipated that view by desiring to say that the Son was fully of the
Father; God of God, and like the Father in every way, while shying
away from essence language which could be misinterpreted and even
used against the church.[33] This anticipation was apparent in Eusebius'
already mentioned explanation of the proceedings where he wrote,

> It was concluded that the expression "being of one substance with the
> Father," implies that the Son of God does not resemble, in any one
> respect, the creatures which He has made; but that to the Father alone,
> who begat Him, *He is in all points perfectly alike*: for He is of the essence
> and of the substance of none save the Father.[34]

Kelly has argued that although later theologians concluded that the
Fathers at Nicaea understood ὁμοούσιος to mean three persons in
one identical substance, that as far as the Fathers themselves were
concerned,

> there are the strongest possible reasons for doubting this. The chief of
> these is the history of the term ὁμοουσιος itself, for in both its secular
> and theological use prior to Nicaea it always conveyed, primarily at
> any rate, the "generic" sense.[35]

The fragility of the coalition became apparent after the Council, when
all four parties later became clearly delineated. Constantine's desire
for peace in the empire was insufficient to hold the Bishops together.
    The history of the rivalry among the parties evolved in a series of
exchanges of power between the party of Athanasius and those who
held Arian views. When Constantine, under his sister's influence,
recalled Arius from banishment, Athanasius objected and was him-

---

[31] Hefele, 285.
[32] Hanson, *The Search*, 346–47.
[33] The Arians subsequently did precisely this. Hefele, 244.
[34] Epistle of Eusebius in Theodoret, *Ecclesiastical History*. Book I, Chap. 11. *NPNF*
Vol. 3, 50. My emphasis.
[35] J.N.D. Kelly, *Early Christian Doctrines*, rev. ed. (San Francisco: Harper and Row,
1978), 234–35, cf., Prestige, ch. 10.

self deposed at the Synod of Tyre in 355 and banished to Treves. In 337 Constantine died and Constantius returned Athanasius to his post. Constantius then came under the influence of the Arians and Athanasius was again deposed by those who supported Eusebius of Nicomedia at the Synod of Antioch in 341. A series of synods met in both East and West.[36] The First Sirmium Creed (351), with its twenty-six anathemas was the first of four produced at that place.[37] It was based upon the Fourth Creed of Antioch (341). This creed rejected both extreme Arian formulae[38] as well as the Nicene formulae.[39] It marked a shift toward an anti-Nicene position, though cannot be said to be pro-Arian.[40] It is well worth noting that it was anathama 25 of this Creed which Clarke cited in proving that the Son was a result of the will of the Father and not of necessity.[41] He was apparently sympathetic to its views. The Second Sirmium Creed (357)[42] is said by Hanson to have been clearly Arian in its drastic subordination of the Son, its insistence on the uniqueness of the Father and its rejection of substance language.[43] In 358 the Emperor Constans called twelve bishops to meet. The leader among these was Basil of Ancyra and this group produced a document which resulted in "the emergence of a new and coherent theological point of view."[44] Basil rejected the apparent Sabellianism of Marcellus of Ancyra as well as the radical Arians.[45] He also, less often, rejected the ὁμοούσιος. His position was that the ὁμοούσιος flirted with corporeal ideas regarding God, and that it was wrong to say that the substance of the Father was identical with that of the Son. Hanson has summarized Basil of Ancyra's contribution by saying, "When all has been said and done, however, this Ancyran document of Basil's represents a new and fruitful departure in the confused melee of theological opinions to which the theology of Arius had given rise."[46]

---

[36] Fisher, 139–143.
[37] This Creed can be found in Athanasius, *De Synodis*, 27.
[38] See Anathemas XIV, XII, XIV.
[39] Fisher, 142, cf., Hanson, *The Search*, 328–29.
[40] Hanson, *The Search*, 329.
[41] Clarke, *SD*, 144.
[42] Sources are Athanasius, *Apol. Sec.* 39; *Apol de Fuga* 5; Hilary *De Synodis* 11. For other sources see Hanson, *The Search*, 343, n. 114.
[43] Hanson, *The Search*, 346.
[44] Ibid., 349.
[45] Ibid., 355.
[46] Ibid., 356.

Basil managed to convince the Emperor to convene a Council which produced the Third Sirmium Creed, which did not survive.[47] Following this, a Fourth Sirmium Creed, (359) known as the "Dated Creed" was produced to bring a compromise between the Homoians (moderate Arians) and the Homoiousians. This Creed avoided the term οὐσία altogether, but said "the Son [is] like the Father in everything as the holy Scriptures declare and teach."[48] Its rejection of the ὁμοόυσιον was much milder than the Second Sirmium Creed of 357.[49] This may have been due to Basil's influence. He added his own gloss to the Creed, which interpreted "like in all things" to say "in all respects, not only according to will but according to *hypostasis* and according to constitution (ὕπαρξις) and according to being (τό εἶναι)."[50] Here Basil's sympathy with the spirit, if not with the letter, of the ὁμοόυσιος was evident.

By the time of the Council of Seleucia in 359 the spectrum of thought on the doctrine of God looked like this:[51]

Neo-Arians	*Homoian Arians*	*Homoiousians*	*Homoousians*
Aetius	Valens	Basil of Ancyra	Athanasius
Eunomius	Ursacians	George of Laodicea	
	Germinus	Silvanus of Tarsus	
	Akakius of Caesarea	Sophronius of Pomeiopolis	
	George of Alexandria	Eleusius of Cyzius	
	Uranius of Tyre	Cyril of Jerusalem	
	Eudoxius of Antioch	Eustathius of Caesarea	

During this period the Neo-Arians[52] were led by Aetius and Eunomius.[53] About the time of Fourth Sirmium Creed (359/60) Eunomius had written,

---

[47] A meager account of this council is in Sozomen IV.15.3. See also Hilary's brief statement in *De Synodis* 78, 79.

[48] Ibid., 363.

[49] Ibid., 364–65.

[50] Ibid., 365.

[51] See Hanson, *The Search*, 372–73. On Cyril's placement see Michael O'Carroll, *Trinitas: A Theological Encyclopedia of the Holy Trinity* (Wilmington Delaware: Michael Glazier, Inc., 1987), 81. Eusebius is not listed because he had died in 339 or 340 (Quasten, Vol. III, 310).

[52] This term comes from Thomas Kopecek, *A History of Neo-Arianism* 2 Vols. in the Patristic Monograph Series No. 8 (Philadelphia: The Philadelphia Patristic Foundation Ltd., 1979).

[53] Aetius' doctrine is expressed in his *Syntagmation* [Little Treatise] in thirty-seven propositions which are a response to Athanasius' *De Decretis*. For an analysis of this

The Son is neither *homoousios* nor *homoiousios* because the former implies an origin and a division of (the Father's) *ousia*, and the latter an equality (of *ousia*). The Son is entirely subordinated to the Father.[54]

Hanson has classified Eunomius as "an individualist, philosophically eclectic theologian ... He used Aristotelian logic to deploy his peculiar brand of rationalist Unitarianism."[55] Aetius did not believe the Son to be like the Father in respect to οὐσία, but instead he resembled the Father by fulfilling the will of God. He believed that for one who was ingenerate, to produce one generate who was identical in substance, was a contradiction in terms. This was expressed in Propositions 1–11 of his *Syntagmation*.[56]

The Homoian position emerged victorious at the Council of Constantinople in 360 which secured the Creed of Nice. For a time this Creed had ecumenical authority, and subsequently became the standard of Arianism.[57] The Creed had dropped the Homoiousian "like the Father in all respects" of the Dated Creed and instead inserted,

> that there should be absolutely no mention of the *ousia* of the Father and the Son ... but we declare that the Son is like (*homoian*) the Father, as also the Holy Scriptures declare and teach.[58]

Hanson has succinctly listed the primary differences between the Neo-Arians and the Homoians:

1. The comprehensibility of God (see Basil Epp. 234); in spite of their belief in the incomparability of the Father they [the Neo-Arians] believed that not only could the Son know him fully, but that any believer could, because "knowing God" meant understanding true doctrine about God; the Homoian Arians believe in the incomprehensibility of God and most of them held that the Son could not fully know him;

---

work see Kopecek, 227–97. The work can be found in Epiphanius, *Panarion* 76. 11.1–12.37. Eunomius' works include the *Apology* (sometimes called the *First Apology*), the *Apology for the Apology* (sometimes called the *Second Apology*), and the *Confession of Faith*. Hanson treats Aetius in pp. 603–611 and Eunomius in pp. 617–18.

[54] Eunomius, *Apology*, 26, 27 in Hanson, *The Search*, 619.
[55] Hanson, *The Search*, 636.
[56] See Kopecek, Vol. 1, 229–32.
[57] Hanson, *The Search*, 382.
[58] Ibid., 380.

2. The immutability of the Son, which the Neo-Arians maintained and the Homoian Arians denied; the Neo-Arians taught that the Father had given the Son an immutability by his will, by grace not by nature;

3. The formula for the Son's likeness to the Father among the Homoian Arians was "like according to the scriptures" among the Neo-Arians, "like according to will," different according to *ousia*;

4. The Neo-Arians constantly employed the vocabulary of Greek philosophy, whereas this is far from prominent in the writings of the Homoians, and least of all in the Latin speaking Homoians.[59]

While the Cappadocian Fathers all affirmed the Nicene language of ὁμοούσιος, it is not certain how they understood it. The position of Basil the Great in the Arian controversy is debated. Zahn, Loofs, and Harnack have suggested that Basil used the orthodox ὁμοούσιος in the sense of ὁμοιούσιος meaning that the οὐσία of the Son was of the same kind as the Father, but that he was not numerically the same.[60] Their thesis is that the Cappadocians adopted an interpretation like that of Basil of Ancyra, who believed that the Son was like the Father "in all things." We have already seen that Kelly holds that this to be the position of the Nicene Fathers themselves. If so, then the Cappadocians were simply following the Nicene Fathers. In regard to Basil's theology, this thesis of a "generic unity" is attractive for two reasons: First, it reflects the fact that Basil was familiar with Origen's subordinationism through his preparation, with Gregory Nazianzus, of the *Philocalia*. Second, it shows his acquaintance with Basil of Ancyra, with whom he traveled to Constantinople to debate the Neo-Arians in 359.[61] Nevertheless the theory is problematic in not taking full account of Basil's defense of the numerical unity of God.[62]

---

[59] Ibid., 635–36.

[60] Johannes Quasten, *Patrology*, 4 Vols. (Westminster Maryland: Christian Classics Inc., 1990. First published, 1950), Vol. III, 230, cf., Hanson, *The Search*, 696. See Adolph von Harnack, *History of Dogma*, trans. from the 3d German ed., E.B. Spiers and James Millar (London, Edinburgh, Oxford: Williams & Norgate, 1898), Vol. IV, 84–85.

[61] Hanson, *The Search*, 680.

[62] Quasten, Vol. III, 230.

Hanson argues that while Harnack's thesis isn't proven it is not dis-
proved by his opponents either.[63] The picture of Basil that emerges
is one of an individual who affirmed the Nicene formula, but was
desirous of bringing the *homoiousians* into alliance.[64] Basil had written,
"that relation which the general has to the particular, such a relation has the *ousia* to the *hypostasis*."[65] In one letter Basil stated that
the phrase used by Basil of Ancyra "like in respect to substance" was
acceptable provided the word "unalterably" was added to it. (Basil,
Ep. 9.3). He recognized that the term ὁμοούσιος had caused orthodox persons trouble, and that it was right to hesitate over it, referring to the Council of Antioch in 268.[66] Like the other Cappadocians,
and the Eastern tradition in general, his focus was on the three divine persons rather than on their unity of substance.[67] Several texts
by both Gregory of Nyssa and Gregory of Nazianzus can also be
interpreted in this generic manner.[68] Hanson recognizes the ambiguity the Cappadocian doctrine of God when he writes,

> We should conclude that while none of the three held a doctrine of
> identity of substance as strict as that of Athanasius none of them be-
> lieved in a thinly disguised form of the *homoiousios*. Far less should we
> assume that they (or any other theologian in the ancient world) held
> the too popular modern theory that God is three persons in our mod-
> ern sense, i.e. three centres of consciousness.[69]

In view of the evidence, however, Hanson may have overstated the
Cappadocian response to the ὁμοιούσιος. In light of Basil's remarks
in particular, it seems they did in fact possess a sympathy for the
generic interpretion of the ὁμοούσιος. This would have been all the
more true if they believed, as Kelly[70] suggests, that the Nicene Fathers had intended it in this way.

The history of the entire Arian controversy can seen as a time of
testing for a variety of theses regarding the emerging doctrine of God.
Ultimately the Neo-Arian and Homoian postions were excluded at
Constantinople in 381. The language of the ὁμοούσιος was validated,

---

[63] Hanson, *The Search*, 698.
[64] O'Carroll, 49.
[65] Basil, *Ep.* 4 in Hanson, *The Search*, 692.
[66] Basil, *Ep.* 52.1 in Hanson, *The Search*, 693–95.
[67] Quasten, Vol. III, 230.
[68] Hanson, *The Search*, 734–35.
[69] Hanson, *The Search*, 737.
[70] Kelly, *Early Christian Doctrines*, 234–35.

but even those in the vanguard continued to use analogies which created ambiguity and could imply a generic understanding of the term. Hanson is right to describe the controversy as "not the story of the defense of orthodoxy, but of a search for orthodoxy, a search conducted by the method of trial and error."[71]

Clarke's Use of Patristic Sources

It was clear to Clarke, that drawing his argument from scripture alone would be insufficient. Although he quoted Chillingworth's famous maxim, "The Bible, I say, the Bible only, is the Religion of Protestants,"[72] he knew that his understanding of the trinity would have to be compatible with that of the early Church. Proofs from the Fathers were a standard part of the Anglican apologetic for any doctrine,[73] and it remained incumbant upon Clarke to provide his doctrine of the trinity with requisite proofs from Patristics. While he acknowledged this to be the case, Clarke nevertheless emphasized the methodological distinction between the weight accorded to scripture and that accorded to tradition.[74]

> And I have illustrated each proposition with some testimonies out of the ancient writers, both before and after the Council of Nice; especially out of Athanasius and Basil; among which are several, not taken notice of either by Petavius or the learned Bishop Bull. Concerning all which, I desire it may be observed, that they are not alleged as *proofs* of any of the propositions (for proofs are to be taken from the scripture alone,) but as illustrations only.[75]

Clarke's thesis contended that the reading of the early Fathers supported his propositions.

> The greatest part of the writers before and at the time of the Council of Nice, were (I think) really of that opinion, (though they do not always speak very clearly and consistently,) which I have endeavoured to set forth in those propositions. At least, whatever metaphysical specu-

---

[71] Hanson, *The Search*, xix–xx.
[72] Chillingworth, *Religion of the Protestants*, chpt. 6, sect. 56 in his *Works*, 480–81, in Clarke, *SD*, introduction, v.
[73] McAdoo, *The Structure of Caroline Moral Theology*, 7–8.
[74] Note that this distinction was maintained as early as St. Thomas. See *Summa Theologiae* Ia, q.1, a.8.
[75] Clarke, *SD*, ix.

lations they indulged in their controversial writings, they never suffered
those speculations to become part of their religion: As appears from
the uniformity of all the creeds both Greek and Latin, in all the Christian churches of the world for three centuries. But as to the writers
after that time, the reader must not wonder, if many passages not
consistent with (nay, perhaps contrary to) those which are here cited,
shall by any one be alleged out of the same authors. For I do not cite
places out of these latter authors, so much to show what was the opinion
of the writers themselves, as to shew how naturally truth sometimes
prevails by its own native clearness and evidence, even against the
strongest and most settled prejudices; and how men are frequently
compelled to acknowledge such premises to be true, as necessarily infer
a conclusion different from what they intend to establish.[76]

Clarke believed the early Fathers supported his Propositions, and that
this was reflected in the Post-Nicene developments.

Clarke cited Patristic sources for twenty-six of his fifty-five Propositions drawn from scripture.[77] Those sources were taken from
twenty-seven authors.[78] When the list of authors is compiled several
things become apparent. First, the number of citations taken from
Latin theologians is greatly overshadowed by the Greek ones. There
is an historical reason for this. The trinitarian controversy erupted in
the East with the theology of Arius in Alexandria. The issues were
debated and settled at Nicaea almost exclusively by Eastern bishops.
Second, there is a link between geography and chronology; the contributions of the Latin Fathers tend to come later, with the exceptions of Tertullian and Novatian. Clarke used early Fathers, who
were predominantly Greek, in support of his propositions. This was
compatible with his general philosophical framework, which, as we
have seen in Chapter One, was deeply influenced by the Cambridge
Platonists.[79] Third, while Clarke alerts us to the fact that he relies
heavily on the work of Athanasius and Basil (which he does) he neglects

---

[76] Ibid.

[77] These are Propositions: IX, XI, XII, XIII, XIV, XVII, XVIII, XXII, XXIII,
XXVI, XXVII, XXX, XXXIV, XXXV, XXXVI, XXXVII, XXXIX, XLI, XLIII,
XLIV, XLV, XLVI, L, LI, LIV, LV.

[78] These authors and citations include: Irenaeus (29), Athanasius (26), Basil (21),
Eusebius of Caesarea (17), Origen (16), Justin Martyr (14), Clement of Alexandria
(12), Novatian (10), Hilary (9), Tertullian (7), Alexander of Alexandria (5), Theophilus (3), Ignatius of Antioch (3), Cyprian (2), Gregory of Nazianzus (2), and one
citation each from Epiphanius, Marius Victorinus, Shepherd of Hermas, Gregory of
Nyssa, Tatian, Theodore of Abucara, Hippolytus, Cyril of Jer., Lactantius, the
Martyrdom of Polycarp, Clement of Rome, and Augustine.

[79] Henry More's Latin edition of his *Opera Omnia* was published in 1679, Cudworth's

to mention how heavily he draws upon Irenaeus, Origen, and Eusebius of Caesarea. The significance of this will become apparent.

I have reduced Clarke's fifty-five propositions to five general theses, under which I have ordered his application of the Patristic materials:

1. In the language of scripture, the term "God" denotes almost always the "Father," even when it denotes the Son, its connotation ultimately leads to the Father.
2. The Son is neither self-existent, nor a creature.
3. The Son is etiologically subordinate to the Father, and biblical statements which ascribe deity to him are to be understood in terms of his exercise of title and power.
4. The Holy Spirit is also derivative of the Father.
5. That supreme worship belongs to the Father alone.

THESIS 1: In the Language of Scripture the term "God" denotes almost always the "Father," even when it denotes the "Son" its connotation ultimately leads toward the "Father"

In support of this thesis, Clarke drew Patristic material under four of his propositions.[80] He began in Proposition IX by stating, "The Scripture, when it mentions the One God, or the Only God, always means the Supreme person of the Father."[81] He cited Irenaeus that, "This God is the Father of our Lord Jesus Christ; and of Him it is, that St. Paul the apostle declares, 'There is one God, even the Father, who is above all, and through all, and in all.'"[82] For Clarke, this one God, who was the Father, was the one referred to when Christians express their monotheism. He quoted Cyprian's statement that, "There is one Lord God of the universe; who cannot but be of unequalled majesty, having all power absolutely and solely in himself."[83] Likewise Origen, "We worship the one God, and his one Son or Word; offering up our prayers to the supreme God, through his only begotten Son."[84] For Clarke, the reason Christians could be trinitarian *and* monotheistic lay in the fact that while the Son was properly called

---

True Intellectual System of the Universe was first published in London in 1678. Therefore both would have been available for Clarke.

[80] These are Propositions IX, XI, XXXII, LV.
[81] Clarke, *SD*, 123.
[82] Irenaeus, *Against Heresies*, Book 2, Chpt. 2 in Clarke, *SD*, 124.
[83] Cyprian, *De Bono Patientiae*, in Clarke, *SD*, 126.
[84] Origen, *Contra Celsus*, Book 8 in Clarke *SD*, 126.

God, he was not, like the Father, unoriginate. If he were, then there would exist two originating principles, which would be ditheism.[85] Only the Father was unoriginate, and this fact preserved the Christian claim to monotheism. To support his view, Clarke drew upon both Western and Eastern theologians. Novatian, the Latin Father wrote,

> God the Father therefore is alone unoriginated- the one God; whose greatness majesty and power, nothing can exceed, nothing can even be compared with it.—The Son indeed as proceeding from God, is also God, constituting a second person, but not therefore hindering the Father from being the one God. For since the principle or first cause of all things, is that which is unbegotten; (Which God the Father only is, as being without any original at all;) this shews that tho' he which is begotten is also God, yet the one God is he whom the Son hath declared to be unoriginated—whilst the Son acknowledgeth the whole power of his divinity to be derived from the Father, he declares the Father to be the one true eternal God, from whom alone that divinity of the Son is derived—the Son indeed is shewn to be God, as having divinity derived and communicated to him; and yet nevertheless the Father is proved to be the one God, as being the communicator of that divinity.[86]

Clarke cited Eusebius of Caesarea to the same end. Eusebius presented one of the stock images for representing the relationship between the Father and the Son: that of a mirror and the object it reflects.

> The Son hath his divinity by derivation from the Father, as being the image of God; so that there is but one divinity considered in both . . . And there is but one God, viz. he who exists of himself without cause and without original, and who is manifested by his Son as by a glass and an image.[87]

Eusebius repeated the point in his *Ecclesiastical Theology*.[88]

The second proposition Clarke drew upon to support Thesis 1 was number XI, "The Scripture, when it mentions God, absolutely

---

[85] It should be noted that this was precisely the argument of the Orthodox Church against the Latin *filioque*.

[86] Novatian, *De Trinitate*, Chap. 31 in Clarke, *SD*, 126–27. It is instructive that when Clarke does draw on a western theologian, it is one with a clearly subordinationist tendency. By doing so he is able to broaden his basis of support within the tradition among his readers, while not sacrificing his perspective.

[87] Eusebius, *Demonstration of the Gospel*, Book 5, Chpt. 4 in Clarke *SD*, 127.

[88] Eusebius, *Ecclesiastical Theology*. Book I, Chpt. 11 in Clarke, *SD*, 127.

and by way of eminence, always means the person of the Father."
Clarke cited Justin Martyr, "The Word is the first power (next after
God, the Father and supreme Lord of all;) and it is the Son."[89] In
order to support his view of the usage of "Father," as equivalent to
"God," Clarke quoted Theophilus, "Of the Trinity namely, of God,
and his Word and his wisdom."[90] Finally he appealed to Theodore
of Abucara, "The apostles and almost all the scriptures, when they
mention God absolutely and indefinitely, and commonly with an article
(ὁ θεός,) and without any personal distinction; mean the Father."[91]

The third proposition Clarke used to support Thesis 1 was number XXXII, "the Person of the Holy Ghost, is no where in scripture
expressly stiled, God or Lord." This was simply a consistent application of what Clarke had already maintained concerning the Son.
Here Ambrose was cited using the corrupted Latin copy of John 3:6
which said, "that which is born of the Spirit, is Spirit, *because the
Spirit is God.*" Ambrose had used this text to argue against the Arians,
saying that they, upon reading the italicized words, struck them out
of their Bibles. Clarke pointed out that the text was, in fact, an inter-
polation, and that, as such, it represented a theologizing not found
in scripture.[92]

Finally in support of Thesis 1, Clarke produced Proposition LV,
where he cited the New Testament titles given to the members of the
trinity when mentioned together. His conclusion from all these Propositions we have listed under "Thesis One" was, "From all which, it
appears, even to a demonstration; (the words, God and Father, being
put promiscuously for each other;) that God, in scripture-language,
does not signify the trinity, but the first person of the trinity."[93]

THESIS 2: The Son is Neither Self-existent nor a Creature

Here Clarke's concern was to steer the middle course between Sabellianism and Arianism. Both schools of thought sought to preserve

---

[89] Justin Martyr, *Apol.* 1 in Clarke, *SD*, 134.
[90] Theophilus, *To Autolycus.* Book II in Clarke, *SD*, 134. This is the first use of the
term trinity (*tpiados*). Quasten, Vol. 1, 239, cf., *ANF* Vol. 2, 101 n. 2.
[91] Theodore of Abucara, *Opusc.* taken by Clarke from Pearson's *Exposition on the
Creed* in Clarke, *SD, 135.* Others cited on this Proposition are Ambrose, Basil, The
Council of Sirmium, and Athanasius.
[92] Ambrose, *On the Holy Spirit.* Book 3, Chap. 11 in Clarke, *SD*, 154. Clarke's
comment here is in keeping with the text critical insights of his age and is reflected
in the writings of Bentley, Mill and Wettstein.
[93] Clarke, *SD*, 191.

monotheism, but through opposite means. The Sabellians absorbed the Word into the Godhead, leaving him merely as mode of God's self expression. The Arians asserted that the Word was part of the created order, and therefore not God. In the former school the Son lost his distinctiveness as a true *hypostasis*, in the latter as true God.

Clarke developed five propositions in support of his thesis that the Son was neither self-existent nor a creature.[94] In Proposition XII Clarke wrote, "The Son is not self-existent; but derives his being, and all his attributes, from the Father, as from the supreme cause."[95] Clarke drew from a host of Patristic sources to bring out different dimensions of this idea. There was an immense distance between the unbegotten Father and the creation, which required a middle nature, a begotten one between them.[96] The very term "Father" implied causality regarding the Son.[97] He quoted Hilary that the notion of the Son's self-existence was impious because it destroyed the unity of God.

> 'Tis most impious to profess the Son to be unoriginate. For then there would no longer be one God; the doctrine of the unity of God being founded necessarily in the nature of one unoriginated God: And the reason why there is but one God, though the Father be God and the Son of God be God; is because one only is unoriginate. The Holy (Catholick) faith therefore forbids us to teach that the Son is unoriginate; that, by holding one only unoriginate, it may maintain that there is but one God.[98]

While Clarke asserted that the Son was in fact originate, he declined to describe the manner in which this occurred. In Proposition XIII Clarke wrote, "In what particular metaphysical manner, the Son derives his being from the Father, the scripture has no where distinctly declared; and therefore men ought not to presume to be able to define."[99] Clarke cited Novatian's argument that as to the manner of the Son's generation the Apostles, the Prophets and even the angels were ignorant.[100] Moreover, Alexander of Alexandria had said that

---

[94] These are XII, XIII, XIV, XVII, and XVIII.
[95] Clarke, *SD*, 136.
[96] Alexander of Alexandria, *Epist. apud Theodoret Hist.* Book 1, Chap. 4 in Clarke, *SD*, 136.
[97] Basil, *Contra Eunomius* 1 in Clarke, *SD*, 137.
[98] Hilary, *De Synodis* in Clarke, *SD*, 137.
[99] Clarke, *SD*, 137.
[100] Novatian, *De Trinitate*, 31 in Clarke, *SD*, 138.

the manner in which the Son received his substance was "ineffable."[101] Clarke cited Eusebius three times in this regard.[102] Basil also had warned against inquiring too much into the matter.

> Thou believest that he was begotten? Do not enquire how. For, as it is in vain to enquire how he that is unbegotten, is unbegotten; so neither ought we to enquire how he that is begotten, was begotten.—Seek not what cannot be found out—Believe what is written; search not into what is not written.[103]

Clarke affirmed that the Son was indeed begotten, and not self-existent, while refusing to investigate the manner of his origination.[104]

Having affirmed that the Son was not self-existent, Clarke then turned to the other side of the problem, and maintained that although the Son was not unoriginate, he nevertheless was not a creature. Here Clarke certainly had the Arian position in view. As we have seen, Arius had been a presbyter in Alexandria, and about 319 challenged the standard theology regarding the Son. The two principle tenets of Arianism were: 1) That the Son was a creature, something made (κτίσμα) out of nothing (ἐξ οὐκ ὄντων) and therefore like the rest of creation. 2) That there was a time when the Son did not exist, when he was not (ὅτι ἦν ποτε ὅτε οὐκ ἦν).[105] Arius stated these views in a letter to his friend Eusebius of Nicomedia,

> And before he was begotten or created or defined or established, he was not. For he was not unbegotten. But we are persecuted because we say, "The Son has a beginning, but God is without beginning." . . . We are persecuted because we say "He is from nothing." But we speak thus inasmuch as he is neither part of God nor from any substratum. On account of this we are persecuted.[106]

---

[101] Alex. of Alexandria, *Epistle ad Alex. apud Theodoret.* Book 1, Chap. 4, in Clarke, *SD*, 139.

[102] Eusebius, *Ecclesiastical Theology.* Book 1, Chap. 12; Book 1, Chap. 8 and Theodoret, *Ecclesiastical History*, Book 1, Chap. 11.

[103] Basil, *Homil.* 29 in Clarke, *SD*, 140.

[104] The position that the Son was not self-existent was characteristic of Arminius' theology and later Arminianism as well. Perhaps this is one reason why the Remonstrants were able to accept the Polish Socinians in worship during Locke's tenure in Holland, as we saw in Chapter One. It seems more likely that Clarke derived his views here based upon his examination of the patristic sources, rather than as a simple adoption of Arminian theology.

[105] William G. Rusch, *The Trinitarian Controversy*, in *Sources of Early Christian Thought Series* (Philadelphia: Fortress Press, 1980), 17.

[106] Arius, *Letter to Eusebius of Nicomedia* trans. by Rusch, 30.

Clarke challenged each of these proposals in Propositions XIV, XV and XVI respectively, although he only cited Patristic sources for the first. In Proposition XIV Clarke wrote, "They are both therefore worthy of censure; both they who on the one hand presume to affirm, that the Son was made out of nothing (ἐξ οὐκ ὄντων); and they who, on the other hand, affirm that he is the self-existent substance."[107] Since he had treated the idea of self-existence under Propositions V and XII, he proceeded to discuss the former assertion. Clarke cited the *Shepherd of Hermas* regarding the fact that the Son was more ancient than all other creatures since he was present with the Father at the beginning of the creation.[108] The Father conversed with the Son before the creation[109] and he was the most ancient of all derivative beings.[110] He not only preceded all other creatures, but unlike them, who were created *ex nihilio*, he was of the Father. He was God from God. Clarke stated that Athanasius himself said, "Who, when he hears Him, whom he believes to be the only true God, say, 'this is my beloved Son'; dares affirm that the Word of God was made out of nothing?"[111] Here then, one of the foundational tenets of Arianism was flatly refuted. Clarke also denied the other foundational tenet of Arius when he wrote in Proposition XV, "The scripture, in declaring the Son's derivation from the Father, never makes mention of any limitation of time; but always supposes and affirms him to have existed with the Father from the beginning, and before all worlds."[112] This was followed immediately in Proposition XVI where Clarke added, "They therefore have also justly been censured, who taking upon them to be wise above what is written, and intruding into things which they have not see; have presumed to affirm that there was a time when the Son was not (ὅτι ἦν ποτὲ ὅτε οὐκ ἦν)."[113] So we see that with the assistance of the Fathers, Clarke held a middle ground between two heresies: Sabellianism on the one hand, and Arianism on the other.

Although the actual manner of the generation of the Son remained incomprehensible, Clarke asserted that it was not by a necessity of nature, which would be aseity, but by God's power and will. Whereas

---

[107] Clarke, *SD*, 140.
[108] Hermas, *Similitudes*, 9 in Clarke, *SD*, 140.
[109] Justin Martyr, *Dialogue with Trypho* in Clarke, *SD*, 140.
[110] Origen, *Contra Celsus*, Book 5 in Clarke, *SD*, 141.
[111] Athanasius, *Defense of Dionysius of Alexandria* in Clarke, *SD*, 141.
[112] Clarke, *SD*, 141.
[113] Ibid.

Clarke was an intellectualist in his understanding of God's relationship to goodness and the natural law, he was a voluntarist in his understanding of the relationship between the first and second persons of the trinity. However, to assert that the Son was generated by the Father's power and will was not to say that the generation occurred at a definite time. Here Clarke carefully drew in part from Origen and in part from Eusebius. He adopted Origen's view of the eternal generation of the Son, but not Origen's position that this generation found its necessity in the Father's nature. On the other hand, he embraced Eusebius' rejection of the necessity of the Son's origination according to nature, but disallowed Eusebius' denial of eternal generation. Both Origen and Eusebius agreed on one point however, that the Son was derived by God's will. For Origen it was derivation by nature *and* will—eternally. For Eusebius it was generation by the will alone—before time.[114] Clarke carefully synthesized the two approaches when he wrote,

> It cannot be denied but the terms (Son and beget,) do most properly and necessarily imply an act of the father's will. For whatever any person is supposed to do, not by his power and will, but by mere necessity of nature; 'tis not indeed he that does it at all, in any true propriety of speech; but necessity only. Nor can it intelligibly be made out, upon what is founded the authority of the Father in the mission of the Son, if not upon the Son's thus deriving his being from the father's incomprehensible power and will. However, since the attributes and powers of God are evidently as eternal as his being; and there never was any time, wherein God could not will what he pleased, and do what he willed; and since it is just as easy to conceive God always acting, as always existing; and operating before all ages, as easily as decreeing before all ages: it will not at all follow, that that which is an effect of his will and power, must for that reason necessarily be limited to any definite time. Wherefore not only those antient writers who were esteemed Semi-Arians, but also the learnedest of the Fathers on the contrary side, even they who carried up the generation of the Son the highest of all; did still nevertheless expressly assert it to be an act of the Father's power and will.[115]

The point was that to maintain the eternal generation of the Son, at the same time insisting that he was derived by the will and power of the Father, was not a contradiction. Clarke appealed to Origen on this point.

---

[114] See Lyman, 258–59.
[115] Clarke, *SD*, 141.

Origen speaks thus concerning the time of the Son's generation; "These words, Thou art my Son, this day I have begotten thee; are spoken to him by God, with whom it is always to day: [sic] For there is no evening nor morning with him: But the time co-extended, if I may so speak, with his unbegotten and eternal life, is the to day in which the Son was begotten: So that the beginning of his generation can no more be discovered, than of that day." And yet none of the antient writers do more constantly and uniformly than Origen, represent the Son as begotten by the power and will of the Father.[116]

While Origen believed the Son to be derived by nature *and* will, Eusebius believed him derived from will alone.[117]

And yet no-body more expressly than the same Eusebius, declares that the Son was generated by the power and will of the Father: The light (saith he) does not shine forth by the luminous body, but by a necessary property of its nature: But the Son, by the intention and will of the Father, received the subsistence so as to be the image of the Father: For by his will did God become the Father of his Son, and caused to subsist a second light, in all things before all ages a real subsistence, by the inexpressible and inconceivable will and power of the Father.[118]

Clarke cited not only from Origen and Eusebius on this point, but from a host of other Patristic sources.[119] Clarke noted that Victorinus had insisted that the Son's generation was not by necessity of nature, but by the will of the Father's majesty.[120] The Father's will was concurrent with his power in the begetting of his Son.[121] As we have seen, Clarke cited the twenty-fifth anathema of the First Sirmium Creed (351).

If any one says, that the Son was begotten not by the will of the Father; let him be anathema. For the Father did not beget the Son by a physical necessity of nature without the operation of his will; but he at once willed, and begat the Son, and produced him from himself, without time, and without suffering any diminution himself.[122]

---

[116] Origen, *Commentary on John*, 31 in Clarke, *SD*, 143.
[117] Lyman believes that Eusebius' purpose here was to heighten the voluntary power of the Father as well as the distinct existence of the Son. Lyman, 259.
[118] Eusebius, *Demonstration of the Gospel*, Book 5, Chap. 1 in Clarke *SD*, 144.
[119] Included are Alexander of Alexandria, Gregory of Nyssa, Justin, Tatian and Hippolytus.
[120] Marius Victorinus, *Against Arius* in Clarke, *SD*, 145.
[121] Basil, *Homily 29* in Clarke, *SD*, 145.
[122] Clarke cites from Hilary, *De Synodis 37*. For a contemporary translation see Hanson, *In Search*, 326–28.

To this Clarke added Hilary's comment that "this canon was therefore made by the council, lest any occasion should seem given to
hereticks, to ascribe to God the Father a necessity of begetting the
Son, as if he produced him by necessity of nature, without the operation of his will."[123] We see, then, that Clarke argued that whether
the generation of the Son was believed to be eternal (Origen), or
before time (Eusebius), or whether the Son was believed to be generated by nature (Origen), or not (Eusebius), he was believed by
everyone to be generated by the will and power of God.

Under what I have called Thesis 2, it was also important for Clarke
to show the Son to be a real person, not merely an abstraction of
the Father. He wrote that before the Council of Nicaea several theologians, namely, Theophilus, Tatian, and Athenagoras, embraced the
distinction between the λόγος ἐνδιάθετος (the internal word) and the
λόγος προφόρικον (the expressed word). Clarke maintained that this
position was a contradiction in terms, and implied that the Son was
merely an attribute of the Father prior to his "expression."[124] Clarke
taught that Irenaeus and Clement of Alexandria spoke on this point
with some ambiguity, but were clear enough in their intention to
understand the Son as a real person.[125] The other writers before the
Council by and large spoke of the Son clearly as a person.[126] Around
the time of the Council the situation became more unclear.

> About the time of the Council they spake with more uncertainty; some-
> times arguing that the Father considered without the Son would be
> without Reason and without Wisdom, (which is directly supposing the
> Son to be nothing but an attribute of the Father:) and yet at other
> times expressly maintaining, that the Son was "neither the Word spo-
> ken forth, nor the inward Word (or Reason) in the mind of the Father,
> nor an efflux of him, nor a part (or segment) of his unchangeable
> nature, nor an emission from him; but truly and perfectly a Son."[127]

For Clarke, even in the chaos, most writers affirmed the personhood
of the Son and this position was later proved by Eusebius in his
Ecclesiastical Theology against Marcellus of Ancyra, who followed Sabellius and Paul of Samosata.[128] Following the Council clarity continued

---

[123] Hilary, *De Synodis* in Clarke, *SD*, 145.
[124] Clarke, *SD*, 146.
[125] Ibid., 146.
[126] Clarke, *SD*, 146–47. Cites Justin's Dialogue with Trypho here.
[127] Ibid., 147. Athanasius, *Exposition of the Faith.*
[128] Eusebius, *Ecclesiastical Theology.* Book I, Chap. 8 in Clarke, *SD*, 147.

to disappear until at last the scholastic theologians obfuscated it altogether.[129] Here again we see the impact of Eusebius' thought on Clarke. The Son was a person and could not be reduced to an attribute of God in any sense. Throughout his work, Clarke sought to hold together the statements that the Son was not self-existent, and yet not a creature. His person existed in a different category altogether. He was God, yet not as the Father. He was the eternally begotten Son, yet not in any way created.

THESIS 3: The Son is Etiologically Subordinate to the Father, and Biblical Statements which Ascribe Deity to Him are to be Understood in Terms of His Exercise of Title and Power

In the Propositions under Thesis 3, Clarke clarified the precise relationship of the Father and the Son. Again we see the subordinating tendency which Clarke derived from the patterns of Origen and Eusebius. He drew Patristic support for eight propositions under this thesis.[130] Proposition XXVI stated, "By the operation of the Son, the Father both made and governs the World."[131] Clarke commented on this Proposition that "There is hardly any doctrine, wherein all the antient [sic] Christian writers do so universally, so clearly, and so distinctly agree; as in this."[132] Here he cited only Irenaeus and Athanasius.[133] First then, the Son was the one through whom the Father created and ruled. In Proposition XXVII, Clarke wrote,

> To the Son are ascribed in Scripture other the greatest things, [sic] and the highest titles; even all communicable divine powers: That is, all powers which include not that independency and supreme authority, by which the God and Father of all is distinguished to be the God and Father of All.[134]

Clarke cited Justin Martyr[135] here, but then added his own explanation.

---

[129] Clarke, *SD*, 147.
[130] The Propositions are XXVI, XXVII, XXXIV, XXXV, XXXVI, XXXVII, XXXIX, XLVI.
[131] Clarke, *SD*, 151.
[132] Ibid.
[133] Irenaeus, *Against Heresies*. Book I, Chap. 19; Book III, Chap. 8; Book III, Chap. 4. Athanasius, *Contra Gentes, Contra Sabell.* in Clarke, *SD*, 151.
[134] Clarke, *SD*, 151.
[135] Justin Martyr, *Apology* 1 in Clarke, *SD*, 151.

In order to understand rightly and consistently, how, and in what sense, in several of these passages, many of the same powers are ascribed to Christ, which in other passages are represented as peculiar characters of the person of the Father; it is to be observed, that with each one of the attributes of the Father, there must always be understood to be connected the notion of supreme and independent; but the titles ascribed to the Son, must always carry along with them the idea of being communicated or derived.[136]

The Son possessed all of the power of God and the titles of God, but these were understood to be his without that supreme independency which belonged to the Father alone as the source of all power and title.

Not only was the Son subordinate in drawing his attributes from the Father, but his existence itself was subordinate, because it was derivative. In Proposition XXXIV Clarke wrote,

The Son, whatever his metaphysical essence of substance be, and whatever divine greatness and dignity is ascribed to him in scripture; yet in this he is evidently subordinate to the Father, that he derives his being, attributes and powers, from the Father, and the Father nothing from him.[137]

Here again we see Clarke relying on the testimony of Origen.

We affirm the Son not to be more powerful, but less powerful than the Father: And this we do in obedience to his own words, "My Father which sent me is greater than I."—But when we consider our saviour as God the Word . . . and Wisdom and Righteousness and Truth; we then indeed exalt his kingdom, over all who are subject to him as having these titles; but not over his God and Father, to whom on the contrary he himself is subject.[138]

Eusebius was also quoted, reflecting again the Origen-Eusebius-Clarke connection.

The Father is perfect of himself, and first, as Father, and as the cause of the Son's subsistence; not receiving any thing from the Son, to the completing of his own divinity. But the Son, as being derived from a

---

[136] Clarke, *SD*, 153.
[137] Clarke, *SD*, 155.
[138] Origen, *Contra Celsus*, Book 8 in Clarke, *SD*, 155. Clarke also cites Alexander of Alexandria, *Epist. ad Alex. apud Theodoret*, who used the same scripture text, but more reservedly. Where Origen said that the scripture "the Father is greater than I" implied that the Son was less powerful, Alexander restricted the application to the arena of the derivation of existence.

cause, is second to him whose Son he is; having received from the Father both his being, and his being such as he is.[139]

Clarke also cited Novatian[140] and Hilary, who, on the basis of derivation, affirmed the superiority of the Father.[141] Clarke quoted Basil in the same vein, "We affirm that according to the natural order of causes and things issuing from them, the Father must have the preeminence before the Son."[142] Thus Clarke used a variety of Patristic sources, both Eastern and Western, while relying chiefly on Origen and Eusebius, to make his point concerning the derivative nature of the Son.

In Proposition XXXV Clarke went on to say that "Every action of the Son, both in making the world, and in all other his operations; is only the exercise of the Father's power, communicated to him after a manner to us unknown."[143] Thus the Son did not act according to his own initiative, but according to that of the Father. While Clarke recognized that the language of the Fathers varied, for him, their teaching remained the same. He noted that for Irenaeus the Father alone was παντοκράτωρ (almighty), who made all things by his Word (the Son) and his Wisdom (the Spirit).[144] Clement of Alexandria referred to the Lord's (the Son's) power as the "operating power" of the Father.[145] Origen distinguished between the Son as the "immediate maker of the world" and the Father as the "principle author of it."[146] For Eusebius, the distinction was spoken of using causal language.

> The evangelist, when he might have said, all things were made by him as the efficient cause; (and again, the world was made by Him;) did not so express it, by Him as the efficient cause; but by (or through) him as the ministering cause; that hereby he might refer us to the supreme power of the Father, as the original of all things.[147]

---

[139] Eusebius, *Demonstration of the Gospel*. Book IV, Chap. 3 in Clarke, *SD*, 156.
[140] Novatian, *De Trinitate*, Chap. 31 in Clarke *SD*, 156.
[141] Hilary, *De Trinitate*, Book, 3 in Clarke, *SD*, 157.
[142] Basil, *Contra Eunomius*, 1 in Clarke, *SD*, 157. In addition Clarke cited from Athanasius, Clement of Alexander, Justin, Constantine, and the Synod of Sardica.
[143] Clarke, *SD*, 159.
[144] Irenaeus, *Against Heresies*. Book 2, Chap. 55 in Clarke, *SD*, 159–160.
[145] Clement of Alexandria, *Stromata*, 7 in Clarke, *SD*, 160.
[146] Origen, *Contra Celsus* Book 6 in Clarke, *SD*, 160.
[147] Eusebius, *Ecclesiastical Theology*. Book 1, Chap. 20, sect. 3 in Clarke, *SD*, 161.

Clarke pointed out that Gregory of Nyssa also used causal language,[148] and that Cyril had written that the Son formed the creation by "appointment of the Father."[149] For Clarke, then, the Son was derived in terms of his being, and his power was communicated by the Father. It was not a different power than the Father's, but the Son served the Father in an instrumental fashion as the one who exercised his power.

Clarke continued along this theme in Proposition XXXVI where he stated, "The Son, whatever his metaphysical nature or essence be; yet in this whole dispensation, in the creation and redemption of the world, acts in all things according to the will, and by the mission or authority of the Father."[150] Here Clarke drew from both Greek and Latin theologians. From the former Clarke cited Justin several times to the effect that the Son was begotten according to the Father's will and served the same.[151] Irenaeus[152] said that the Son "performs the good pleasure of his Father."[153] Clement of Alexandria wrote that the Son "ministers to the will of the Father who is Good [sic] and supreme over all."[154] Clarke stated that, for Origen, the Father was the primary author of the world because it was created by the Son at the Father's "command."[155] For Athanasius the Son acted according to the "good pleasure of the Father."[156] Basil wrote that,

> by the will of the Father, the ministering Angels exist; by the immediate operation of the Son, they are brought into being; by the presence of the Spirit, they are perfected . . . You observe then three things; the Lord, which commands; the Word, which operates; the Holy Spirit, which confirms and strengthens.[157]

Clarke also drew from the Latin Fathers. Tertullian wrote, "The Son always appeared, and the Son always acted, by the authority and will of the Father; because the Son can do nothing of himself, but

---

[148] Gregory of Nyssa, *Epist.* 43 in Clarke, *SD*, 161–62.

[149] Cyril, Hieros. *Catech.* 11 in Clarke, *SD*, 162.

[150] Clarke, *SD*, 164.

[151] Justin Martyr, From his *Apology* and *Dialogue with Trypho* in Clarke, *SD*, 164.

[152] Although Irenaeus is from Lyon in Gaul, he was raised in Asia Minor, was acquainted with Polycarp, and wrote in Greek. (Quasten, Vol. 1, 287).

[153] Irenaeus, *Against Heresies.* Book 3, Chap. 8 in Clarke, *SD*, 165.

[154] Clement of Alexandria, *Stromata* 7 in Clarke, *SD*, 166.

[155] Origen, *Contra Celsus.* Book 6 in Clarke *SD*, 166.

[156] Athanasius, *Contra Gentes*, in Clarke, *SD*, 167.

[157] Basil, *On the Holy Spirit*, Chap. 16 in Clarke, *SD*, 167.

what he seeth the Father do."[158] Clarke quoted Cyprian along the same line.

> That very power or authority by which we are baptized and sanctified, Christ received from the same Father; whom he acknowledged to be greater than himself; by whom, he prayed to be glorified; whose will he fulfilled, even unto the obedience of drinking that cup, and of undergoing death.[159]

Clarke also quoted Novatian, who expressed the point most clearly. "The Son does nothing of his own will, nor of his own motion, nor comes of himself, but obeys all his Father's will and commands— The minister of the will of the Father, from whom he derives his being."[160] It is apparent that Clarke drew on a broad spectrum of Patristic sources to argue that the Son acted in everything according to the will and authority of the Father.

In Proposition XXXVII, Clarke stressed that all of the Son's actions were determined by the goal of the glorification of the Father. "The Son, how great soever the metaphysical dignity of his nature was, yet, in the whole dispensation, entirely directed all his actions to the glory of the Father."[161] Here he used both Origen[162] and Athanasius, and concluded, "But this is so evidently the whole tenor of scripture, and the unanimous sense of all antiquity; that it would be very needless to enlarge upon it."[163]

Clarke turned, in Proposition XXXIX, to the problem of how the Son and the Father could both be referred to as God and yet monotheism be maintained.

> The reason why the scripture, though it stiles the Father God, and also stiles the Son God, yet at the same time always declares there is but one God; is because, there being in the monarchy of the universe but one authority, original in the Father, derivative in the one God (absolutely speaking) always signifies him in whom the power or authority is original and underived.[164]

---

[158] Tertullian, *Against Praxes*, Chap. 15 in Clarke, *SD*, 166.
[159] Cyprian, *Epist*, 73 in Clarke, *SD*, 166.
[160] Novatian, *De Trinitate*, Chap. 31 in Clarke, *SD*, 167.
[161] Clarke, *SD*, 168.
[162] Origen, *Contra Celsus*, Book 6 in Clarke, *SD*, 168.
[163] Clarke, *SD*, 169.
[164] Ibid.

The term "monarchy" could be understood in the Patristic period in two ways. It could simply be a synonym for the "oneness" of God, or it could refer to the operation of God in his rule of the world.[165] The latter related specifically to the person of Christ and his relationship to the Father. Two early interpretations of the latter form of Monarchianism were rejected by the early church. The first was Modalistic Monarchianism represented most acutely by the already mentioned Sabellius.[166] This form of Monarchianism preserved the unity of the Godhead at the expense of the individuality of the Son. The three "forms" of the Father, Son, and Holy Spirit were just that; forms only, and behind each form stood the same person, portraying different roles in creation, redemption, and sanctification.[167] Kelly has suggested that this form of Monarchianism was popular and widespread. Behind it were the twin convictions of the oneness of God and the full deity of Christ.[168] The second form of Monarchianism rejected by the early church was Dynamic Monarchianism. Paul of Samosata was the greatest proponent of this strain. Here Christ was simply an earthly man who was permeated by divine influences. He responded obediently to them and, as a result, was exalted to fellowship with God.[169] Paul's views were, as we have seen, rejected by the three Antiochene synods and he was finally deposed in 269.[170] In contrast to Modalistic Monarchianism, this form was "a relatively isolated phenomenon with a predominantly rationalist appeal."[171] This brief sketch of Monarchiansim is necessary in order to understand the context within which Clarke worked out his own monarchian program, in which he was desirous to avoid the two heresies. He was conscious of trying to maintain the unity of the Godhead while

---

[165] Prestige, 94–95.

[166] This form of Monarchianism was condemned by Pope Calixtus in 220. Briggs, 83.

[167] Ibid., 113. Prestige points out here that no ancient Father before Basil uses the term *prosopon* in the sense of "mask." It did not mean a transitory or superficial presentation, but simply an individual.

[168] Kelly, 119.

[169] Ibid., 115.

[170] Briggs, 83. On the connection among Lucian the Martyr, Arius and Paul, Prestige writes, "But even when it has been granted that the eclectic system of Arius contained elements closely resembling Paul's teaching, the fact remains that Arianism, and presumably Lucianism, owed its distinctive character to its acceptance of an extreme form of subordinationism, which was undoubtedly derived from Origen, the teacher whose followers had condemned Paul." (Prestige, 116).

[171] Kelly, 119.

at the same time giving genuine individuality to the person of the Son, without compromising his divinity.

Clarke's Monarchianism relied upon the ancient images of the relationship of Father and Son drawn from both domestic and governmental spheres. The relationship was like that of a father in his own house with his son and heir present in the same house. They were not two masters, because their authority was one. In the same way, a king may sit on his throne and his son administer the government, yet there are not two kings, for the son administered by his father's authority.[172] Clarke began by citing Justin to the effect that the Son was God in his person.[173] With this established, he went on to describe, in the words of Tertullian, how a monarchy within the Godhead could be compatible with the idea of one God.

> And if the monarch has a Son; yet his dominion is not presently divided, and ceases to be a monarchy, though He takes his Son into the government with him. The government is still principally his, from whom it is communicated to his Son; and so long as it is His, it is nevertheless a monarchy, for being administred [sic] by two persons so united . . . The notion of a monarchy is then only destroyed, when another dominion is supposed to be set up, independent, and of itself, and so rivalling the first: But I who derive the Son from no other original, but from the substance of the Father; and suppose him doing nothing but by the will of the Father, and receiving all his power from the Father; how can I destroy the belief of the monarchy, which I preserve in the Son, delivered from the Father to him?[174]

Clarke followed Origen here again in negotiating the way between Arianism and the doctrine of Paul of Samosata. Origen wrote,

> Hence we may save the scruple of many pious persons, who, through fear lest they should make two Gods, fall into false and wicked notions; (either on the one side denying the real personality of the Son distinct from the Father; and so, while they (rightly) acknowledge his divinity, making him (erroneously) to be in reality nothing but a mere name: Or else on the other side, denying (erroneously) his divinity, while they (rightly) acknowledge his real personality and that his subsistence is truly and properly distinct from that of the Father:) This scruple, I say, of many pious persons, may thus be solved. We must tell them, that he who is of himself God, is that God; (as our saviour,

---

172 Clarke, *SD*, 169.
173 Justin, *Dialogue with Trypho* in Clarke, *SD*, 169.
174 Tertullian, *Against Praxus*, Chaps. 3 & 4 in Clarke, *SD*, 169–70.

in his prayer to his Father, says, "that they may know Thee the only true God;) but that whatever is God, besides that self-existent person, being so only by communication of his divinity, cannot so properly be stiled that God, but rather a divine person, &c."[175]

Once again, Eusebius was also relied upon to answer the Sabellian challenge that the distinct personhood of the Son would compromise the unity of God. Clarke quoted Eusebius,

> But you are afraid perhaps, lest acknowledging two distinct subsistences, you should introduce two original principles, and so destroy the monarchy of God. Know then, that if there is but one underived and unbegotten God, and the Son is begotten of him, there can be but one Head, one monarchy, one dominion: seeing that even the Son himself acknowledgeth the Father to be his original cause; "for the head of Christ," saith the Apostle, "is God."[176]

Athanasius was cited in the same regard.[177] Basil, who had worked out the relationship between οὐσία and ὑπόστασις in the form which would eventually become dogma at Chalcedon,[178] was used to summarize Clarke's position.

> We express each of the persons singly; One God and Father, One only-begotten Son, and one Holy Spirit—For when we worship the Son as God of God, we at the same time both acknowledge the distinctiveness of the persons, and yet preserve the monarchy of the universe, taking heed not to divide our notion of God into a number of independent persons. But how then (you will say,) if there be two distinct persons, do we not make two Gods? Why just as the King and the image (or representative) of the King, do not make two Kings;— because whatever honour is paid to the image, redounds to the original.—The way therefore to the true knowledge of God is, to ascend from the one Spirit, through the one Son, to the one Father; and on the other side, the goodness and holiness of the divine nature, and royal dignity, is communicated from the Father, through the only-begotten, unto the Spirit. Thus both distinctiveness of the persons is acknowledged, and yet the monarchy of the universe (as piety requires) is preserved by us.[179]

---

[175] Origen, *In Joh.* p. 46. Clarke is citing from Huetius' *Origeniana* in Clarke, *SD*, 170–71.

[176] Eusebius, *Ecclesiastical Theology*. Book 1, Chap. 20, sect. 15 in Clarke, *SD*, 173.

[177] Athanasius, *Contra Arianos*, Orat. 4 in Clarke, *SD*, 175.

[178] Michael O'Carroll, *Trinitas: A Theological Encyclopedia of the Holy Trinity* (Wilmington, Delaware: Michael Glazier, Inc., 1987), 49.

[179] Basil, *On the Holy Spirit*, Chap. 18 in Clarke, *SD*, 176.

It is crucial to note here the theological lineage of Basil. Hanson writes,

> Basil emerged from a background, not of the strongly pro-Nicene theology of Athanasius, but of the school of Basil of Ancyra and beyond him, as we have seen, of Gregory Theodorus and of Origen. It is not therefore surprising to find that he does not treat *homoousios* as an indispensable watchword. He does not make it a prominent part of his defence of N [Nicaea] against Eunomius.[180]

The important element to see in Basil, which I believe Clarke took over from him, is the "derivative" sense which Athanasius attached to Ὁμοόυσιος when applied to the Son.[181]

> Basil produced a doctrine of God as a single *ousia* with three distinct sets of recognizable proprieties or peculiarities (γνωπίστικαι ἰδιότητες), each set forming an authentically existing *hypostasis*, the whole bound together inseparably in a common *ousia* or nature, no *hypostasis* being subordinate to or less than the others, but the Second and Third deriving from the First as their source or ultimate principle.[182]

The Son is God in the fullest sense, but that fullness is derived from the Father as alone self-existing. Here then, we can see a subordinating (derivative) element beginning with Origen, moving through Eusebius, Basil of Ancyra, through Basil the Great and eventually being picked up by Clarke.

The way in which the monarchy was administered was described by Clarke in the final Proposition under this Thesis as "economy." Proposition XLVI states,

> For, the great oeconomy, or the whole dispensation of God towards mankind in Christ, consists and terminates in this; that all authority and power is originally in the Father, and from him derived to the Son, and exercised according to the will of the Father by the operation of the Son and by the influence of the Holy Spirit; and all communications from God to the creature, are conveyed through the intercession of the Son, and by the inspiration and sanctification of the Holy Spirit: So on the contrary, all returns from the creature, of prayers and praises, of reconciliation and obedience, of honour and duty to God; are made in and by the guidance and assistance of the Holy Spirit, through the mediation of the Son, to the supreme Father and author of all things.[183]

---

[180] Hanson, *The Search*, 693.
[181] Ibid., 695.
[182] Ibid., 699.
[183] Clarke, *SD*, 186.

Modern scholarship has noted that Tertullian[184] and Hippolytus used the term "economy" to describe the functional constitution of the trinity.[185] For Tertullian the divine triad devolved out of the divine unity itself. In the triadic structure the unity is "distributed" or "dispensed," "organized" or "methodized."[186] The term "economy" carried not only the sense of distribution, but of "constructive order or system."[187] Clarke cited Athanasius,[188] Justin[189] and Irenaeus[190] to the effect that there was an ordering within the divine economy. It was through this economy that the monarchy of God was managed, and remained intact.

THESIS 4: The Holy Spirit is also Derivative of the Father

Under this heading Clarke offered only three Propositions.[191] He had made his case in principle regarding the Son, and in these propositions he merely made application to the Spirit. Proposition XXII stated, "In what particular manner, the Holy Spirit derives his being from the Father, the scripture hath no where at all defined, and therefore men ought not to presume to be able to explain." Here he cited only Basil, who never referred to the Spirit as "God" in his *De Spiritu Sancto*.[192] We have also noted this Cappadocian's Origenist legacy from his early years, which he never entirely abandoned. He never applied the ὁμοούσιος to the Spirit.[193] His derivative theology, which maintained both the supremacy of the Father as well as the individuation of the Spirit, insisted that these two statements were all that could be made concerning the their relationship.

> The very motions of our own mind, whether the soul may be said more properly to create or to beget them; who can exactly determine? What wonder then is it, that we are not ashamed to confess our ignorance concerning the Holy Spirit? For, that he is superior to created beings, the things delivered in Scripture, concerning him, do sufficiently

---

[184] Tertullian *Against Praxeas*, especially Chaps. 2 and 3. *ANF*, Vol. III, 598–99.
[185] Prestige, 97–111.
[186] Ibid., 102.
[187] Ibid.
[188] Athanasius, *Contra Sabellianos*, and *Contra Arianos*, Orat. 3 in Clarke, *SD*, 186.
[189] Justin Martyr, *Apology*, 2 in Clarke, *SD*, 186.
[190] Irenaeus, *Against Heresies*. Book 5, Chap. 36 in Clarke, *SD*, 187.
[191] These are XXII, XXIII, and XLI.
[192] Quasten, Vol. III, 231.
[193] Hanson, *The Search*, 694.

evidence: But the title of unoriginated, this no man can be so absurd as to presume to give to any other than to the supreme God, nay, neither can we give to the Holy Spirit the title of Son; for there is but one Son of God, even the only-begotten . . . Neither let any man think, that our refusing to call the Spirit a creature, is denying his personality, (or real subsistence:) For it is the part of a pious mind, to be afraid of saying any thing concerning the Holy Spirit, which is not revealed in scripture; and rather to be content to wait till the next life, for a perfect knowledge and understanding of his nature.[194]

Next, Clarke was careful to maintain the self-existence of the Father over against the Spirit in the same way he had concerning the Son. In Proposition XXIII he wrote,

They who are not careful to maintain these personal characters and distinctions, but, while they are solicitous (on the one hand) to avoid the errors of the Arians, affirm (in the contrary extreme) the Son and Holy Spirit to be (individually with the Father) the Self-existent Being: These, seeming in words to magnify the name of the Son and Holy Spirit, in reality take away their very existence; and so fall unawares into Sabellianism (which is the same as Socinianism.)[195]

Interestingly, Clarke cited two texts from the Fathers which have no bearing on the Spirit at all. He was repeating the point made earlier, that the Son was not *autoousia*, and the reader was expected, by extrapolation, to make application to the Spirit.[196] He proceeded to warn against the dangers of Sabellianism if the proper distinction between the divine persons was not maintained. He cited Athanasius and Basil in this regard.[197] Only Gregory of Nazianzus was quoted directly on the Spirit.

And Nazianzen, speaking of the same opinions, (Orat. 1) calls those men (ἄγαν ὀρθοδόξας) over-orthodox, who, by affirming the Son and the Holy Spirit to be unoriginated, did consequently either destroy their personality, that is, their existence; or introduce three co-ordinate self-existent persons, that is, (πολυωρξίαν) a plurality of Gods.[198]

Lastly Clarke pointed out that the Spirit acted only by the will and power of the Father. Proposition XLI stated,

---

[194] Basil, *Contra. Eunomius*, Book 3 in Clarke, *SD*, 148.
[195] Clarke, *SD*, 148–49.
[196] In this way Clarke used Novatian, *De Trinitate*, chap. 18; Origen, *Contra Celsus*. Book 8 in Clarke, *SD*, 149.
[197] Athanasius, *Contra Sabellianos*; and Basil, *Monachis Suis*, Epist. 73 in Clarke, *SD*, 149.
[198] Gregory of Nazianzus, *Orations*, 1 in Clarke, *SD*, 149.

The Holy Spirit, whatever his metaphysical nature, essence or substance be; and whatever divine power or dignity is ascribed to him in
scripture; yet, in the whole dispensation of the gospel, always acts by
the will of the Father, is given and sent by him, intercedes to him, &C.[199]

Clarke quoted Irenaeus twice in this regard. The second quotation
read,

The Father supporting both the whole creation and his own Word,
and the Word supported by the Father, do (each of them) bestow
the Spirit upon all, according to the will of the Father. And so the
Father is shewn to be the one God, who is above all, and through all,
and in all.[200]

To this quotation Clarke added "Above all, by himself, as the same
author afterwards expounds it; through all, by his Son; and in all, by
his Spirit."[201] With the Propositions I have grouped under *Thesis 4*,
Clarke did nothing more than take several of the key points he made
regarding the Son and stated that they were true of the Holy Spirit
as well. It is to be noted that he has continued to rely on Eastern
theologians who follow out of the tradition of Origen, especially the
Cappadocians, Basil and Gregory Nazianzus.

THESIS 5: That Supreme Worship Belongs to the Father Alone

Clarke was not merely concerned with theology in the abstract, but
with its practical implications for the life of the church. Under this
Thesis I have brought together those Propositions where Clarke used
Patristic support to bring his theological conclusions to bear on
worship.[202] It is worth noting that these Propositions appear relatively late in Part Two of his *Scripture-Doctrine*. Clarke waited to lay
out the crucial elements of his trinitarian program before drawing
conclusions about worship.

In Proposition XLIII Clarke stated, "Upon these grounds, [all that
has been said before] supreme honour or worship is due to the person
of the Father singly, as being alone the supreme and original author
of all being and power."[203] Clarke defended his proposition by say-

---

[199] Clarke, *SD*, 179.
[200] Irenaeus, *Against Heresies*, Book 5, Chap. 18 in Clarke, *SD*, 179.
[201] Clarke, *SD*, 179.
[202] These Propositions include numbers XLIII, XLIV, L, LI, and LIV.
[203] Clarke, *SD*, 179.

ing, "'tis plain that the person of the Father, being alone self-existent, independent, unoriginated, and absolutely supreme, can alone be honoured or worshiped as self-existent, independent, unoriginated, and absolutely supreme."[204] He cited Alexander of Alexandria to the effect that there should be reserved to the unbegotten Father a peculiar dignity as a result of his aseity.[205] Once again he relied on Origen's distinction in worship between the Supreme God, who is the Father, and the Son. "Now to ascend to the Supreme God, is to pay him our whole, entire, undivided worship, through his Son."[206] The emphasis here was on the Father as the final *telos* of worship, and on the necessity of worship being directed *through* the Son. Clarke quoted Basil, who also made a distinction between Father and Son in worship, which fit with the derivative nature of his understanding of the ὁμοούσιος.

> As an archangel is (προτιμότερος) more honourable, and has (μεῖζον ἀξίωμα) greater dignity, than an angel; though both are of one angelick nature: So, (though he viz. Basil, supposes the Father, the Son and the Holy Spirit, to be all likewise of one divine nature; yet) the Son, is second to the Father, both in order, because he is from him; and in dignity, because the Father is the original and cause of the Son's being, and the Son is the passage and conductor by and through whom men are brought to God even the Father:—That the Spirit is second likewise (both in order and dignity) to the Son is the doctrine of piety.[207]

Clarke's first point under "Thesis 5" then, was to establish the supremacy of the Father in worship.

Having established in principle the supremacy of the Father in worship, Clarke moved on in Proposition XLIV to specify how this principle was worked out in prayer. "For the same reason, all prayers and praises ought primarily or ultimately to be directed to the person of the Father, as the original and primary author of all good."[208] Here Clarke cited Justin and Irenaeus to show that prayer has been understood in the church to proceed to the Father *through* the intercession or priestly work of the Son.[209]

---

[204] Ibid., 180.
[205] Alexander of Alexandria, *Apud Theodoret.* Book I, Chap. 4 in Clarke *SD*, 180.
[206] Origen, *Contra Celsus.* Book 8 in Clarke, *SD*, 180.
[207] Basil, *Contra Eunomius*, Book 3 in Clarke, *SD*, 180.
[208] Clarke, *SD*, 181.
[209] Justin Martyr, *Apology*, 2. Irenaeus, *Against Heresies*. Book 4, Chap. 33, Al. 17 in Clarke, *SD*, 181.

Once again, Clarke relied on Origen to demonstrate his point. He said of Origen's opinion,

> Origen, in his book concerning prayer, has a long discourse on purpose to endeavour to prove, that all prayers ought to be offered to God the Father only, and not directly to the Son (who is appointed our high-priest by the Father,) or to the Holy Spirit (who receives his being form the Father,) but *by* or *through* them.[210]

Origen introduced a distinction into worship. After stating that prayer went to the "Supreme God," he wrote,

> Yet we may also offer up supplications and intercessions and thanksgivings and prayers, to the Word himself; if we can distinguish between that which is prayer strictly and directly, and that which is so figuratively and obliquely.[211]

It is clear that, for Clarke, this "distinction" in Origen's mind really had to do with the fact that prayer was offered to the Son "first," only in the formal sense, as our intercessor.[212]

In the same way, in Proposition XLV Clarke stated that not only praise and prayer, but any honor given to the Son and Spirit belonged ultimately to the Father.

> And upon the same account, whatever honour is paid to the Son who redeemed, or to the Holy Spirit who sanctifies us, must always be understood as tending finally to the honour and glory of the Father, by whose good pleasure the Son redeemed, and the Holy Spirit sanctifies us.[213]

On this Proposition Hilary alone was quoted.

> The Son hath nothing but what is derivative; and the greatness of the honour of Him which is begotten, is to the glory of Him which begat: There is no room therefore to object, that we derogate from the majesty of the Father; seeing that whatever majesty we shall ascribe to the Son, must all redound to the magnifying of the power of Him, who begat a Son of divinity and majesty.[214]

Commenting on Propositions XLIV and XLV Clarke made the observation that whether one holds the orthodox doctrine, or a Sabellian

---

[210] Clarke, *SD*, 181, citing Origen, *De Oratio*, sects. 50, 51, 52.
[211] Origen, *Contra Celsus*. Book 8 in Clarke, *SD*, 182.
[212] Ibid.
[213] Clarke, *SD*, 185.
[214] Hilary, *De Trinitate*. Book 4 in Clarke, *SD*, 185.

one in the speculative theology, the practical implication for worship was the same.

> For if on the one hand, the Father, the Son, and the Holy Spirit, be understood to be three real persons or intelligent agents; then, it being manifest that the two latter must of necessity be subordinate, (because other wise there would be three supreme intelligent agents, that is, three Gods;) 'tis manifest likewise, that to the former only can be paid honour absolutely supreme. And if on the other hand, they may be understood to be, not really, but figuratively three persons, viz. God, and the internal reason and wisdom of God; then 'tis also manifest, that to Him only, who is the real person, and not to his reason or wisdom, ought prayers properly to be put up.[215]

In Proposition L Clarke acknowledged that there were places in scripture which referred specifically to the worship of the Son. These, he maintained, were not in deference to his metaphysical nature, but to his role as the Mediator.

> After and upon account of the accomplishment of which dispensation, [his suffering and death] he is described in scripture as invested with distinct worship in his own person; his original glory and dignity being at the same time revealed, and his exaltation in the human nature to his mediatorial kingdom declared: Himself sitting upon his Father's throne, at the right hand of the majesty of God; and receiving the adoration and thanksgivings of his church, as the alone mediator between God and men.[216]

Justin, Irenaeus and the writer of *The Martyrdom of Polycarp* all asserted that the Son was to be worshiped.[217] He cited Clement of Alexandria, Tertullian and Eusebius (whose words he favors) regarding the equalization of the Son in worship with the Supreme Lord.[218]

Nevertheless, this worship was due the Son because of deeds and qualities relative to us, not his essence. In Proposition LI Clarke wrote,

> This honour, the scripture directs to be paid to Christ; not upon account of his metaphysical essence or substance, and abstract attributes; but of his actions and attributes relative to us; his condescension in becoming man, who was the Son of God; his redeeming, and interceding

---

[215] Clarke, *SD*, 185.
[216] Clarke, *SD*, 187.
[217] Clarke cites from *The Martyrdom of Polycarp*; Justin, *Dialogue with Trypho* and *Apology*, 2; Irenaeus, *Against Heresies*, Book 1, Chap. 2.
[218] Clarke, *SD*, 189.

for, us; his authority, power, dominion, and sitting upon the throne of
God his Father, as our lawgiver, our king, our judge, and our God.[219]

Here Clarke argued that the worship due to the Son is due to him
as person, not to a φύσις, ὑπόστασις, or οὐσία.[220] "Every act of Duty,
respect, honour or worship, is entirely personal; corresponding to the
individual power, dominion or authority, of the respective person to
whom it is paid."[221] Clarke cited Justin regarding on this point.

> Next after the Unbegotten and ineffable God, we worship and love
> Him who is the Word of God; because that for our sakes he became
> man, and was made partaker of our sufferings, that he might heal us.[222]

In Proposition LIV Clarke addressed the issue of worshiping the Holy
Spirit.

> For putting up prayers and doxologies directly and expressly to the
> person of the Holy Spirit, it must be acknowledged there is no clear
> precept or example in scripture. The same must be confessed concern-
> ing the practice of the primitive church in the three first centuries, so
> far as appears from the remaining genuine writings of those ages.
> Concerning the use of tradition in these matters, see Basil, *De Spiritu
> Sancto*, Cap. 27 and 29.[223]

It is now evident that in the propositions listed under Thesis 5, Clarke
ordered worship in accordance with the doctrine of God he had
worked out earlier. The supreme honor in worship was due to the
Father alone. All prayer and praise were ultimately directed to him.
Not only prayer and praise, but all honor and glory redounded to
the Father. The Son was worshiped in his role as the person of
the Mediator, not according to an impersonal essence. There was no
biblical nor traditional justification for praying to or glorifying the
Holy Spirit.

Clarke's Use of His Contemporaries' Readings of the Patristics

Just as Clarke had realized that he must, at least, show reasonable
support for his doctrine from among the church Fathers, he also

---

[219] Ibid.
[220] Ibid.
[221] Ibid.
[222] Justin, *Apology*, 2 in Clarke, *SD*, 188.
[223] Clarke, *SD*, 191.

knew that he would have to demonstrate that he was not a voice crying in the contemporary wilderness. The main exponent of orthodox trinitarianism in Clarke's time was Bishop Bull who, published his *Defensio Fidei Nicaenae* in 1685.[224] Bull was the Bishop of St. David's, and his *Defensio* was originally published to counter the charge that he was a Socinian due in part to the substantial role works played in his theology. The *Defensio* became the first in something of a trilogy, being followed by his *Judicium Ecclesiae Catholicae* (1694), which was a response to Episcopius' view that the Nicene Fathers did not consider a belief in Christ's true and proper divinity as an indispensible term of catholic communion. Bull's third work was the *Primitiva et Apostolica Traditio*, which was dircted against Zwicker's position that Christ's divinity, pre-existence, and incarnation were inventions of the early heretics.[225] Together these works formed a refutation of the continental Arminians, Episcopius and Curcellaeus, who maintained that the Fathers before Nicaea held a doctrine different than that adopted by the Council, and that of the Jesuit Patristic scholar Petavius,[226] who held that the position of the Ante-Nicene Fathers was not uniform.[227] Bull's thesis was that there was no difference between the doctrine of the Ante-Nicene Fathers and the Creed of the Council of Nicaea.[228] Fisher has evaluated Bull charitably.

---

[224] Note that Fisher's date of 1689 is incorrect. Fisher, 370.

[225] Dictionary of National Biography, Vol. VII, 237.

[226] Dionysius Petavius [Denis Petau], *Opus de Theologicus Dogmatibus*. Edited by Ludovicus Guerin. 8 Vols. (Paris-Brussels: Barri-Ducis, MDCCCLXIV). Petau was a Jesuit and one of the leading Patristic scholars of the seventeenth century. Of the ten books planned for his dogmatic theology, only five appeared: *De Deo, De Trinitate, De angelis, De mundi opificio* and *De Incarnatione*.

[227] Franks, 151.

[228] *Filium Dei Deo Patri homoousian, sive constantialem, hoc est, non creaturae alicujus aut mutabilis essentiae, sed ejusdem prorsus cum patre suo naturae divinae et incommutabilis, proinde Deum verum de Deo vero esse, catholicorum doctroum, qui tribus primis saeculis floruerunt, constans concorsque fuit sententia.* George Bull, *Opera Omnia, Defensio Fidei Nicenae* (London: Samuel Bridge, 1703), Sect. II, Cap. 1, p. 25.
In another place, Bull outlined his thesis, more comprehensively.
"The unanimous sense of the catholic doctors of the church, for the first three ages of Christianity, concerning the article of the Trinity, is in short this:

I. That there are in the Godhead three (not mere names or modes, but) really distinct *hypostases* or persons, the Father, the Son or the Word of God, and the Holy Ghost.

II. That these three persons are one God; which they thus explain:
  1. There is but one fountain or principle of divinity, God the Father, who only is *Autotheos*, God of and from himself; the Son and Holy Ghost deriving their

Bull sought to show that the Ante-Nicene Fathers were orthodox. His learning was great, and he was a strong reasoner. He claimed somewhat more for the correctness of the pre-Arian Fathers than the scholarship of the present day is able to sanction.[229]

Clarke never came out and flatly accused Bull of being wrong. Instead, he used a number of Bull's subordinationist statements to prove his own quite different conclusions.[230]

In addition to Bull, Clarke drew heavily upon Bishop Pearson's *An Exposition of the Creed*,[231] and William Payne's *The Mystery of the Christian Faith*.[232] Beyond these, he cited from a number of scattered authorities and contemporaries.[233] Clarke cited Bull thirty-one times, Pearson nine times, and Payne five times. With all three theologians, he did the same thing. He used their comments on the Patristic materials to buttress his own conclusions.

---

divinity from him; the Son immediately from the Father, the Holy Ghost from the Father and the Son, or from the Father by the Son.

2. The Son and the Holy Ghost are so derived from the fountain of the divinity, as that they are not separate or separable from it, but do still exist in it, and are most ultimately united to it.

"All the Fathers insist upon this, that if there were more than one fountain of the divinity, or if the three persons were each of them a self-dependent principle of divinity, or if the three persons were separate from each other, then there would be three Gods. But being there is but one fountain of the divinity, the Father, the Son and the Holy Ghost deriving their divinity from that fountain, and that so, as still to exist in it, and be inseparably united to it, there is but one God. That this is the unanimous consent and constant doctrine of the primitive Fathers, I have full shewed in my *Defensio Fidei Nicenae*."

George Bull, *The Works*. Collected and revised by Edward Burton (Oxford: At the University Press, MDCCCXLVI), Vol. II, Discourse I, pp. 1–2.

[229] Fisher, 370. For a similar evaluation see Hefele, 233, n. 1.

[230] On a subordinationist strain in Bull's thought see Hagenbach, 328–29.

[231] John Pearson, *An Exposition of the Creed*. Third edition (Oxford: Printed by J.F. for Joh. Williams, 1699). The creed here is the Apostle's Creed.

[232] William Payne, *The Mystery of the Christian Faith and of the Blessed Trinity Vindicated, and The Divinity of Christ Proved. In Three Sermons preached at Westminster Abbey upon Trinity-Sunday, June the 7th and September 21, 1696* (London: Printed for Richard Cumberland at the Angel in St. Paul's Church-Yard, 1697). These sermons were preached in defense of Thomas Sherlock, whose orthodoxy was under attack by Dr. Robert South. Sherlock, who emphasized the individuality of the persons of the Trinity, was accused of Tritheism by his opponents. *Dictionary of National Biography*, Vol. XLIV, 123–24; Fisher, 370–71. See below, Chp. 5.

[233] These include: Valesius, *Not. ad Eusebius*; Dr. Cave, *Dissertation Against Le Clerc in Defense of Eusebius' Orthodoxy*; Zanchy(i) *De Trib Elohim*; Hooker, *The Mystery of Godliness*; Jackson's *Adnotationes ad Novatianum*; Dr. Mede *Discourse on 2 Peter* 2:1; Archbishop Wake, *Commentary on the Church Catechism*; Calvin, *In Valentin. Gentile* and Flacius Illyricus, *Clavis Script. in voce, Deus*.

Under the Propositions relating to what I have called Thesis 1: that, "In the Language of scripture, the term 'God' denotes almost always the 'Father.' Even when it denotes the 'Son,' its connotation ultimately leads to the Father," Clarke used Bp. Pearson who wrote, "That one God is Father of All; and to us there is but one God, the Father."[234] Next, under this heading, Clarke focused on the issue of aseity. Here he quoted Bull's introduction,

> When he (Socinus) affirms that all the Antients, till the time of the Nicene Council, believed the Father of Jesus Christ to be alone the one true God; if this be understood of that preheminence [sic] of the Father, by which He alone is of himself (by self-existence) the true God; we confess that this assertion is most true.[235]

He moved on to cite Payne, that lack of clarity on this point had resulted in the charge of polytheism by the Church's enemies.[236]

Under Thesis 2: that "The Son is neither self-existent, nor a creature," only Bull was quoted. He wrote, "They who contend that the Son can properly be stiled God of Himself, [or Self-existent;] their opinion is contrary to the catholick doctrine."[237] The point for Bull was that the Creed said the Son was "God from God" not "God of himself" and he warned all students who would ignore such a distinction.[238]

Thesis 3 states that, "The Son is etiologically subordinate to the Father, and biblical statements which ascribe deity to him are to be understood in terms of his exercise of title and power." Under this heading Clarke cited extensively from Bull, and once each from Payne and Pearson. The contributions are drawn up under Propositions XXXIV, XXXV, XXXVI, and XXXIX. One of Clarke's more revealing selections was a text where Bull wrote affirming Eusebius' understanding of this principle. We have already noted Clarke's sympathy for Eusebius' line of thought. Bull wrote,

> That prudent man (viz. Eusebius) took care here (viz. in his Creed,) as almost every where else, to guard against the Sabellians; in so asserting the true divinity of the Son, as at the same time to reserve entire to

---

[234] Pearson, 26.
[235] Bull, *Defensio*, Proem. sect. 4 in Clarke, *SD*, 130. See also *SD*, 136 for Clarke's use of Bull on the same Thesis.
[236] Payne, *Sermon on Trinity-Sunday, June the 7th, 1696*, 18 in Clarke, *SD*, 131.
[237] Bull, *Defensio*, Sect. 4, Chap. 1, par. 7 in Clarke, *SD*, 137.
[238] Ibid., par. 8.

> God the Father the prerogative of being alone God of Himself, (or,
> God self-existent,) and thereby to distinguish the Father from the Son.
> In which, the Nicene Council agreed with him.[239]

The puzzling thing to note here is that Clarke must have been aware
that, even if the Council agreed with Eusebius, which it probably
did, the words of the Creed did not. It seems then, that Clarke's use
of Bp. Bull on this point was his way of implying that the conclusions expressed in the language of the Creed must have been interpreted by the Fathers in a way unlike the contemporary Athanasian
interpretation.

In Proposition XXXV Clarke focused on the notion that the Son's
power was ultimately the Father's. Bull was used to reflect the same
distinction.

> That the Father alone operates of himself (by his own proper power,)
> what catholick can deny? For 'tis the peculiar property of the Father,
> to exist and operate of himself; But the Son receives from the Father,
> as from his original, both his being and power of acting: Upon which
> account he is also said to work his works as it were in imitation of the
> Father, John v., 19.[240]

For both Bull and Clarke, the Son was the minister of the Father,
where the power of the Son was, there was the power of the Father.[241] In Proposition XXXVI, where Clarke shifted emphasis from
the power of Christ to his will and mission, he took issue with Bull's
Latin translation of Clement of Alexandria's *Stromata* 4. Clement had
written, "The Lord Jesus, who, *by the will of the Almighty*, is inspector
of our hearts." Bull had translated the italicized phrase *omnipotente sua
voluntate, etc.*, "who by his *own* almighty will." Clarke argued that this
translation was wrong for two reasons. First, God was not omni-
scient by his will, but by his nature. Second, God did not know our
hearts by his will, but by his power.[242] Clarke here established the
idea that Christ always acted in accordance with the Father's will.
He later chose another text on this point, where he believed Bull
had contradicted his former position, "That the Father, as the chief

---

[239] Bull, *Judicium Ecclesiae Catholicae*, chap. 6, par. 5 in Clarke, *SD*, 159. On Proposition XXXIV see also *SD*, 158.
[240] Bull, *Defensio*, Sect. 2, Chap. 13, par. 10 in Clarke, *SD*, 163.
[241] Ibid., Sect. 4, Chap. 2, par. 2.
[242] Clarke, *SD*, 166.

author giving his commands, created all things by his Son executing the command and will of the Father."[243]

Regarding the second clause of the Proposition, pertaining to the mission of Christ, Clarke used Pearson.

> Upon this pre-eminence (as I conceive) may safely be grounded the congruity of the divine mission. We often read that Christ was sent; from whence he bears the name of an apostle himself (Heb. III. 1.) named so, because as the Father sent him, so sent he them . . . But we never read that the Father was sent at all; there being an authority in that name, which seems inconsistent with this mission.[244]

With these two points, Clarke argued that both the power and will of the Son were subordinate to the Father in that they were derived from the mission he established.

Finally, under the general theme of subordination, under Proposition XXXIX, Clarke used several authors to reinforce his notion of monarchy. He quoted Bull to the effect that two self-originating principles was Ditheism. Bull agreed with Clarke in the etiological subordination of the Son.

> But now on the contrary, if we allow that subordination, by which the Father alone is God of himself, and the Son is God from God the Father; then those antient writers thought, that both the pre-eminence of the Father, and the monarchy of the universe, would be preserved entire.[245]

Here Clarke also cited the Patristics scholar Valesius, who, in his *Notes on Eusebius*, wrote, "All the primitive Christians in their discourses concerning God, ascribe the monarchy to God the Father; but the oeconomy, or administration and dispensation to the Son and Holy Spirit."[246] Clarke then argued from Dr. Payne to show how this might be so.

> But our Saviour says, he and his Father are one; and three may be one, as well as two. We must therefore consider the true sense and

---

[243] Bull, *Defensio*, Sect. 2, chap. 5, par. 6 in Clarke, *SD*, 168.

[244] Pearson, *Exposition*, 36.

[245] Bull, *Defensio*, Sect., 4, Chap. 4, par. 2 in Clarke, *SD*, 177.

[246] Henricus Valesius, *Notes on Eusebius*, p. 5 Valesius was one of the leading patristic translators and scholars of his time. He published a number of Greek texts and Latin translations of leading church historians of the patristic period. His editions were reprinted in Migne's *PG* and became the basis of the early study of church history. It is likely that Clarke would have relied heavily upon the authoritative work of Valesius in his understanding of Eusebius.

meaning of the words; which was not to teach us a new way of num-
bering, or to destroy the nature of numbers; ... There are several sorts
of unity: There is an unity of consent and agreement, which may be
amongst a great many; of power and authority, which may be possessed and executed by several persons, who may be all—one sovereign
and royal monarch ... the unity of God consists in this, that the person stiled in scripture the one God, is the Father;—that the Son and
Holy Spirit are in the Father, as in the fountain of their being; and are
naturally and inseparably united to him; and that he is the self-existent
unoriginated principle, the root and fountain of the other two; and
therefore they are one with him, because, though having real being
and subsistencies of their own, yet they are from him and in him.[247]

Finally, under our "Thesis 5": that "Supreme Worship Belongs to
the Father alone," Clarke drew support under two Propositions. Under
Proposition XXXIX he took issue with Bishop Bull. Bull had argued
that with regard to the worship of the Son a distinction was necessary between his human and divine natures. First, Bull argued, we
worship the Son in his humanity, according to his mediatorial capacity, and thus all worship was directed through him to the Father.
But regarding his deity, "if we consider Christ as God, without regard to his mediatorial office; we may again consider him in two
distinct respects: Either as God, absolutely; or relatively, as God, or
the Son of God."[248] If the Son was considered under the former
respect, he deserved the exact same worship as the Father. Under
the latter respect (relatively as he is in the Son), as derived from the
Father, "then it is certain again, that all the honour and worship,
which we pay to him, must redound to the Father, and be referred
ultimately to the Father, as the fountain of divinity."[249] Clarke believed that this latter distinction between the Son considered absolutely and relatively was arbitrary. It produced a coordinate worship
which did not ultimately terminate in the Father, and

has not only no manner of foundation in the nature of things, (for
Christ is manifestly no otherwise God, than as he is God of God;) ...
but is contrary even to the doctrine of Athanasius ... and directly
contrary to this excellent author's [Bull's] own express doctrine, in the
whole Fourth Section, and in other places.[250]

---

[247] Payne, *Sermon on Trinity Sunday, June 7, 1696*, 20–21 in Clarke, *SD*, 177–78.
[248] Bull, *Defensio*, Sect. 2, Chap. 9, par. 15 in Clarke, *SD*, 182.
[249] Ibid, *SD*, 183.
[250] Ibid.

In addition to Bull, Clarke cited other contemporary sources.[251]

Not only were prayer and praise to be offered to the Father only, but under Proposition XLV, all honor ultimately went to the Father as well. Here again, Clarke used Bull to make his case.

> 'Tis certain that all the honour and worship, which we pay to him as he is the Son, and derives his original from the Father, must redound to the Father, and be referred ultimately to the Father, as the fountain of divinity.[252]

In summarizing Clarke's use of his contemporaries it is clear that he relied heavily on Bishop Bull for supporting the foundational argument for the *Scripture-Doctrine*, namely that the Son did not enjoy aseity. Although Bull's intention in writing the *Defensio* had been to show that all the Ante-Nicene Fathers were what was later termed "orthodox," Clarke subverted this intention and used Bull's work to support his own reading of the situation. Pearson was utilized by Clarke for the same purpose, and also to support Clarke's contention that the terms "God" and "Father" were equivalent in scripture language. Pearson was also used to establish the Father as the origin of the mission of the Son. Payne was used because he was sympathetic to Sherlock's emphasis on starting with the individual persons of the trinity, and recognizing the distinctions among them. This was compatible with the Eastern approach to understanding the Godhead; an approach which Clarke shared. Overall, then, Clarke exploited the contemporary material at his disposal well. He drew upon several authors who were sympathetic to his reading of the Fathers, and from one whose subordinationism he enlisted toward ends quite against the author's intentions.

By way of concluding this chapter we are now in a position to begin to evalute the scholarly consensus outlined in the Introduction. The general consensus among scholars has been that Samuel Clarke held an Arian doctrine of God. Referring to Clarke's *Scripture-Doctrine* Fisher wrote, "A defense of Arianism, to be sure, in the highest form, by such a man, excited a commotion."[253] Shedd made the same assumption. "Clarke's views were, in reality, a reproduction of the

---

[251] Mede, *Discourse on 2 Peter ii, 1* and Wake, *Commentary on the Church Catechism*, 130–31 in Clarke, *SD*, 184.

[252] Bull, *Defensio*, Sect. 2, Chap., 9, par. 15 in Clarke, *SD*, 185.

[253] Fisher, 371.

Origenistic and High-Arian doctrine of subordination, as distinguished from the Athanasian."[254] Sheldon was more circumspect in writing, "Samuel Clarke, in his *Scripture-Doctrine of the Trinity* (1712) pushed the aspect of subordinationiem far toward the borders of Arianism. His position, as gathered from this work, might be described as a position of indecision between Origen and Arius.[255] More recently Asch described Clarke as semi-Arian, but this is because, "his position differed from that of Arius in that Clarke believed that there was no time at which the Son and the Holy Spirit had not existed, and Arius held that there was."[256] It is obvious that Asch means "semi-Arian" in the common usage as "partly Arian." The term is not capitalized, and her dissertation shows no acquaintance with the Semi-Arian or *Homoiousian* party of the fourth century. She does, at least, suspect that Clarke's doctrine is not thoroughly Arian. My conclusion regarding Clarke and the Patristic sources is, that rather than describing Clarke's work as "a position of indecision between Origen and Arius" (Sheldon), *The Scripture-Doctrine of the Trinity* represents a reassertion of the trajectory of thought found in Eusebius of Caeserea. Eusebius received from Origen's school a certain subordinationism, primarily related to the derived nature of the Son. Both Clarke and Eusebius affirmed that the generation of the Son was ultimately beyond human knowledge. Eusebius wrote,

> The Holy Scriptures teach Him to be begotten of the Father, by a mode of generation which is incomprehensible and inexplicable to all created beings.[257]

Likewise Clarke in his Proposition XIII,

> In what particular metaphysical manner the son derives his being from the Father, the Scripture has no where distinctly declared; and therefore men ought not to presume to be able to define.[258]

Both Clarke and Eusebius insisted on what was generally understood in the Ante-Nicene era, but not in Clarke's, that the Father alone was underived and without cause. As we have seen above, Clarke

---

[254] Shedd, Vol. I, 386. For similar assessments see Hodgson, 222; Payne, 100.
[255] Sheldon, Vol. II, 99.
[256] Asch, 157.
[257] Epistle of Eusebius, cited in Theodoret *Eccleisiastical History* I, XI, *NPNF*, Vol. III, 50.
[258] Clarke, *SD*, 137.

even cited Eusebius as a source on this point.[259] Also, both Clarke
and Eusebius stressed the mediatorial role of the Son. This idea was
thematic in Eusebius[260] and was expressed in his Oration in the *Life
of Constantine,*

> He was the light associating with the Father beyond the universe,
> mediating, and screening the unbeginning and unoriginated Ideal (ἰδεάν)
> from the substance of all produced things (γενητόν), and he, springing
> up from the ineffable and unbeginning Godhead, issues forth from the
> place above the heaven and all that is within heaven, shining with the
> rays of wisdom greater than those of the sun.[261]

While he was uncomfortable with the language of the ὁμοούσιος,
Eusebius was willing to embrace it as a bastion against Arianism.
His own creed had used "likeness" language, which was picked up
by Basil of Ancyra in the Dated Creed. Eusebius was representative
of the majority of bishops at Nicaea who were brought rather unhap-
pily to assent to that Creed. That majority would later ascend under
the leadership of Basil of Ancyra and produce the Third Sirmium
Creed in 358, which was a ὁμοιούσιος statement. This position was
softened by the Fourth Creed of 359, which Basil signed, but added
his gloss. The Homoiousians were eventually eclipsed by the Homoians
at Constantinople in 360. These in turn were eventually overturned
by the Cappadocian theologians, who reflect in certain ways the line
of thought expressed by Origen, Eusebius and Basil of Ancyra. Concerning them, Hanson writes,

> Though Basil wrote several letters to Athanasius in Alexandria show-
> ing the greatest respect for him and Gregory of Nazianzus delivered a
> eulogy on him after his death, none of the Cappadocian theologians
> derived their theological tradition directly from him. Their intellectual
> pedigree stemmed from the school of Basil of Ancyra ... The doctrine
> of "like in respect of *ousia*" was one which they could accept or at least
> take as a starting point, and which caused them no uneasiness.[262]

We can now see where Clarke's thought is aligned within the Patristic
debate. He was certainly no Arian as he expressly denied the two

---

[259] On this point see also Eusebius, *Ecclesiastical Theology*, Book I, Chap. 2. in
Clarke, *SD*, 127.
[260] Hanson, *The Search*, 57.
[261] Eusebius, *Life of Constantine*, "Oration", 1.6. *NPNF*, I, 583. This translation is
taken from Hanson, *The Search*, 57–58.
[262] Ibid., 678.

Arian tenets. The Son was not a creature, nor was there "a time when he was not." Clarke was not a Homoian because he believed, not merely that the Son was like the Father, but "like in all things" excepting ingenerateness. On the other hand it is clear that Clarke was uncomfortable with the problems of the language of ὁμοόυσιος. He maintained that the Son was the express image of the Father but fell short of affirming an numerical identity of substance, which he believed to be Sabellianism. His position, and his understanding of the Patristics is best summarized in his letter to Robert Nelson.

> And that article in the Nicene Creed, (of one substance with the Father,) is now (through the ambiguity of the Latin and English translation,) by most men taken much otherwise, than the Council intended it: For the greater part of modern Christians, (if we may judge by the writings of eminent divines,) understand it (as if it had been ταυτούσιος) to signify, of one individual substance with the Father; Whereas all learned men know, that the Greek word (ὁμοόυσιος) never had any such signification, and that the Council meant no such thing; but, of the same kind of substance with the Father: (ἐκ τοῦ ὀυσιίς τοῦ πατρὸς, so the Council of Nice explained themselves, though those words are now left out of the Creed;) The Son was, they said, γεννηθεὶς ἐκ τοῦ πατρὸς, τουτέσιν ἐκ τοῦ οὐσιός τοῦ πατρὶς [sic], begotten of the Father, that is, from the substance of the Father: And therfore was not (which notion was then universally condemned) himself that individual substance from which he was begotten. But their meaning was; he was produced, not from any other substance, (as man was formed from the dust of the earth,) but, after an ineffable manner, from the substance of the Father only. Which sense of theirs, is now generally mistaken.[263]

It is clear that Clarke's position and concerns reflect the influence of Origen's theology and bear a striking resemblance to the opinions of Eusebius of Caesarea and later Basil of Ancyra. If Clarke was in fact a Eusebian, and therefore, by extension, a *homoiousian*, several things follow. The first is that he is not an Arian. We have seen that Clarke denied the two essential tenets of Arianism. The second thing which follows is that the context of theological options against which Clarke's thought is evaluated must be understood to be more sophisticated than simply Sabellian (Socinian), Arian or Orthodox. Here the work of contemporary scholars has been crucial in reacquainting us with the nuances of fourth-century thought. The ὁμοιόυσιος position was

---

[263] Clarke, *A Reply to the Objections of Robert Nelson, Esq; and of an Anonymous Author, against Dr. Clarke's Scripture-Doctrine of the Trinity* in *Works*, Vol. IV, 263.

held by a variety of Fathers whom the tradition holds to be orthodox, and that position was specifically mentioned by Athanasius as
being within the bounds of theological truth. Concerning those who
held that position he wrote,

> those, however, who accept everything else that was defined at Nicaea,
> and doubt only about the Coessential, [ὁμοούσιος] must not be treated
> as enemies; nor do we here attack them as Ariomaniacs, nor as oppo-
> nents of the Fathers, but we discuss the matter with them as brothers
> with brothers, who mean what we mean, and dispute only about the
> word. For, confessing that the Son is from the essence of the Father,
> and not from another subsistence, and that he is not a creature nor
> work, but His genuine and natural offspring, and that he is eternally
> with the Father as being his Word and Wisdom, they are not far from
> accepting even the phrase, "coessential." Now such is Basil who wrote
> from Ancyra concerning the faith.[264]

The historians of doctrine who mention Clarke, make the assumption that Sabellian (Socinian), Arian and Orthodox are the only options
for expressing the doctrine of God, without exploring a major position which in fact represented the majority position at the Council,
and afterward became central in setting up the Cappadocian settle-
ment. While Clarke clearly demurred from "coessential" language as
problematic, he affirmed that the Son was generated from the Father,
and defined this to mean, "immediate derivation of being and life
from God himself."[265] We have already seen Clarke refute the Arian
ideas that the Son was a creature or work[266] and that there was a
time when he was not.[267] Therefore, according to Athanasius' own
words "he is a brother who disputes only about the word."

Finally, if we examine the options during the Arian controversy,
and look for parallels in Clarke's time, our position is confirmed. Hanson writes that the position of the Neo-Arian Eunomius has parallels in its rationalism with the thought of John Toland.[268] We have
seen in Chapter One, that Toland (at least the early Toland who
wrote *Christianity Not Mysterious*) was a Deist. For both the Deists and
Neo-Arians, Christ was a man, and not God in any sense, except
by example. The Homoians believed that Christ was like God, but

---

[264] Athanaisus, *De Synodis*, 41. *NPNF* Vol. IV, 472.
[265] Clarke, *SD*, 138.
[266] Ibid., Proposition XIV, 140.
[267] Ibid., Propositions XV and XVI, 141.
[268] Hanson, *The Search*, 632.

not derived in any way from his substance. Like the Socinians they held that he resembled God through his obedience and was exalted to Sonship because of it. His pre-existence as the Son of God was denied. The Homoiousians, as we have seen, affirmed a likeness according to substance, but recoiled from a numerical identity of substance, fearing Sabellianism. They affirmed the eternal pre-existence of the divine Son. This was Clarke's position. The Homoousians affirmed all of the previous, and in addition went so far as to identify the essence of the Father as being numerically the same as that of the Son. This was the traditional "orthodox" theology of Clarke's time.

Neo Arians	→ *Deists*
Homoian Arians	→ *Socinians*
Homoiousians	→ *Clarke*
Homoousians	→ *"Orthodox" Majority*

The theologians of Clarke's period, as well as those of the nineteenth century, tended to reduce the options under the doctrine of God to Sabellian (Socinian) Arian, and Orthodox. Under this reductionist framework, the "Semi-Arian" or ὁμοιούσιος position was lost. It was wrongly held to be tantamount to Arianism. This perception, as we have seen, was foreign even to Athanasius himself.[269] Contemporary scholars, like Hanson, Kopecek, Kelly and Prestige have reacquainted us with the rich diversity of views held by the early Fathers, thus vindicating the work of some of the earlier scholars like Petavius, who challenged the standard thought of his day. Contemporary scholarship has revealed that Clarke's reading of history was more accurate than Bull's. The ὁμοιούσιος position was a vital one, held by most of the bishops at Nicaea, considered within the realm of orthodoxy by Athanasius, and fundamental to the theology of the Cappadocians, particulary, Basil the Great. Clarke's thought represents a re-emergence of the views of Origin, Eusebius of Caeserea, and, in a sense, of the Eastern tradition in general. Clarke was not an Arian, nor an Athanasian, but a Eusebian. His work must be understood and studied within the multi-faceted context of the Arian contro-

---

[269] This position was typified by Clarke's adversary Daniel Waterland, whose views will be examined in the last chapter.

versy which in many ways paralleled the trinitarian controversy of his own time. While Clarke relied most heavily on scripture and the Fathers for his trinitarian formulation, there is another, more immediate source from which he may have drawn inspiration. This other source is the subject of the next chapter.

CHAPTER FOUR

CLARKE AND NEWTON

In addition to using a wide range of Patristic sources, we have seen that Clarke used contemporary sources as well, including: Bull, Chillingworth, Pearson, More, Payne and others. These were employed to lend support to Clarke's interpretation of the Fathers. One name which is listed nowhere in the *Scripture-Doctrine* is Isaac Newton. This chapter raises the question of whether or not there is a likelihood that Newton was an influential source for Clarke's trinitarian thought. We have already established that Newton and Clarke were intimate friends, that they shared a variety of interests, and were partners in several intellectual projects. Since they collaborated on so many things, is it possible that Newton and Clarke shared the same perspective on the trinity, and that Newton was an unheralded source of Clarke's thought?

The idea that Clarke and Newton held similar views on the trinity is not new. When Emlyn heard the first course of Boyle Lectures in 1704, he began to suspect Clarke's orthodoxy since Clarke placed such a radical emphasis on the necessity of God's unity in the seventh proposition of his *Demonstration*.

> The self-existent Being, must of necessity be but one. This evidently follows from his being necessarily self-existent. For necessity absolute in itself, is simple and uniform and universal, without any possible difference, difformity, or variety whatsoever: And all variety or difference of existence, must needs arise from some external cause, and be dependent upon it, and proportionable to the efficiency of that cause, whatsoever it may be. Absolute necessity, in which there can be no variation in any kind of degree, cannot be the ground of existence of a number of Beings, however similar and agreeing: Because without any other difference, even number is itself a manifest difformity or inequality (if I may so speak) of efficiency of causality.[1]

Newton, in the *General Scholium*, which he subsequently inserted into the second edition of his *Principia*, also emphasized the unity of the Godhead. So close were Clarke and Newton that the Calvinist John

---

[1] Clarke, *Demonstration* in *Works*, II, 541.

Edwards remarked that "the learned knight seems to me to lay open his heart and mind, and tell the world what cause he espouses at this day viz. the very same which Dr. Clarke and Mr. Whiston have publicly asserted."[2]

Stewart[3] has analyzed in detail the relationship between Clarke's trinitarian conclusions, with their emphasis on unity in the Godhead, and Newton's understanding of absolute space. Referring to the first course of Boyle Lectures he writes,

> From this Clarke launched into the *a priori* argument based on the necessity of a universal self-existent Being whose attributes must be eternity, infinity and unity. This theological view obviously bears a close resemblance to the Newtonian view of absolute space, a doctrine founded upon immateriality, which in turn may have led the way to Clarke's metaphysical view of the Trinity.[4]

When Butler pressed Clarke during the trinitarian debate on the necessity of unity without division his responses indicated this reliance on Newton's understanding of absolute space and time.[5] The absolutes of self-existence and non-origination belonged to the Father alone. The other attributes of the Godhead could be shared among the persons, but not these. In this way, Clarke believed he had found the distinction between the relative and the absolute in the trinity and this distinction was a necessary corollary of the Newtonian understanding of absolute space and time.[6]

Edwards and Butler suspected a link in the thought of Newton and Clarke, and the conclusion they drew was that both men were Arians.[7] This, as we have seen with respect to Clarke, and will see with respect to Newton, is also the verdict of more recent scholarship. While this conclusion is questionable, the instinct of Edwards and Butler was right. There are in fact several connections. Newton's and Clarke's trinitarian understandings are linked not only at the point of their mutual commitments in natural philsophy, but in a number of other ways. For this reason, the thought of Newton must

---

· [2] John Edwards, *Some Brief Critical Remarks on Dr. Clarke's Last Papers* (1714), 42. Cited in Ferguson, *Heretic*, 215.

[3] Larry Stewart, "Samuel Clarke, Newtonianism, and the Factions of Post-Revolutionary England (1689–1720)," *Journal of the History of Ideas* 42 (1981): 53–72.

[4] Ibid., 56.

[5] Ibid., 58.

[6] Ibid., 57.

[7] The trinitarian controversy will be examined in the last two chapters.

be examined, and compared with Clarke. Only then can the question of influence and source be raised. An overview of Newton's theological views was presented in Chapter One. The present chapter will be devoted to examining Newton's trinitarian scheme and comparing it with Clarke's. It will close by addressing the question of influence.

Newton's Trinitarian Views and the Historians

Historians of Newton's thought have been wide ranging in their assessment of his understanding of the trinity. David Brewster, in his *The Life of Sir Isaac Newton* (1831) was fully convinced that Newton was an orthodox trinitarian. However, he recognized that "a traditionary belief has long prevailed that Newton was an Arian."[8] Two reasons were used to defend his conclusion that Newton was orthodox. The first was a letter from John Craig, a friend of Newton's, written shortly after Newton's death to John Conduitt, the husband of Newton's niece. In this letter Craig remarked that Newton's theological opinions "were sometimes different from those which are commonly received" but that he hoped Conduitt would publish Newton's theological papers "that the world may see that Sir Isaac Newton was as good a Christian as he was a mathematician and philosopher."[9] The second reason with which Brewster defends his conclusion is his acknowledgment that the doctrine of the trinity itself had variations.

> I had no hesitation when writing the *Life of Sir Isaac Newton* in 1830, in coming to the conclusion that he was a believer in the Trinity; and in giving this opinion on the creed of so great a man, and so indefatigable a student of scripture, I was well aware that there are various forms of Trinitarian truth, and various modes of expressing it, which have been received as orthodox in the purest societies of the Christian Church.[10]

L.T. More in his biography, *Isaac Newton*, gently chided Brewster for not publishing some of the crucial manuscripts which eventually became part of the Keynes collection.[11] From these additional manu-

---

[8] Brewster, *Memoirs*, Vol. 2, 339. Here he cites Dr. Thompson who wrote that Newton did not believe in the trinity (Thompson, *History of the Royal Society*, 284).
[9] Ibid., Vol. 2, 316.
[10] Ibid., Vol. 2, 340.
[11] More, 631.

scripts More reached the conclusion that Newton was an Arian. He proceeded to say that Newton was not only an Arian, but a Unitarian because of the manner in which he understood Jesus' role as prophet.[12]

More recently, John M. Keynes, the famous British economist, who considered it a great "impiety" that Newton's non-scientific manuscripts were dispersed at the Sotheby's auction in 1936, and who recovered about half of them, thus creating the "Keynes" collection at Cambridge, offered a different view of Newton.

> Very early in life Newton abandoned orthodox belief in the Trinity. At this time the Socinians were an important Arian sect amongst intellectual circles. It may be that Newton fell under Socinian influences, but I think not. He was rather a Judaic monotheist of the school of Maimonides. He arrived at this conclusion, not on so-to-speak rational or skeptical grounds, but entirely on the interpretation of ancient authority. He was persuaded that the revealed documents give no support to the Trinitarian doctrines which were due to late falsifications. The revealed God was one God.[13]

It is the consensus of contemporary scholarship that Isaac Newton was an Arian rather than a Socinian.[14] This perspective is clearly expressed by Richard Westfall who writes, "Well before 1675, Newton had become an Arian in the original sense of the term. He recognized Christ as a divine mediator between God and man, who was subordinate to the Father who created him."[15] Yet, Frank Manuel in his *The Religion of Isaac Newton* (1974) advises that we not try to

---

[12] Ibid., 644.

[13] J.M. Keynes, "*Newton the Man*" in *The Royal Society Newton Tercentenary Celebrations 15–19 July 1946* (Cambridge: At the University Press, 1947), 27–34. This was a lecture prepared by J.M. Keynes, who died before it was to be delivered. It was read to the Society by Mr. Geoffrey Keynes. Keynes offers a tantalizing invitation to consider Newton not as "the first of the age of reason," but rather as the "last of the magi." He argues that Newton saw the world as a "riddle" or "cryptogram set by the Almighty." This is all the more an intriguing approach for those who live in a time when Stephen Hawking, who holds Newton's Lucasian chair at Cambridge, and was born on the anniversary of Newton's birth, is seeking the holy grail of the Unified Theory.

[14] See Richard Westfall, "The Rise of Science," 230; Force, "The Newtonians and Deism", 60; Richard Popkin, "Newton as a Bible Scholar" in *Essays on the Context, Nature and Influence of Isaac Newton's Theology*. Edited by James E. Force and Richard H. Popkin (Dordrecht: Kluwer Academic Publishers, 1990) 107; Reventlow, 341; Christianson, 249; Gjertsen, 591. Gjertsen seems to have taken his taxonomy of trinitarian belief from L.T. More, 630 n. 41.

[15] Richard Westfall, *Never at Rest: A Biography of Isaac Newton* (Cambridge: Cambridge University Press, 1980), 315.

push Newton into a theological categorization too quickly. He reminds us that Newton was, if nothing else, an original thinker.

> It is an error to seize upon his antitrinitarianism in order to pigeonhole him in one of the recognized categories of heresy—Arian, Socinian, Unitarian, or Deist.[16]

So what did Isaac Newton believe about the trinity? In exploring his writing on the subject we will be guided by two principles mentioned above. The first is Brewster's insight, buttressed by the work of Hanson and Kelly, that the trinitarian doctrine has in fact been understood with a certain degree of variety within the sphere of orthodoxy. The second is from Manuel, that we must resist the temptation to make Newton "fit" some predetermined category or school of trinitarian thought. We will begin by looking at the resources available for studying Newton's thought on the trinity.

Although, as we have seen in Chapter One, Newton wrote at least one million words on theology and scripture, and perhaps much more, a large part of that corpus dealt either directly or indirectly with the trinity. There are a number of folio pages in the Yahuda collection which deal with the history of the early church during the time of the Council of Nicaea.[17] Many of these pages center on the derivation of early trinitarian theology as reflected in quotations from the early Fathers. Likewise, Newton's notes on prophecy also address this issue. In the same collection there is a Latin version of the first part of the *"Two Notable Corruptions of Scripture."*[18] In the Babson Collection there is a Latin text on the theology of Athanasius, a discourse on true religion, and a short fragment with a note on the history of the early church.[19] The long Bodmer manuscript on the history of the church likely has the trinity as a focal area, if Newton's other notes on the early Church are any indication. A number of useful manuscripts come from the Keynes collection at Cambridge. MS. 2 is a theological notebook that contains scriptural citations which begin by following a quasi-credal structure and then transition to a series

---

[16] Manuel, *Religion*, 58.
[17] Yahuda MSS. 2.2, 2.3, 2.5, 5.3, 11, 12, 14, 15, 19, 22, and 29. (Richard Westfall, *"Newton's Theological Manuscripts"* in *Contemporary Newtonian Research*. Edited by Zev Bechler (Dordrecht: D. Reidel Publishing Company, Hingham, MA, 1982), 141–143.
[18] Yahuda MS. 20.
[19] Babson MSS. 436, 438 and 704 respectively.

of subject headings.[20] Also contained in this manuscript are two sections in Latin on the trinity which are primarily citations drawn from the Fathers. Finally there are some brief notes on the terms *homoousia, ousia, hypostasis, substantia and personis*. MS. 4 is a number of pages of notes from Petavius' *De Theologicus Dogmatibus*. MS. 6 is seven points on religion and MS. 8 is twelve articles on religion. MS. 9 is a series of sheets on true religion.[21] MS. 10 is entitled *Paradoxical Questions concerning the morals and actions of Athanasius and his Followers*.[22] MS. 11 is entitled *Quaeries Regarding the word* ὁμοόυσιος.[23] There is also an important manuscript at the Clark Library (Los Angeles) titled, "Paradoxical questions concerning the morals and actions of Athanasius & his followers," which is much more extensive than Keynes MS. 10.[24] These then, are the primary sources from which Newton's trinitarian theology must be drawn.[25]

Newton and Clarke

The thought of Newton and Clarke on the trinity can be arranged under five headings: 1. Their rejection of the mixture of philosophical language and biblical revelation. 2. Their denial of the textual grounds for the standard trinitarian argument and their interpretation of key texts. 3. Their reading of the history of the period surrounding the Nicene Creed. 4. Their view of the relationship of the Father and the Son. 5. Their understanding of what the Church Fathers intended by their employment of the *ousia* word group.

1. *Their Rejection of the Mixture of Philosophical Language and Biblical Revelation*

Newton and Locke had shared in their rejection of innate ideas, and consequently notions like "substance." For Newton, we could only

---

[20] For example, Newton begins with *Deus Pater, Deus Filius, Christi Incarnati, Christi Passio, Descendus, et Resurrectio, Christi Satisfactio and Redemptionare, Spiritus Sanctus Deus* and then moves into topics like *Angeli Mali et boni, Praedestinatio, De Antchristo* etc.

[21] This is available in Brewster, *Memoirs*, Vol. II, 349–50.

[22] Ibid., 342–46.

[23] Ibid., Appendix No. 30.

[24] Westfall dates this MS. from the 1680's. The Clark Library card catalog dates it from the 1690's.

[25] It should be noted here that Keynes only recovered about one half of the

have true knowledge of what was present to our senses. The idea of substance, while it might exist, was epistemologically inaccessible, especially the substance of God. Newton believed that the church proceeded best when it followed revelation and not philosophy as the sole source of its doctrine. The philosophical category of "substance" had no place in the Church's formulation of doctrine, and was the source of her subsequent difficulties. In the "General Scholium" of the second edition of the *Principia* Newton wrote,

> We have ideas of his [God's] attributes, but what the real substance of any thing is we know not. In bodies, we see only their figures and colours. We hear only the sounds. We touch only their outward surfaces. We smell only the smells, and taste the flavours; but their inward substances are not to be known either by our senses, or by any reflex act of our minds: much less, then, have we any idea of the substance of God.[26]

This idea was reinforced in his analysis of the language the early bishops allowed in the theological debate regarding Paul of Samosata's introduction of the term ὁμοόυσιος.

> Had they interdicted the novel language of both parties, & only established the declared language in wch they received the faith from ye beginning & upon pain of excommunication commanded all men to acquiece in that languuage without farther disturbing the Churches about questions or opinions not proposed in the language of the scriptures they had quieted the Empire & the Church.[27]

In the first of his "seven points on religion," Newton stated "That religion and philosophy are to be preserved distinct. We are not to introduce divine revelations into philosophy, nor philosophical opinions into religion."[28] In his *Quaeries Regarding the Word* ὁμοόυσιος, Newton asked "Whether Christ sent his apostles to preach metaphysics to the unlearned common people, and to their wives and children?"[29]

"Portsmouth Papers" of Newton, eleven of which are theological. The majority of Newton's theological papers are in the Yahuda collection in Jerusalem, and there are several in the Babson collection formerly held in Wellesley, Massachusetts, but recently transferred to the Dibner Institute at M.I.T. It is possible that there are still individual papers, privately held, which have yet to come to light and could bear on the subject.

[26] Newton, *Principia*, Vol. 2, Bk. III, 312, 13.
[27] Yahuda MS. 15 fol. 190. Newton makes a similar point concerning the mixture of philosophical opinion and religion in his "seven points on religion" Keynes MS. 6.
[28] Newton, Keynes MS. 6.
[29] Newton, Keynes MS. 11 in Brewster, *Memoirs*, Vol. II, Appendix XXX, 532.

As we saw in Chapter One, this distinction between religion and philosophy was the program outlined by Francis Bacon in his *Of the Advancement of Learning*.[30] It was also the program followed by Newton while President of the Royal Society.

When we view Clarke's thought alongside Newton's it is immediately apparent that there are striking resemblances in their understandings of the trinity. Just as Newton rejected the intrusion of philosophical metaphysics into the formation of Christian doctrine, so did Clarke. In the Introduction to his *Scripture-Doctrine of the Trinity* Clarke stated that during the first three centuries of church history the creeds of all the churches held a uniform sense, and were free from "matters of philosophical controversy."[31] It was during the fourth century that "metaphysical uncertainties began to be determined in Creeds."[32] For him, like Newton, the Bible alone set the standard of doctrine and faith.[33] It was the intrusion of philosophical reasoning into the doctrines of the Church, which impaired its unity.

> And indeed, with regard to scholastick and philosophical inquiries concerning metaphysical natures, essences, substances and subsistencies; with other the like notion; which (in the language of the excellent Arch-Bishop Tillotson) men "have spun, as spiders do cobwebs, out of their own brain;" this manner of judging is so right and true, that had these things never been meddled with, and had men contented themselves with what is plainly revealed in scripture (more than which, they can never certainly know;) the peace of the Catholick Church, and the simplicity of Christian faith and worship, had possibly never been disturbed.[34]

"Essences, substances and subsistencies" belonged to the language of philosophy, and therefore were foreign to theology. Clarke confined the scope of theological discourse relative to the trinity as an analysis of,

> the distinct powers and offices of the Father, the Son and the Holy Spirit, in the creation, government, redemption, sanctification, and salvation of man; and the proper respective honour due consequently from us to each of them distinctly, that we may not worship we know not what."[35]

---

[30] Bacon, *Advancement*, 45–46.
[31] Clarke, *SD*, Intro., iv.
[32] Ibid.
[33] Ibid., v.
[34] Ibid., xii.
[35] Ibid., xiii.

This repudiation of metaphysical speculation in doctrinal formulation was repeated in the body of the *Scripture-Doctrine* itself. Proposition IV of Part II stated,

> What the proper metaphysical nature, essence, or substance of any of these divine persons is, the scripture has nowhere at all declared; but describes and distinguishes them always by their personal characters, offices, power, and attributes.[36]

As a direct result of this principle, Clarke held concerning the Son's and the Spirit's manner of derivation from the Father that "Scripture has no where distinctly declared; and therefore men ought not to presume to be able to define."[37]

2. *Their Denial of the Textual Grounds for the Standard Trinitarian Argument and their Interpretation of Key Texts*

Not only was Newton uncomfortable with the traditional metaphysical foundation of the trinitarian doctrine, he found that the biblical texts used to substantiate it were faulty. At first he shared his insights with his close friend Locke.

> Amongst Locke's friends were many Unitarians. Sir Isaac Newton, his junior by ten years, was an intimate friend. He sent Locke his critical discussions of the two Trinitarian proof-texts (1 John v.7; and 1 Timothy iii.16), a mark of extreme confidence in so cautious a person.[38]

These insights were to be published anonymously by Locke's friend LeClerc, whom he had met in Holland, but at the last minute Newton withdrew them in a panic.[39] Referring first to the Johannine comma, Newton wrote,

> Whereas all the Greek Manuscripts of the New Testament, and all the ancient versions, that have been made of it into any language whatever ... are quite silent in regard to the testimony of the "three in Heaven"; and all the councils, fathers, commentators and other writers, at least of the first four centuries of the church ... do plainly shew,

---

[36] Clarke, *SD*, 122–23.
[37] Ibid., Prop. XIII, 137; Prop. XXII, 148.
[38] McClachlan, 101. Gjertsen has commented on the relationship of Locke and Newton, "Judging by Newton's surviving letters to Locke, the relationship between them was one of the freest and relaxed to be found in the whole correspondence." (p. 322).
[39] Manuel, *The Religion*, 12. According to Manuel, scientific controversy was one thing for Newton, but religious controversy gave him deep anxiety.

that it stood in their books "it is the Spirit that beareth witness; because the Spirit is truth: For these are three that bear record, the Spirit the Water and the blood: and these three agree in One:"[40]

Moving to his second text, 1 Timothy 3:16 he continued,

What the Latins have done to the text of the first epistle of Saint John v.7. the Greeks have done to that of St. Paul's first epistle to Timothy iii.16. For by changing *ho* into OC, the abbreviation of *Theos*, they now read, "Great is the mystery of Godliness: *God* was manifested in the flesh." whereas all the churches for the first four or five hundred years; and the authors of all the ancient versions, Jerome, as well as the rest, read, "Great is the mystery of Godliness, which was manifested in the flesh."[41]

Just as Clarke's views on philosophy and theology were like Newton's so was his understanding of both the textual difficulties Newton mentioned and his exegesis of crucial trinitarian biblical texts.

As we have seen, Newton wrote his *Two Notable Corruptions* on the texts of 1 Tim. 3:16 and the Johannine comma, 1 John 5:8. In that work Newton took the position that Erasmus' Greek text of 1516 was inaccurate and as a result these texts could not serve as pillars in bearing the weight of the trinitarian argument. Clarke commented on the textual problem of 1 Tim. 3:16 when he wrote,

It has been a great controversy among learned men, whether [θεός] or [ὅς] or [ὁ,] be the true reading in this place. All the old versions have it, *qui* or *quod*. And all the antient Fathers, though the copies of many of them have now in the text itself, [θεός, Deus;] yet from the tenour of their comments upon it, and from their never citing it in the Arian controversy, it appears they always read it *qui* or *quod*; till the time of Macedonius, under the Emperor Anastasius, in the beginning of the sixth century.[42]

On the Johannine comma he wrote,

Not [Εἷς *unus*] One and the same person; but [ἓν *unum*] one and the same "thing" in effect; one and the same testimony. Though it ought not indeed to be concealed, that the whole passage here printed in a different character [namely "in Heaven; the Father, the Word, and the Holy Ghost; and these three are One . . ."], since it has never yet been proved to be found in the text of any greek manuscript, before the invention of printing; nor in the text of any antient [sic] version; nor

[40] Isaac Newton, *Two Letters of Isaac Newton to Mr. LeClerc*, 4.
[41] Ibid., 84–85.
[42] Clarke *SD*, 47–48.

was cited by any of the numerous writers in the whole Arian controversy; ought not to have much stress laid upon it in any question.[43]

In the same way, both Clarke and Newton collected numerable texts
that bore on the relationship of the members of the trinity.[44] The
first text Newton listed under *Deus Pater* was 1 Cor. 8:6 which spoke
of the one God, distinguishing between the Father *of* whom are all
things and the one Lord Jesus Christ *by* whom are all things. He
quoted this text again in Article 12 of his manuscript titled "On our
Religion to God, to Christ, and the Church."[45] This text was a central pillar in Clarke's argument with Daniel Waterland regarding the
fact that the Son was not self-existent.[46] More illustrative of their
parallels in interpretation is their treatment of John 10:30 "I and the
Father are One." In the second of two memoranda cited by More,
Newton wrote,

> Jesus therefore by calling himself the Son of God and saying I and the
> Father are one meant nothing more than that the Father had sancti-
> fied him and sent him into the world.[47]

It is clear from this passage that Newton did not understand the text
to mean that Jesus and the Father were ontologically one. Rather,
the implication seems to be that the Father had set him aside (sanctified) for a purpose, and that their unity was to be discovered in
that purpose. Clarke likewise rejected an ontological interpretation
here, holding that the oneness Jesus spoke of was a simple metaphor
like that of John 17:22 where Jesus prayed that the disciples "may
be one, even as we are one." In refuting the argument of the author
of *The True Scripture Doctrine &c.* Clarke referred to the idea that what
was behind this verse was a unity of power, and that the Jews were
angry because Jesus had "assumed to himself the power and authority of God."[48] He reminded his readers that the greek term ἑις (*Unus*),
meaning "one and the same person" is not used here, but rather ἑν,

---

[43] Ibid., 121, for a similar assessment see pp. 237–38.

[44] This is Clarke's entire method of Part One of the *SD*, in which he collected
1,251 texts on the trinity. Newton, in Keynes MS. 2, collected a multitude of texts
under the headings of *Deus Pater, Deus Filius, Spiritus Sanctus Deus.*

[45] Keynes MS. 9 in Brewster, *Memoirs*, Vol. 2, 350.

[46] Clarke, *The Modest Plea &c. continued* in *Works*, IV, 469.

[47] In More, 643.

[48] Clarke, *A Letter to the Author of the True Scripture Doctrine &c.* in *SD*, Vol. IV, 435–
36. Although Clarke is citing his opponent here, it is clear that he is citing him to
make his own case.

unum, meaning "one and the same thing."[49] Thus we see that Newton and Clarke viewed both the textual problems and some crucial biblical passages associated with the doctrine of the trinity in the same way.

3. *Their Reading of the History of the Period Surrounding the Nicene Creed*

The third reason Newton struggled with the classical trinitarian formulation was his understanding of church history. Early on he believed that the results of Nicaea were skewed by Athanasius, and that his interpretation of the creed represented an aberration of the true views of the early Fathers. In fact, Newton believed that it was Athanasius who introduced the errors into the above mentioned texts.[50] Here Newton's preoccupation with prophecy influenced his reading of church history, so that the fourth century was seen as the time in which false teaching was introduced into the church. He believed that the central message of the book of Revelation was that of the great apostasy in the fourth century when Athanasius and the Roman Church imposed a false doctrine of the trinity upon the Church.[51] Concerning Newton's view of history William Whiston, his close friend and successor to the Lucasian chair wrote,

> Nay, I afterwards found that Sir Isaac was so hearty for the Baptists, as well as for the doctrines of Eusebius and Arius, that he sometimes suspected they were the two witnesses in the Revelation.[52]

Newton's antipathy toward Athanasius is well documented. MS. 10 of the Keynes collection is entitled "Paradoxical questions concerning the morals & actions of Athanasius & his followers."[53] In this

---

[49] Clarke, *SD*, 55.

[50] Popkin, "Newton as a Bible Scholar," 110.

[51] Westfall, "Isaac Newton's *Theologiae Gentilis Origines Philosophicae*," 17.

[52] McClachlan, 129, quoting Whiston, *Authentic Records*, Pt. II, 1075. Also Whiston's *Memoirs*, first edition, 206. Whiston's comment on Newton's being an Arian must be tempered here by a statement in the *Biographica Britannica* on Newton which says that Newton was so angry with Whiston's accusation that he was an Arian, that he blocked Whiston's admission to the Royal Society on this account. See Brewster, *The Life of Sir Isaac Newton* (New York: Printed and published by J & J Harper, 1831), 255. Whiston, however, in his *Memoirs* gives other reasons. L.T. More, 630 and 631, n. 43, believes that Brewster is wrong here, and has conflated different comments by Whiston in order to preserve Newton's orthodoxy.

[53] This is available in Brewster, *Memoirs*, Vol. 2, 342f. This is not to be confused with the MS. in UCLA's Clark Library by the same title, which runs upward of one hundred folio pages.

piece Newton accused Athanasius of lying, murder, adultery, and seizing the See of Alexandria "by sedition and violence against the canons of that church." Moreover, in Newton's mind, Athanasius' being deprived of his See at the Council of Tyre had nothing to do with the controversy over doctrine, but with his outrageous tactics as Bishop.[54] Based upon new manuscript evidence, contemporary scholarship has come to a similar conclusion.[55] Beyond this, Newton maintained that Athanasius had labored to prove that Arius had died outside of the fellowship of the church by concocting the story that he died "in a bog-house" just before being received back into communion, and that this ignominious death represented God's judgment against his cause.[56] Newton cited the early historians Socrates, Sozomen, and Rufinus to show that in fact Arius had traveled from Constantinople to Tyre and Jerusalem then to Alexandria "before he died & was one of those whome the Council of Jerusalem received into its communion."[57]

More importantly, we discover in this same manuscript, clues to Newton's understanding of the history of the church directly following Nicaea. In the Keynes "Paradoxical Questions" he asked "Whether the Council of Tyre & Jerusalem was not an Orthodox authentick Council bigger than that of Nice."[58] Newton asserted that this Council was every bit as significant, and more so, than Nicaea for determining the mind of the Church regarding the trinity. He defended it at length,

> This council has been reputed Arian & on that account of no authority, but the accusation was never proved & an accusation without proof is of no credit . . . Now all the evidence that this Council was Arian is only this, that they received Arius into communion & banished Athanasius . . . For they did not receive Arius without his disowning those things for wch [sic] he had been condemned at Nice, nor condemned Athanasius for his owning the Nicene decrees: & 'tis not ye receiving or condemning men but ye receiving or condemning opinions that can make any Council heretical. So far was this Council from being Arian that the Bishops thereof in almost all their following Councils declared against Arianism & anathematized the opinions for

---

[54] Newton, Keynes MS. 10, Questions I, XI, XIII.
[55] Hanson, *The Search*, 239ff., esp. 254–55.
[56] Newton, Keynes MS. 10, Question I.
[57] Ibid., Newton cites: Socr. l.1 c. 26, 27, 33, 37, 38; Sozom. l.2, c. 27, 28, 29; Rufin. l.1. c. 11.
[58] Ibid., Question III.

wch [sic] Arius had been condemned . . . we have no other means of
knowing men's faith but by their profession & outward communion &
way of worship, & by all these characters the Fathers of the Council
were Orthodox. They constantly professed against Arianism & were in
communion with the churches of all the World & worshipt as other
churches of that age did.[59]

At stake for Newton was his conviction that the Nicene formulation
was in fact *not* understood by the majority of bishops in the way in
which Athanasius, and subsequent generations, interpreted it.

> That the church in ye times next after Constantius were so far from
> making one singular substance that they decryed it for heresy and
> Sabellianism notwithstanding any distinction of persons what ever. See
> ye creed of Lisenius[60] sent to Athanasius and [the] Council of Alex-
> andria's epistle to ye Antiochians.[61]

Perhaps even more telling of Newton's perception of the trinitarian
doctrine in the early church was his extensive use of the Patristic
scholar Petavius. F.X. Murphy writes that it was Petavius who first
called the attention of theologians to the "hesitations, misconceptions,
and inexactitudes of many of the early Fathers with regard to the
theology of the Trinity in the early church."[62] As a result he was
accused by the Jansenists and by Bp. Bull, in his *Defensio fidei Nicaenae*,
of making the majority of the Fathers of the first three centuries
deny the divinity of the Son. Actually, Petavius' work was of "crucial
significance" in the history of doctrine.[63] We saw earlier that the
work of contemporary scholars like Hanson, Kelly and Prestige have
confirmed Petavius' understanding of the Patristic material.

   Newton's papers contain an entire manuscript of notes taken from
Petavius' *De Theologicus Dogmatibus*. Petavius was perceived as an enemy of orthodoxy by Bull and Waterland because he called into
question their view of a monolithic adherence by the Ante-Nicene
Fathers to what became the Nicene formula. Petavius recognized and
discussed under the heading of the third chapter of *De Trinitate* certain

---

[59] Ibid., Question III.
[60] Spelling is unclear in the MS. due to Newton's handwriting.
[61] Newton, Keynes MS. 2.
[62] Francis X. Murphy, "Petavius" in the *New Catholic Encyclopedia*. 16 Vols. Edited
by the editorial staff at the Catholic University of America (N.Y.: McGraw Hill
Book Co., 1967), Vol. 11, 199–200. Petavius' rising historical consciousness was
paralleled in biblical studies in the work of R. Simon and others.
[63] Ibid., 200.

disagreements among the Fathers,[64] and Newton drew his notes in
Latin most heavily from this third chapter.[65]

When Clarke's thought is compared with Newton's on this subject
once again the parallels are striking. Clarke mentioned the name of
Petavius rarely because using Petavius would not have strengthened
his argument in the eyes of his adversaries. Nonetheless, it is clear
that Clarke had read and studied him. In describing his method in
the Introduction of the *Scripture-Doctrine*, Clarke mentioned that he
had drawn heavily from Athanasius and Basil, and that he has found
some citations "not taken notice of either by Petavius, or the learned
Bishop Bull."[66] In his *Reply to Nelson* he cited Nelson himself who had
written,

> Dr. Clarke, who had so ample a collection of testimonies concerning
> the Trinity before him in this Treatise (of Bishop Bull's,) as well as in
> Petavius; hath not made that use of them, which this indefatigable and
> judicious collector (Bp. Bull) did.[67]

Clarke, while allowing that he did not draw the same conclusions
from the collections as others, repudiated Nelson's accusation.

When we look at Clarke's conclusions regarding the period surrounding the Council, we find that they are quite similar to those we
have found already in Petavius and Newton. Clarke held (against
Bull, but with Petavius and Newton) that the language of the Ante-
Nicene Fathers, while favoring his position, was not always consistent. He wrote,

> The greatest part of the writers before and at the time of the Council
> of Nice, were (I think) really of that opinion, (though they do not al-
> ways speak very clearly and consistently,) which I have endeavoured to
> set forth in those Propositions.[68]

For Clarke this point was exemplified by the difference of opinion
among the Fathers as to whether the Son as *Logos* was a real person
or not. Prior to the council, Theophilus, Tatian and Athenagoras

---

[64] "*Exponuntur veterum quorumdam, qui ante Ariana tempora in Christiana professione floruerunt, de Trinitate sententiae ab catholica regula, saltem loquendi usu, discrepantes; ut Justini Martyris, Athenagorae, Tatiani, Theophilli, Irenai, Clementis Romani.* (*Theologica Dogmata*, Vol. II, p. 353)."
[65] Newton, Keynes, MS. 4, et passim. Newton also cited Petavius in Keynes MS. 2.
[66] Clarke, *SD*, Introduction, ix.
[67] Clarke, *A Reply to Mr. Nelson* in *Works*, IV, 256. See also p. 145 for a direct quote from Petavius' *De Trinitate*.
[68] Clarke, *SD*, Introduction, ix.

had spoken of the *Logos* as the internal reason of God (λόγος ἐνδιάθετος) while Irenaeus and Clement of Alexandria had spoken ambig-
uously, with the other writers speaking more or less clearly of the
Word as a distinct person.[69]

Around the time of the Council the language grew more uncertain,
with some supposing the Son (as God's wisdom and power) to be
merely an attribute of God, while others held him to be a "real
person." Following the Council of Nicaea,

> they spake still more and more confusedly and ambiguously; til at last
> the schoolmen ... made this matter also, as they did most others, ut-
> terly unintelligible.[70]

A second illustration of Clarke's position, that the Fathers surrounding Nicaea were not "orthodox" as defined by Bull and Waterland,
came into view in his understanding of essence language, which will
be treated more fully below. Here we only need note the flavor of
his reading of the period in his *Letter to the Reverend Dr. Wells*. Clarke
criticized Wells' statement that "in the Godhead there are three persons
of the same Divine *individual* essence," saying,

> Besides, it is a phrase not only not used in Scripture, nor in the three
> first centuries, nor in the fourth, (unless it be the true rendering of the
> word μονοόυσιος or ταυτοόυσιος, which was then universally condemned
> as heretical;) but seems to be the invention of the schools, in latter
> ages.[71]

4. *Their Views of the Relationship of the Father and the Son*

Newton's trinitarian position is clarified by examining his understanding
of the relationship between the Father and the Son. To date, the
assumption among scholars seems to be that Newton's earliest convictions, as represented in his notebook from the seventies, held fast
throughout his life. Westfall writes, "The convictions that solidified
as he collected the notes remained unaltered until his death."[72] An
exception to this was Dr. Johnson's comment a century after Newton that, "Sir Isaac Newton set out an infidel, and came to be a

---

[69] Ibid., 146.
[70] Ibid., 147.
[71] Clarke, *A Letter to the Reverend Dr. Wells* in *Works*, IV, 239.
[72] Westfall, *Never at Rest*, 312.

very firm believer."[73] While Johnson overstated the case, he points
us in the most profitable direction for evaluating the mixed evidence
on Newton's beliefs; that Newton's thought on the trinity underwent
development through the years.

As we have seen, the majority of scholars have perceived Newton
as an Arian. This position is expressed most fully by More. He bases
his conclusion on two previously unpublished MSS., and two short
memoranda. In the first of these unpublished manuscripts Newton
laid down fourteen *Argumenta* in Latin, which, More argues, demonstrate that for Newton, the Son was neither coeternal with, nor equal
to, the Father. He lists the most important points as follows.

2. Because the Son is called the Word: John 1.1.
4. Because God begot the Son at some time, he had not existence
   from eternity. Prov. viii. 23, 25.
5. Because the Father is greater than the Son. John XIV, 28.
6. Because the Son did not know his last hour. Mark XIII, 32–
   Matt. XXIV, 36–Rev. 1.1 and V.3.
7. Because the Son received all things from the Father.
9. Because the Son could be incarnated.[74]

In the second manuscript Newton offered seven *Rationes* against the
traditional formulation.

1. *Homoousian* is unintelligible. 'Twas not understood in the Council of Nice (Euseb. apud Soc. . . . .) nor ever since. What cannot
   be understood is no object of belief.
6. The Father is God, creating and a person; the Son is God,
   created and a person; and the Holy Ghost is God, proceeding
   and a person; *et tamen non est nisi unus Deus.*
7. The Person is intellectual substance [*substantia intellectualis*], therefore the three Persons are three substances.[75]

Besides these two unpublished manuscripts, More cites two memoranda which, he says, "can mean only that he [Newton] did not
believe in the divinity of Jesus."[76] The first states that God had the
prophecy [of the Book of Revelation] originally in his own breast,

---

[73] James Boswell, *The Life of Samuel Johnson, L.L.D.* (New York, n.d.), 274, cited in
Westfall, *Never at Rest*, 317.
[74] More, 642.
[75] Ibid., 642–43.
[76] Ibid., 643.

and that Christ received it from God, and delivered it to John, who gave it to the churches in a continual subordination. "And to deny this subordination would be to deny Jesus Christ as he is a Prophet." The second states that Newton understood Jesus saying "I and the Father are one" to mean nothing more than that "the Father had sanctified him and sent him into the world," and that when he called himself the Son of God or God, that this was simply in the Old Testament sense by which he defended his statement. More takes this to be evidence of Unitarianism.[77]

As we saw in Chapter Three, the two terms of Arianism are a denial of the eternity of the Son (there was a time when he was not), and a belief that the Son was a creature (that he was created out of nothing). There seems to be evidence for both of these propositions in the passages quoted by More. In the fourth of the fourteen *Argumenta* above, Newton claimed that since the Son was begotten at some time, that he had not existed from eternity. Likewise in number six of the seven *Rationes* Newton writes that the "Son is God *created* and a person." This evidence alone might well lead us to More's conclusion that Newton was an Arian.[78] In addition, Westfall cites MS. 14 from the Yahuda collection as evidence of Newton's Arianism.

> Now the term λόγος before St. John wrote, was generally used in ye sense of the Platonists, when applied to an intelligent being, & ye Arrians understood it in ye same sence [sic], & therefore theirs is the true sense of St. John.[79]

Westfall gives the date of Yahuda 14 as sometime between 1672 and 1675.[80] Taken together, this evidence points toward Newton's Arian convictions in the early period of his reflection.

But Manuel, in his *The Religion of Isaac Newton*, quotes one of Newton's Mint papers where he chastised Athenagoras for calling Christ the "Idea" of all things, taking him for the Logos of the Platonists. For Newton, this made Christ the λόγος ἐνδιάθετος of the Father, making him "generated not from all eternity but in the beginning of the creation, the eternal Logos being then emitted or projected

---

[77] Ibid.

[78] Unfortunately More does not tell us where he found these manuscripts. It would be helpful to review the contexts of Newton's comments for further elucidation of his meaning.

[79] Yahuda 14, fol. 25, cited by Westfall, *Never at Rest*, 316.

[80] Ibid., 315.

outwardly like the Aeons of the Gnosticks and Logos of the Cata-
phrygians and Platonists."[81] Newton went on to condemn Athenagoras
for making the Holy Ghost "an emanation of the Father, not a necessary and eternal emanation but a voluntary and temporary one."[82]
How can we explain the apparent shift in Newton's thought from
saying that the Arians had rightly understood John through the Platonic interpretation of the logos, and his rejection of Athenagoras for
adopting the same interpretation? Moreover, he quite clearly rejects
one of the fundamental tents of Arianism here, i.e. "that there was
a time when he was not," by holding for a "necessary and eternal
genration." The most logical explanation seems to be that, during
the twenty-one years or more[83] which separated these two statements,
Newton's thought on the trinity had matured. This idea is supported
by the intensive study of the early history of the Church, and particularly the patristic texts, which Newton undertook in the late seventies and eighties. At least thirteen of the Yahuda manuscripts on
the Fathers and early church history come from this period.[84] Thus
while the manuscript evidence More and Westfall have selected indicates that Newton denied the eternal generation of the Son, in fact,
Newton, later, explicitly condemned Athenagoras for alledgedly holding just such a position. Therefore, to say that Newton held the Arian
tenet that "there was a time when he was not" can only be said
relative to his early writing. As for Newton's statement about the
Son being "God created" this need not be interpreted strictly, but
may be understood simply as a linguistic contrast to the uncreatedness
of the Father. Newton might just of well have said "begotten," except that he would have destroyed the literary parallelism. We must,
after all, remember that he says the Son is *God* created, and Newton
was clearly a sophisticated enough theologian to know that God was
not a created being.

How then, did Newton understand the relationship between the
Father and the Son? Here there is a link between Newton's natural

<hr />

[81] Manuel, *Religion*, 71–72.
[82] Ibid., 72. Mint Papers, V. fol. 37r. Here Manuel rightly warns us against an all
too "facile identification of Newton with the philosophical doctrines of the Cambridge Platonists." We have already seen that one of the primary differences between
the Platonists and the Latitudinarians was over the latter's rejection of Platonic
Idealism.
[83] Newton began his work at the mint in 1696, thus the paper cited by Manuel
cannot be any older than this.
[84] Yahuda 2.1, 2.2, 2.5, 5.2, 5.3, 11, 12, 13.1, 14, 15, 18, 19, and 29.

philosophy and his trinitarian conception. The link is in the term "dominion." We have seen in Chapter One how Newton envisioned God's relationship to creation in terms of dominion. This is the same relationship he projected into the relationship between the Father and Son. They could be co-equal only in the sense that the Son derived his authority from the Father. Otherwise the ultimate authority and unity of the Father as the *principium* of the universe would be jeopardized. Newton saw the Father as giving his power, dominion, and authority to the Son and this alone was what qualified the Son for worship.

> The heathens and Gnosticks supposed not only their Gods but even the souls of men and the starrs to be of one substance with the supreme God and yet were Idolators for worshipping them. And he that is of this opinion may believe Christ to be of one substance with the Father without making him more than a mere man. Tis not consubstantiality but power and dominion which gives a right to be worshipped.[85]

Newton balanced his subordinationism by speaking of a monarchial unity.

> And therefore as a father and his son cannot be called one King upon account of their being consubstantial but may be called one King by unity of dominion if the Son be Viceroy under the father: so God and his son cannot be called one God upon account of their being consubstantial.[86]

In his reading of the history of doctrine Newton concluded that both Arius and the Homoousians had been guilty of introducing "metaphysical opinions" into the church's teaching. The former had been dispelled by anathematization, and the latter by the repeal of the homoousian language of Nicaea by several subsequent councils. For him, the truly biblical alternative, that of a subordinationism in monarchial unity, was taught by the Eastern churches.

> The Homousians made the father and son one God by a metaphysical unity, the unity of substance: the Greek Churches rejected all metaphysical divinity as well that of Arius as that of the Homousians and made the father and son one God by a Monarchical unity, an unity of Dominion, the Son receiving all things from the father, being subject to him, executing his will, sitting in his throne and calling him his

---

[85] Newton, Yahuda MS. 15.7, fol. 154r in Manuel, *The Religion*, 60.
[86] Newton, Yahuda MS. 15.7, fol. 154r in Manuel, *The Religion*, 58.

God, and so is but one God with the Father as a king and his viceroy are but one king.[87]

This approach was borne out in Newton's exegesis as well. In commenting on the famous passage in Philippians 2 regarding the Son's not grasping for equality with God, Newton commented,

> Rapine must here being applied to something wch it is capable of rapine that is not to ye substance or essence of a [c]aptor, but to something that is acquirable by him. For the substance essence or internal nature of a man is without ye limits of what he may commit rapine in. As its [sic] improper to call any thing as stone blind wch is incapable of seeing so its improper to say any thing is not acquired by rapine wch is not acquirable by rapine. And therefore ye το εἶναι ἴσα θεῷ is to be understood not of ye [here the word "essential" is scratched out] congenit or natural divinity of [our] saviour but his glory and exaltation [and] dominion which he acquired by his death that wch St. Paul expresses in ye next words.[88]

Thus for Isaac Newton, the trinity was valid when conceived with a monarchian idea of dominion as the key to understanding the union of the Father and the Son.

Newton applied this Monarchianism consistently in his view of right worship. Several articles from his "On our Religion to God, to Christ, and the Church"[89] illustrate the point.

> Art. 1. There is one God the Father, ever living, omnipresent, omniscient, almighty, the maker of heaven and earth, and one Mediator between God and man, the man Christ Jesus.

> Art. 6. All the worship (whether of prayer, praise, or thanksgiving) which was due to the Father before the coming of Christ, is still due to him. Christ came not to diminish the worship of his Father.

> Art. 7. Prayers are most prevalent when directed to the Father in the name of the Son.

> Art. 8. We are to return thanks to the Father alone for creating us, and giving us food and rainment and other blessings of this life, and whatsoever we are to thank him for, and desire that he would do for us, we ask of him immediately in the name of Christ.

> Art. 9. We need not pray to Christ to intercede for us. If we pray the Father alright he will intercede.

---

[87] Ibid., 58.
[88] Newton, Keynes MS. 2.
[89] Newton, Keynes MS. 9. In Brewster, *Memoirs*, Vol. II, Appendix No. XXX.

Art. 10. It is not necessary to salvation to direct our prayers to any other than the Father in the name of the Son.

Art. 11. To give the name of God to angels or kings, is not against the First Commandment. To give the worship of the God of the Jews to angels or kings, is against it. The meaning of the commandment is, Thou shalt worship no other God but me.

Art. 12. To us there is but one God, the Father, of whom are all things, and one Lord Jesus Christ, by whom are all things, and we by him.—That is, we are to worship the Father alone as God Almighty, and Jesus alone as the Lord, the Messiah, the Great King, the Lamb of God who was slain, and hath redeemed us with his blood, and made us kings and priests.

Here we see reflected Newton's concern for the proper ordering of trinitarian worship according to his monarchial scheme in which the Son serves as intermediary. Ultimately it is the Father, and the Father alone, in whom all worship terminates. Even the traditional understanding of the intermediary role of the Son is somewhat diminished in Newton's scheme, especially in articles nine and ten. There we find that while we may call Jesus "God" without transgressing the first commandment, he is not to be worshiped as "God Almighty," but only in relationship to his office as Monarch: as "Lord, the Messiah, the Great King, and the Lamb of God." Christ is not worshiped on the basis of his ontology according to Newton's theology, but on the basis of his christological office. Newton could not abide worship grounded in the traditional understanding of consubstantiality, which he believed to be based in philosophy, not in scripture, and referred to it as "this strange religion of ye west," and "the cult of three equal Gods."[90]

When we look to Clarke's thought on the relationship between the Father and the Son, we see a similar pattern. Newton had defined "person" as "intellectual substance" (*substantia intellectualis*) and therefore held that "the three persons are three substances."[91] Throughout the *Scripture-Doctrine* Clarke defined person as "intelligent agent,"[92] and while he granted that it might be theoretically possible for two intelligent agents to subsist in one substance, he held that in the case of God this would yield two Gods.

---

[90] Newton, Yahuda MS. 1.4 fols. 50 and 11, fol. 7. in Westfall "The Rise of Science" 231–32, n. 45.
[91] *Rationes* No. 7 in More, 643.
[92] Clarke, *SD* in *Works*, Vol. IV, 122.

> If two or more intelligent agents can be the same being, or subsist in the same individual substance, provided the Agents be not all of them self-existent as well as the substance; (which is manifest polytheism;) this will no way affect the truth of any of Dr. Clarke's propositions.[93]

In terms of the Godhead, Clarke held to the same understanding as Newton, that the three persons are three individual substances.

As we saw in Chapter Three, Clarke, like Newton, held that the Father alone was, absolutely speaking, God of the universe.[94] The Son derived his being from the Father.[95] For both men, the key to understanding the relationship between the Father and Son was the term "monarchy." In Proposition XXXIX of the *Scripture-Doctrine* Clarke wrote,

> The reason why the Scripture, though it stiles the Father God, and also the Son God, yet at the same time always declares there is but one God; is because, there being in the Monarchy of the universe but one authority, original in the Father, derivative in the One God (absolutely speaking) always signifies Him in whom the power or authority is original and underived.[96]

For Clarke, every action of the Son, both in making the world and in all else he did was an exercise of the Father's power.[97] The Son acted only according to the will, mission and authority of the Father.[98] Here Clarke cited the Patristic scholar Valesius, in his *Notes upon Eusebius* that "All the primitive Christians in their discourses concerning God, ascribe the monarchy to God the Father; but the Oeconomy, or administration and dispensation, to the Son and Holy Spirit."[99] The connection between the principle of monarchy and Clarke's (and Newton's for that matter) doctrine of persons becomes clear where Clarke writes,

> For if on the one hand, the Father, the Son, and the Holy Spirit, be understood to be three real persons or intelligent agents; then, it being manifest that the two latter must of necessity be subordinate, (because otherwise there would be three supreme intelligent agents, that is, three

---

[93] Clarke, *Modest Plea*, in *Works*, IV, 468.
[94] Clarke, *SD* in *Works*, Vol. IV, 123.
[95] Ibid., 136.
[96] Ibid., 169.
[97] Ibid., 159.
[98] Ibid., 164.
[99] Ibid., 177.

Gods;) 'tis manifest likewise, that to the former only can be paid honour absolutely supreme.[100]

Newton and Clarke also both agreed that the Son was not merely the internal reason or wisdom of God, λόγος ἐνδιάθετος, but a real person. Clarke stated in Proposition XVIII,

> The [λόγος, the] Word or Son of the Father, sent into the world to assume our flesh, to become man, and die for the sins of mankind; was not the [λόγος ἐνδιάθετος, the] internal reason or wisdom of God, an attribute or power of the Father; but a real person, the same who from the beginning had been the word, or revealer of the will, of the Father to the world.[101]

Furthermore, both men held the same view of worship. All worship was to terminate in the person of the Father. This was promulgated in Clarke's *Scripture-Doctrine* Propositions XLIII–LII. In these Propositions Clarke clarified precisely the rationale for the worship of the Father and the Son. As we have seen above, supreme honor was to be paid to the Father alone as the sole author of Being and power.[102] For the same reason, all prayers and praise were ultimately to be directed to him.[103] The Son did not have distinct worship paid to him prior to the incarnation, but appeared simply as the *shekinah* or habitation of God's glory, although he was with God and had glory with the Father.[104] During the incarnation he divested himself of the divine glory, and as a result of the fulfillment of his office in his suffering and death, he was invested with distinct worship in his own person.[105] Therefore the honor and worship paid to Christ was not based upon his metaphysical substance, but his "actions and attributes relative to us."[106] Yet even this honor must be understood as redounding to the Father.[107] Clarke summarized the grand sweep of his conception of the relationship of the Father and the Son in Proposition XLVI.

> For the great oeconomy, or the whole dispensation of God towards mankind in Christ, consists and terminates in this; that as all authority

---

[100] Ibid., 185.
[101] Ibid., 146.
[102] Ibid., 179.
[103] Ibid., 181.
[104] Ibid., 187.
[105] Ibid.
[106] Ibid., 189.
[107] Ibid., 190.

and power is originally in the Father, and from him derived to the
Son, and exercised according to the will of the Father, by the operation of the Holy Spirit; and all communications from God to the creature, are conveyed through the intercession of the Son, and by the
inspiration and sanctification of the Holy Spirit: So on the contrary, all
returns from the creature of prayers and praises, of reconciliation and
obedience, of honour and duty to God; are made in and by the guidance and assistance of the Holy Spirit, through the mediation of the
Son, to the supreme Father and author of all things.[108]

5. *Their Understanding of What the Fathers Intended by the* Ousia *Word Group*

The final point in determining Newton's understanding of the trinity
is his understanding of the *ousia* word group. More has written,

> His purpose was not to do away entirely with the interpretation of the
> Athanasian doctrine of one substance, but to show that the argument
> over *homoousios* was not an important, or rather not a fundamental
> doctrine. He would have us believe that the church was all the while
> Arian.[109]

While, as we have witnessed, we may have cause to doubt the last
clause of this statement, the first part appears to be true. In his
"Observations on Athanasius' Works," Newton held that the linguistic distinction between *ousia* and *hypostasis* was relatively late, and that
at the time the Nicene Creed was formulated the terms were virtually interchangeable.[110] On one of the pages of Keynes MS. 2, under
the heading *De Homoousia, usia, hypostasi, substantia et personis*, Newton
noted that the term ὁμοόυσιος was "condemned by ye Council of
Antioch against Paul of Samosata."[111] Under the same heading he
noted that,

> Jerom [sic] in his Epistle to Damascus (Epist. 57) scrupling at ye use
> of thre [sic] *hypostases* as Arian, does notwithstanding expound substance
> of ye [illeg.] & makes thre [sic] hypostases to signify three kinds of
> substances or *usias*. Epiphanius *hares.* 69 & 70 making out one *hypostasis*
> in ye Deity, at ye same time expounds it of generical unity. So Atha-
> nasius with also ye Councils of Alexandria allowing ye language of

---

[108] Ibid., 186.

[109] More, 643.

[110] Newton, Keynes MS. 2, "*Distinctio inter ousian and hypostasin non coepit ante tempora Julian (vide Orat. 5 contra Arianos).*"

[111] Newton, Keynes MS. 2.

hypostasis makes a general union and similitude of substance as you may see in his *Epistle to ye Antiochians* (p. 577) & that to ye Africans.[112]

It is here, in this unpublished passage, that we are able to begin to discern the contours Newton's interpretation of ὁμοόυσιος. The term "generical unity" is the key. Newton was saying that ὑπόστασις and οὐσία were used interchangeably, and that they referred, not to a numerical identity of substance, but to a generic unity; a oneness in kind. This is reinforced by Newton's interpretation of Athanasius' two epistles, where the term ὑπόστασις (which is equivalent to οὐσία) is said to make a "general union and similitude of substance."[113] Thus the substances are identical in kind, but not in number.

> The homousians taught also that the Son was not μονοόυσιος or ταυτοόυσιος to the father but ὁμοόυσιος, & that to make them μονοόυσιοι or ταυτοόυσιοι or, to take the three persons for any thing else then personal substances tended to Sabellianism.[114]

This, of course, was the position which was held by the Homoiousian party as we saw in Chapter Three. We are suggesting then, that rather than being an Arian, Newton resembles more closely the position of the Homoiousians in the fourth century.

This suggestion is supported by Newton's "*Quaeries Regarding the Word* ὁμοόυσιος."[115] The pertinent ones are cited below.

Quaere 2. Whether the word ὁμοόυσιος ever was in any creed before the Nicene; or any creed was produced by any one bishop at the Council of Nice for authorizing the use of that word?

Quaere 3. Whether the introducing the use of that word is not contrary to the Apostles' rule of holding fast the form of sound words?

Quaere 4. Whether the use of that word was not pressed upon the Council of Nice against the inclination of the major part of the Council?

Quaere 6. Whether it was not agreed by the Council that the word should, when applied to the Word of God, signify nothing more than

---

[112] Newton, Keynes MS. 2.
[113] Ibid.
[114] Yahuda MS. 15 fol. 182.
[115] Newton, Keynes, MS. 11. See Brewster, *Memoirs*, Vol. II, Appendix XXX, 532–34.

that Christ was the express image of the Father? and whether many of the bishops, in pursuance of that interpretation of the word allowed by the Council, did not, in their subscriptions, by way of caution, add τουτ' ἐστιν ὁμοιόυσιος.

Quaere 7. Whether Hosius (or whoever translated that Creed into Latin) did not impose upon the Western Churches by translating ὁμοόυσιος by the words *unius substantiae*, instead of *consubstantialis*? and whether by that translation the Latin Churches were not drawn into an opinion that the Father and Son had one common substance, called by the Greeks *Hypostasis*, and whether they did not thereby give occasion to the Eastern Churches to cry out, presently after the Council of Sardica, that the Western Churches were become Sabellian?

Quaere 8. Whether the Greeks, in opposition to this notion and language, did not use the language of three *Hypostases*, and whether in those days the word *Hypostasis* did not signify a substance?

Quaere 9. Whether the Latins did not at that time accuse all those of Arianism who used the language of three *Hypostases*, and thereby charge Arianism upon the Council of Nice, without knowing the true meaning of the Nicene Creed.

Quaere 10. Whether the Latins were not convinced, in the Council of Ariminum, that the Council of Nice, by the word ὁμοόυσιος, understood nothing more than that the Son was the express image of the Father?—the acts of the Council of Nice were not produced for convincing them. And whether, upon producing the acts of that Council for proving this, the Macedonians, and some others, did not accuse the bishops of hypocrisy, who, in subscribing these acts, had interpreted them by the word ὁμοιόυσιος in their subscriptions?

Quaere 11. Whether Athanasius, Hilary, and in general the Greeks and Latins, did not, from the time of the reign of Julian the Apostate, acknowledge the Father, Son, and Holy Ghost to be three substances, and continue to do so till the schoolmen changed the signification of the word *hypostasis*, and brought in the notion of three persons in one single substance?

Quaere 12. Whether the opinion of the equality of the three substances was not first set on foot in the reign of Julian the Apostate, by Athanasius, Hilary, &c.?

Newton attributed the "orthodox" formula of "three persons in one substance" to confusion on two levels in the early history of the Church. On the first level was the confusion over the interpretation of the term ὁμοούσιος which, he argued, was understood by the Nicene Bishops in the sense of ὁμοιούσιος. Discussing the meaning of ὁμοούσιος Newton wrote in the 90's,

> For the word signifies either that a thing is of the same substance wth another or that it is of a like substance. For ὁμος sometimes signifies *like* & that in composition as well as alone, as in the words ὁμοπαθὴς, *obnoxious to like passions* ὁμόνεκρος, *like a dead body as to corruption*, ὁμόφλοιος *having a like bark*, & in this sense ὁμοούσιος signifies nothing more than ὁμοιούσιος *of like substance.*[116]

Newton cited with approval from Hilary's *de Synodis* on this point.

> For if we preach one substance according to ye property & similitude of nature, so that the similitude may not define the species, that is limit it to a singularity, but signify the genus, we preach it religiously provided that by one substance we understand the similitude of property so that their being one do [sic] not signify a singular substance but two equals.[117]

The fact that this was the meaning intended by the Council was certified for Newton by Eusebius of Caesarea's letter to his church.[118] In order to guarantee this interpretation, certain of the Fathers had subscribed the creed with a specific mention that by ὁμοούσιος they meant ὁμοιούσιος.

> So then ye Nicene Fathers first in their debates agreed that ὁμοούσιος signified nothing more then that ye Son was of like substance with ye father, that is, that he was ὁμοιούσιος to him & then by way of caution exprest this interpretation in their subscriptions.[119]

He cited Epiphanius to the effect that the term ταυτοούσιον was not used, which would indicate the same numerical substance and would be Sabellianism.[120] For Newton, this interpretaton of the word ὁμοούσιος had been proven beyond doubt.

---

[116] Newton, Clark MS. "Paradoxical Questions . . ." fol. 48, Newton's emphasis.
[117] Ibid., fols. 45–46, see Hilary, *de Synodis*, XXVII, 67.
[118] Ibid.
[119] Ibid., fol. 51.
[120] Newton, Keynes MS. 2, citing Epiphanius, *Hæres.* 76, n. 7.

The Council of Nice in decreeing ye Son homoousios to ye father understood that he & ye father were two substances of one nature or essence as Curcellaeus & Cudworth have proved beyond all cavil.[121]

The natural rise of the homoiousian party in the East was, for Newton, the logical outgrowth of the true convictions of the Nicene Fathers.

All this plainly respects ye Council of Nice: for that was ye great & orthodox synod, the only synod wherein ye homoousios was subscribed & ye synod wherein it was interpreted of similitude in that ye Son was not like the creatures made by him but like the father only, as you may see in ye above mentioned letter of Eusebius [of Caesarea]. Whence it is plain not only that the Nicene fathers subscribed after this manner but also that the Greek Churches during the reigns of Constantius & Valens did own this Council & by vertue [sic] of these subscriptions plead it on their side & that it was from thence that ye language of ὁμοιούσιος had its rise & was spread so easily over all the east.[122]

On the second level was the problem of the translation of terms from Greek into Latin, which created in the Western church the idea that the Father and Son shared the same numerical substance, an idea rejected by the Greeks. Writing after 1710, Newton delivered a learned summation of the events surrounding Nicaea.

The word ὁμοούσιος wch was used by the Nicene Council in this Creed & wch is here translated *consubstantial,* was by the Latins improperly translated *unius substantiae.* For *unius substantiae* may signify two things of one & the same common substance: but the words ὁμοούσιος & consubstantial were always taken by the ancient Greeks & Latins for two substances of one & the same essence nature or species. For Eusebius of Caesarea writing to his Church in the time of this Council & giving them an account of what passed in it concerning the faith, told them that it was agreed by the Council that the son's being consubstantial to the father signified nothing more then [sic] that the Son of God had no similitude wth the creatures wch were made by him, but was in all respects like ye father & from no other substance then the father's. And the Nicene fathers a considerable number of them in subscribing the decrees of the council by way of explanation that the son was ὁμοιούσιος to the father.[123]

It is clear that Newton, at least by the 1690's, was familiar with the nuances of terms employed by the early Church. The fact that he maintained that the Nicene Fathers held to a *homoiousian* interpreta-

[121] Newton, Clark MS. "Paradoxical Questions," fol. 44.
[122] Ibid., fol. 50.
[123] Yahuda MS. 15 fol. 49.

tion of the formula, which meant that the Son was an "express image" of the Father (Quaeries 6 and 10), indicates that he was deeply familiar with the debates. He blamed the undermining of this position on Athanasius.

> And lastly though this Council [Nicaea] allowed the interpretation of homoousios by similitude & the fathers by way of caution exprest this interpretation in their subscriptions yet, by the clamours of Athanasius & his party it is since grown ye semiarrian [sic] heresy for any man to make this interpretation. Whether Athanasius therefore & his friends have not done violence to this Council I leave to be considered.[124]

The "Quaeries on the word ὁμοόυσιος," together with the evidence from Keynes MS. 2, Yahuda MS. 15, and especially the Clark Library MS. on the "Paradoxical Questions" support the theory that Newton himself, no later than the 1690's, held a *homoiousian* position regarding his interpretation of the Nicene Creed.

It is quite possible that those who have come to the conclusion that Newton was either "orthodox" (Biot, Brewster) or an Arian (More, and contemporary scholars) are simply interpreting his position in light of an inadequate framework of options. More illustrates this kind of framework:

> The anti-Trinitarians can be classed under three main divisions: the Arians who denied that the Son was coeternal with the father, though he was begot before time began and by him the Father created all things ... the Socinians who believe that he did not exist before his appearance on earth, but that he was an object of prayer; the Humanitarians, or Unitarians, who believe him to be a man, and not an object of prayer.[125]

It may be that Newton himself, in the early 1670's, wrote out of a similar framework, and, within that limited set of options, saw the Arian position as the most consistent. It seems clear however, that by the 1690's (or, if Westfall's date of the Clark MS. is correct, by the 1680's), as a result of his rigorous investigation of the early church and Patristics, Newton's trinitarian theology was sufficiently nuanced so as to have adopted the homoiousian position over and against both Athanasianism and Arianism. Rather than squeezing Newton into the standard seventeenth century schools of thought on the trinity, I am suggesting that the key to his thought is found in the categories

---

[124] Newton, Clark MS., "Paradoxical Questions," fol. 90.
[125] More, 630, n. 41.

of the fourth century, upon which he had developed an expertise, specifically among those who held the *homoiousian* interpretation of the Nicene Creed, with which he had now become quite familiar and sympathetic. If the Newton historians of the nineteenth and twentieth centuries have found it "a blot on his record"[126] that Newton was unwilling to join Whiston's attempt to restore "primitive Christianity" or to defend him when he was ousted from Cambridge, perhaps it was, after all, not due to Newton's being "all too human"[127] but because he believed Whiston, as an avowed Arian, had gone too far. Newton was neither "orthodox" (according to the Athanasian creed) nor an Arian. He believed that both of these groups had wandered into metaphysical speculation. He was convinced that his position was the truly biblical one, in which the Son was affirmed to be the express image of the Father, and that this position was best represented by those Bishops at Nicaea who held the Son to be of the same kind of substance as the Father, but not numerically the same. It seems clear at this point that in his maturity Issac Newton held a view on the trinity which, albeit heterodox, was not Arian.

As with the other five points discussed, Clarke and Newton were in agreement about the interpretation of the *ousia* word group during the fourth century. We have seen in Newton's *Quaeries Regarding the Word* ὁμοόυσιος his opinion that the early Fathers did not interpret the term to mean that the Father and the Son were the same identical substance, but rather that the Son was the express image of the Father. Likewise we have seen in the Clark Library manuscript his implicit support of both the early Bishops who subscribed the term with ὁμοιόυσιος by way of interpretation, and those early councils which interpreted the term in the same way.

In Chapter Three, I argued that Clarke's understanding of the trinity was derived along the eastern lines of Origen, Eusebius of Caesarea, Basil of Ancyra and Basil the Great. One of the main features of this line of thought was that these theologians held that the Son was "out of the same substance of the Father" and that they understood this to mean not the same identical substance as the Father, but "of the same stuff," or, the express image of the Father. This was also Clarke's understanding of the *homoousios*. Whereas Newton was more negative about the employment of the term itself (see Quaeries 1–3), Clarke, although he saw it as philosophical language,

---

[126] Keynes, "Newton the Man," 31.
[127] Manuel, *Religion*, 62–63.

was more willing to work with it when it was rightly understood. This right understanding was to be derived from the interpretation which, Clarke believed, the Council of Nicaea itself provided.

> And that article in the Nicene Creed, [of one substance with the Father,] is now (through the ambiguity of the Latin and English translation,) by most men taken much otherwise, than the council intended it; For the greater part of modern Christians, (if we may judge by the writings of eminent divines,) understand it as if it had been ταυτοούσιος) to signify, of one *individual* substance with the Father; Whereas all learned men know, that the Greek word [ὁμοούσιος] never had any such signification, and that the Council meant no such thing; but, of the same *kind* of substance with the Father: [ἐκ τοῦ οὐσιά τοῦ πατρὸς, so the Council of Nice explained themselves, though those words are now left out of the Creed;] The Son was, they said, γεννηθεὶς ἐκ τοῦ πατρὸς, τουτέσιν ἐκ τοῦ οὐσίας τοῦ πατρὸς, that is from the substance of the Father: And therefore was not (which notion was then universally condemned) himself that individual substance from which he was begotten. But their meaning was; he was produced, not from any other substance, as man was formed from the dust of the earth,) but, after an ineffable manner, from the substance of the Father only. Which sense of theirs, is now generally mistaken.[128]

Along the same line, Clarke quoted Cudworth's *Intellectual System* in which Cudworth had argued that St. Cyril and St. Gregory of Nyssa "were far from thinking the three hypostases of the trinity to have the same *singular* existent essence."[129] Clarke proceeded to cite Cudworth to the effect that this doctrine of three persons being the same individual substance was not held by any public authority in the Christian church except the Lateran Council, that no such thing was believed by the Nicene Fathers, and that the truth of this was seen in the fact that those orthodox anti-Arian Fathers also condemned Sabellianism, which was the same as this doctrine of three distinct persons in one substance. Not only that, but the Greek writers never used ὁμοούσιος other than to signify "the agreement of things *numerically* differing from one another."[130] Finally Clarke wrote that, according to Cudworth, the Nicene Fathers who used the word ὁμοούσιος against the Arians, also disclaimed the words ταυτοούσια and μονοούσια.[131]

In conclusion then, it may be said that, on the major aspects of

---

[128] Clarke, *A Reply to Mr. Nelson*, in *Works*, IV, 263.
[129] Clarke, *A Letter to the Reverend Dr. Wells* in *Works*, IV, 239.
[130] Ibid.
[131] Ibid.

their trinitarian formulation, the thought of Samuel Clarke and Isaac
Newton was virtually identical. Both disdained philosophical speculation, relying on Scripture as the source from which they drew their
conclusions. However, both were willing to enter into the philosophical debate, if only to show that the "orthodox" position was untenable.
Both demonstrated knowledge of certain textual problems regarding
the reliability of the "trinitarian texts" and understood the exegesis
of key biblical texts in the same way. Their reading of the history of
the Church around the period of the Nicene Creed was the same,
except perhaps that Clarke held to a stronger belief that the Ante-
Nicene Fathers were more uniform in their understanding of the relationship between the Father and the Son than Newton might have
allowed. Clarke and Newton also viewed the relationship between
the Father and the Son along the same lines. Theirs was a subordinationist paradigm with unity being determined along a monarchial
axis, rather than by an ontological identification. Worship of the Father
and Son was also to be understood along this line, and the Son was
to be worshiped, not because of his ontology, but because of his
office. Lastly, both Newton and Clarke held the same view regarding
the *ousia* word group used by the Fathers. The Son was the "express
image" of the Father, and the two could be said to be of the same
substance, if that be understood to mean the "same kind of substance" and not "the same identical (numerical) substance."

Newton's Influence on Clarke

The crucial question which must be asked for our purposes has to
do with the question of influence. Was Isaac Newton a (the) major
source for Samuel Clarke's trinitarian thought? We have already seen
in Chapter One that Clarke and Newton were intimate friends. They
collaborated on several projects including the translation of Newton's
Optics into Latin, and the debate over natural philosophy with Leibniz.
Newton served on the vestry of Clarke's church, and Clarke was
nominated to fill Newton's post at the mint when Newton died. The
two lived within walking distance of each other in London. All this
is mentioned to reinforce the fact that Newton and Clarke shared a
deep personal friendship which was rooted in their intellectual interests. Newton was a scientist deeply interested in theology, and Clarke
was a clergyman deeply interested in natural philosophy. The prob-

lem in making a definitive statement regarding Newton's influence on Clarke is that there is, to my knowledge, no extant correspondance between them. Thus any conclusion we might reach on this issue must necessarily be tentative and based on circumstantial evidence and inference.

In determining the question of Newton's influence on Clarke the first and most critical issue is when Newton reached his conclusions on the trinity. Modern scholarship is agreed that Newton's career cannot be divided between a vibrant youthfulness dedicated to strict scientific reasoning, and a dotage spent in wanderings into apocalyptic, prophecy and cabbala, separated by the watershed event of a nervous breakdown.[132] As Newton worked in the theological realm, his trinitarian thought seems to have developed from an earlier Arian tendency, as represented in Yahuda 14 (1672–75) to the homoiousian position reflected so clearly in the Clark Library MS. (1690's) and Yahuda 15 (post 1710). This notion of development modifies the approach of Westfall and Christianson, that Newton's conclusions on the trinity were Arian, and were set early.[133] The reason for these developments is probably his extensive historical studies of the late seventies and eighties, as represented by the Yahuda Manuscripts. In addition to his historical studies, Newton was involved in textual study. His *Two Notable Corruptions* was sent to Locke in 1690.[134] The fact that Newton worked on the trinity early on is further supported by the dates Manuel has assigned to some of the trinitarian manuscripts.[135] Newton's trinitarian conclusions changed between the 1670's and the 1690's and appear to be settled after that.[136]

Second, Newton was more than thirty years Clarke's senior, which would establish a natural mentoring relationship. In the field of natural philosophy, Clarke was clearly Newton's disciple, having defended his cause against Leibniz, and having used the Boyle Lectures as a platform for expounding the new natural philosophy.

Third, Newton's knowledge of divinity was well respected among

---

[132] Manuel, *Religion*, 14. This view of the distinct periods in Newton's life was first promulgated by J. Biot in the early nineteenth century.

[133] Westfall, "The Rise of Science," 230 suggests Newton's trinitarian thought was set by 1675; Christianson, 253, suggests a date of 1673.

[134] More, 632.

[135] Keynes MSS. 2, 4, and 10 Manuel assigns to the late seventies and eighties. A number of the Yahuda MSS. on the history of the early church are dated from the same period. Keynes MSS. 6, 8, 9 are dated after 1710.

[136] Yahuda 15 (post 1710) articulates the same view as the Clark MS. (1690's).

divines in the Church of England.[137] As we saw in Chapter Two, Newton was offered the Mastership of Trinity College by Archbishop Tenison.[138] For all these reasons it would seem natural to assert that in theology as in natural philosophy, Clarke simply imitated his mentor. Yet, this would be a hasty conclusion.

Clarke's *Scripture-Doctrine* was a comprehensive study of the doctrine of the trinity, something which Newton never undertook. While both Clarke and Newton clearly used the readily available thesaurus of studies which questioned the standard trinitarian formulation, Clarke was clearly conversant in a wider range of materials. Also Clarke was more precise in his formulations than Newton, and showed more concern to demonstrate that his view was the correct interpretation of the early Fathers.

Clarke's work was his own. He had doubts about the traditional understanding of the trinity as early as the Boyle Lectures (1704–05). Given his relationship with Newton, it is probable that these doubts were discussed at length, and likely that Newton suggested lines of inquiry to Clarke; lines along the history of the Church in the fourth century and relavent Patristic material; lines which he himself had explored twenty years prior.

Just as Clarke represented Newton in the debate with Leibniz, so he may also have represented Newton's views in his treatise on the trinity. If this is the case, the views were clearly his own as well. For all of these reasons, Newton must be seen as a key source for Clarke's trinitarian theology, which he may never had made public without Newton's hidden support and encouragement. Conversely, it may be that Samuel Clarke's *Scripture-Doctrine of the Trinity*, is the closest we will ever come to knowing the mature mind of Isaac Newton on so sublime a subject.

---

[137] North, *Isaac Newton*, 58.
[138] Cited in More, 608.

PART THREE

CONTROVERSY

CHAPTER FIVE

THE LITERATURE OF THE
TRINITARIAN CONTROVERSY

As a result of his successful Boyle Lectures in 1704 and 1705, Clarke
had established a reputation as a leading light in the Anglican church.
Ferguson has suggested that Clarke would one day have become
Archbishop of Canterbury.[1] A major publication, on a major doctrine
of the faith, by a leading figure in the church, would not go unnoticed.
The situation was intensified by the fact that there existed in England at the time a great controversy over the doctrine of the trinity.

The trinitarian controversy in England can be dated from Bull's
Defensio in 1685. Bull was responding to the continental Arminians,
to the Socinians Sandius and Zwicker, and to the Jesuit Petavius. It
is difficult to discover a precise reason for the revival of interest in
the trinity in England. Abbey and Overton have suggested that it
may have been a result of the influx of anti-trinitarians who were
banished from Poland under the Order of Council in 1660.[2] Whatever the reason, a number of authors began to produce works on
this fundamental article of faith. In 1690 Dr. Sherlock, Dean of
St. Paul's produced his *Vindication of the Holy and Ever-blessed Trinity*.
His doctrine hinged on the idea that in God there were three substances undivided, each being conscious of each other's thoughts and
states. For his trouble Sherlock was deemed a Tritheist and received
the censure of the Convocation of Oxford University.[3] Dr. Robert
South, Rector of Islip, near Oxford, and an enemy of Sherlock's,
launched an acrimonious assault against Sherlock in his *Animadversions upon Dr. Sherlock's Book*. South was, in turn, accused of Sabellianism. Despite the fact that the Toleration Act of 1689 did not
protect those who held anti-trinitarian views, the debate continued
until it became so hostile that finally, in 1695, Archbishop Tenison
intervened, convincing King William to issue instructions to the Bishops

---

[1] Ferguson, *Heretic*, 33.
[2] Charles Abbey and John Overton, *The English Church in the Eighteenth Century*, 2d
ed. (London: Longmans, Green, and Co., 1887), 198.
[3] Fisher, 370–71, Abbey and Overton, 200 and Ferguson, *Heretic*, 49.

that no doctrine concerning the trinity should be produced other than that contained in scripture and in keeping with the Creeds and Thirty-Nine Articles.[4] Others who wrote on the trinity during this time were John Wallis, Edward Stillingfleet, John Owen and the Non-Conformist, John Howe.[5] It was into this volatile mixture of opinion that Clarke set down his *Scripture-Doctrine of the Trinity* in 1712. The results were explosive. Regarding its significance, Abbey and Overton have written, "We may take the appearance of Dr. Clarke's book as the commencement of a new era in this controversy."[6]

As soon as Clarke published his *Scripture-Doctrine of the Trinity*, several responses appeared. The first was an anonymous work entitled *Essay towards an Impartial Account of the Holy Trinity, and the Deity of our Saviour, as contained in the Old Testament. In which are Some Remarks on the Scripture account lately published by Dr. Clarke.*[7] This tract called into question several issues raised by Clarke. The first was the question of how Christ could be worshiped, as in the New Testament, if he were not consubstantial with the Father. Secondly, the tract emphasized the mediatorial office of Christ which would ultimately be given up, leaving this subordinating distinction behind. Thirdly, in response to Clarke's insistence that the Son proceeded from the Father, and was therefore derived, the author of the tract insisted that the derivation was personal and therefore consistent with God's unity.

Also published in 1712 was Dr. John Edwards' *Some Animadversions on Dr. Clarke's Scripture-Doctrine, (as he styles it) of the Trinity, briefly shewing that his quotations out of the Fathers are forced; his texts produced from Scripture are wrested; his arguments and inferences are weak and illogical: His whole performance falls short of his design.*[8] Edwards criticized Clarke's use of scripture where Clarke had chosen passages stating the oneness of God to prove the superiority of the Father. Edwards reminded Clarke that what was in view in these texts was external, viz., God's superiority regarding false gods, and not an internal differentiation within

---

[4] Ferguson, *Heretic*, 50–51.

[5] Fisher, *History of Christian Doctrine*, 370–71.

[6] Abbey and Overton, 205.

[7] Anonymous, *An Essay towards an Impartial Account of the Holy Trinity, and the Deity of our Saviour, as contained in the Old Testament. In which are some Remarks on the Scripture Account lately published by Dr. Clarke* (London: 1712).

[8] John Edwards, *Some Animadversions on Dr. Clarke's Scripture-Doctrine, (as he styles it) of the Trinity, briefly shewing that his quotations out of the Fathers are forced; his texts produced from Scripture are wrested; his arguments and inferences are weak and illogical: His whole performance falls short of his design* (London: for the author, 1712).

the nature of the Godhead. Even in texts where Jesus had spoken to the Father out of his limitation and dependence, it was his human nature which was in view, not his divine nature. Edwards also believed that Clarke made the Son a creature, and denied his eternity. Asch reminds us that Edwards overlooked the fact that Clarke had spoken *for* the eternity of the Son in several propositions.[9]

After waiting in vain for a response to his work, Edwards followed up the next year with his *A Supplement to the Animadversions on Dr. Clarke's Scripture-Doctrine etc.* Here Edwards sought to ascertain the roots of Clarke's theology, which he titled "Arian," a title which Waterland was later to popularize regarding Clarke's work, and which scholarship has since tacitly accepted.

> First, I am to assign the rise of the Arian persuasion among Christians not omitting at the same time its growth and its origin and increase, first from the school of Plato, secondly from the unwary and unsafe language of some of the Fathers, third from the notion which some of the ancient doctors of the church entertain'd concerning the paternity of the first person in the Trinity.[10]

Believing that he had discovered the roots of Clarke's teaching, Edwards proceeded to establish that Christ was fully God. He showed that the Son was a natural emanation of the Father, and must therefore have been of the same substance. The Son was also self-existent. If the Father and Son were of the same nature, and the Father was self-existent, then it followed that the Son must be also, and could not be derived.

In the following year (1713), Dr. Edward Wells, Rector of Cotesbach in Leicestershire joined the debate with his *Remarks on Dr. Clarke's Introduction to His Scripture-Doctrine of the Trinity*. Wells focused on the Introduction to Clarke's work because he felt an anonymous work entitled *The True Scripture Doctrine of the Holy Trinity, the Eucharist and the Satisfaction made for us by our Lord Jesus Christ*, had already treated the main body of Clarke's argument thoroughly, but had neglected Clarke's Introduction, which Wells felt was dangerous in itself. Wells criticized Clarke at several points. First, Clarke had failed to include the Old Testament in his biblical survey. Wells asserted that there was much in the Old Testament which bore on the trinity, and that

---

[9] Asch, 135.
[10] John Edwards, *A Supplement to the Animadversions on Dr. Clarke's Scripture-Doctrine of the Trinity* (London: Printed for N. Cliffe and D. Jackson, 1713), 3–4.

by omitting it, Clarke had skewed the evidence. Wells went on to take issue with Clarke's statement that scripture was the only rule of faith. He included reason as also necessary for faith. Reason was required for formulating the logical implications of scripture. In saying this, Wells clarified that he was well aware of the amount of reasoning present in Clarke's proposal. In addition, Wells reminded Clarke of the weight of the testimony of the early church and its theologians. According to Wells, when one relied on private judgment over and against the wisdom and council of the early church, preserved through the providence of God, one was in danger of subjectivism.[11]

The anonymous book mentioned by Wells as having given a satisfactory response to Clarke was authored by Dr. James Knight. Clarke treated this work lightly, and had not even deemed it worthy of a response.[12] Knight followed up with his satirical *A Letter to the Reverend Dr. Clarke* in 1714 and with his more direct *The Scripture Doctrine of the Most Holy and Undivided Trinity*, published the same year. The latter work contained a prefixed letter from Robert Nelson, who had been Bishop Bull's biographer. Clarke had used Bull's *Defensio Fidei Nicaenae* to support his position in the *Scripture-Doctrine*, and Nelson gently reminded him of Bull's orthodoxy when he referred to him as "that great defender of the Nicene faith."[13] Nelson went on to encourage Clarke to consider this work of his learned friend, James Knight.

Knight's work challenged Clarke's thesis in three chapters. These treated the persons of the trinity respectively. Knight drew on the Old Testament, New Testament, and Patristic sources to show that, contrary to Clarke's conclusions, the Church's doctrine of the trinity was biblical and especially in keeping with the early teaching of the Fathers.

> I have made it my endeavour, to shew in some instances, the little ground which the Dr. had for placing those authors on the side of his opinion; being verily persuaded, that such as are cited in these following papers, give great light to the doctrine of our Church, and confirm its antiquity as deduced from Scripture.[14]

---

[11] Asch, 92, 101, 103, 126.

[12] In fact, Clarke did not respond to anything in writing prior to Dr. Wells *Remarks*.

[13] [James Knight], *The True Scripture Doctrine of the most Holy and Undivided Trinity, Vindicated from the Misrepresentations of Dr. Clarke* (London: Printed for Richard Smith, 1714), from Robert Nelson's prefix to the letter, xi.

[14] Ibid., Preface, 2.

Knight selected forty texts from Clarke's list of 1,251 and attempted to demonstrate that his hermeneutics were erroneous, arguing that these examples of Clarke's approach to the texts made all of his interpretation suspect. His main objections to Clarke were:

1) That Clarke believed that when the terms "one" and "only" God are used in scripture, that they refer to the Father alone.

2) That Clarke used the terms "being" and "person" synonymously.

3) That Clarke inferred from the terms "self-existent" and "unoriginated" that which is derogatory to the true divinity of the Son.[15]

In 1714 another refutation of Clarke was produced entitled *Speculum Clarkianum or, Cl__k against Cl__k. Being a Confutation of His Scripture-Doctrine of the Trinity Out of His own previous Writings*. The author called himself "Philotriados." In his pamphlet "Philotriados" set out to prove that Clarke was inconsistent through a comparative examination of his *Scripture-Doctrine*, *Boyle Lectures*, and *Paraphrases on the Evangelists*.

The next response to the *Scripture-Doctrine* came from Dr. Gastrell, Bishop of Chester. He had already written on the trinity in 1696, and had been a Boyle lecturer in 1697. Where Knight argued from scripture and Patristics, Gastrell argued from reason in his *Remarks upon Dr. Clarke's Scripture-Doctrine of the Trinity. By the Author of, Some Considerations concerning the Trinity and the Ways of managing that Controversy*.[16] He challenged Clarke's fifty-five propositions in Part II of the *Scripture-Doctrine*. Gastrell offered and defended two propositions of his own. The first was that the Father, Son and Holy Spirit were not three different beings, and secondly, that they were one God. When the term "God" was used, it applied not only to the Father, but equally to the Son and Spirit.[17] Asch's view of the exchange between Clarke and Gastrell is more irenic than Ferguson's. Asch portrays Gastrell in a mediating role, while Ferguson views him in an adversarial one. While Gastrell did see some merit in Clarke's argument, it is clear that he stood opposed to Clarke's fundamental principles.[18]

---

[15] Asch provides helpful discussion on these points, pp. 129–132.
[16] Francis Gastrell, *Remarks upon Dr. Clarke's Scripture-Doctrine of the Trinity. By the Author of, Some Considerations concerning the Trinity and the Ways of managing that Controversy* (London: 1714).
[17] Ferguson, *Heretic*, 75–76.
[18] Asch, 111–112 cf., Ferguson, *Heretic*, 74–77.

Clarke responded to Gastrell's remarks in his *Answer to the Remarks &c.*,[19] which in turn prompted Edwards to rejoin the debate with his *Some Critical Remarks on Dr. Clarke's last Papers.*[20] It was in the post-script of this work that Edwards joined the names of Clarke and Isaac Newton. As we saw in Chapter Four, Edwards believed there was a link between Clarke's and Newton's thought on the trinity. In fact, he believed that it was Clarke who influenced Newton in the *General Scholium* of the second edition of the *Principia Mathematica* where Newton moved toward the notion of God's dominion being supreme, making the Father supreme, and implying the possibility of lesser Gods, viz., the Son and Spirit. As we have seen, however, Newton had formulated his conclusions by 1690, and therefore it is impossible that he derived his ideas from Clarke. A more likely hypothesis is that with Clarke's having published the *Scripture-Doctrine* the year before the second edition of the *Principia* was published (1713), Newton was encouraged to make public opinions he had held for thirty years or more. An overview of the relation between Clarke and Newton has already been seen in the first chapter, and an analysis of their respective thought on the trinity was offered in chapter four. As for Edwards' tract, Clarke offered no response.

Dr. Edward Potter of Cambridge also challenged Clarke in 1714 in his *A Vindication of our Blessed Saviour's Divinity; chiefly against Dr. Clarke.* Potter centered on the issue of Christ's divinity. For Potter, Clarke's central flaw was his confusion of the terms "being" and "person." Clarke had stated that to say God was one being, and three persons was illogical. In response Potter accused Clarke of metaphysical speculation, a charge which Clarke had used earlier against others. Potter argued that scripture made two truths known: That there was one God; and that this one God existed in three persons. Potter iterated earlier criticism that Clarke, in ardent defense of God's unity, really opened himself to the charge of diluting God's unity by denying that the Son and the Spirit shared totally in the nature of the Father, and were therefore rightfully also called God.

Following Potter's criticism, and resembling it, there appeared in 1714, bearing the imprimatur of Bernard Gardiner, Vice-Chancellor

---

[19] Clarke, *Works*, IV, 327–358.

[20] John Edwards, *Some Brief Critical Remarks on Dr. Clarke's last Papers; which are his reply to Mr. Nelson, and an Anonymous Writer, and the Author of Some Considerations, etc. Shewing that the Doctor is as deficient in the Critic Art as he is in Theology* (London: 1714).

of Oxford, *Dr. Clarke's Scripture-Doctrine of the Trinity Examined.*[21] The author was Edward Welchman. Like Gastrell, Welchman took issue with Clarke's fifty-five propositions in Part II of the *Scripture-Doctrine.* He cited Clarke's XXVIIth proposition, that all titles and powers belonged to the Son, except absolute supremacy and independency which were not communicable. For Clarke, to say these were communicable, was a contradiction in terms. Welchman wrote,

> Then it seems we must look upon the Son as only an inferior and dependent God, that is, no God at all. For absolute Supremacy and Independency are included in the very notion of God. As for the contradiction the Dr. talks of, I see not where it lies, as express as it is. That absolute supremacy and independency should be communicated, without a communication of the essence, from which they are inseparable, were indeed a contradiction. But where the very essence, to which they belong, is communicated, as in the present case, to say they also are communicated, is so far from being a contradiction, that I am sure it is one, to say they are not.[22]

In the same year, 1714, the controversy created so much notoriety that a Convocation of the Church of England was held in June to investigate Dr. Clarke's views.[23] When an *Extract* of Clarke's views and several critiques were laid before the Lower House, it concluded that an inquiry was necessary. Clarke submitted his *Reply* to the *Extract* on June 26 in which he defended his position to the Bishops. About a week after Clarke sent his *Reply* to the Bishops, he sent a shorter *Paper* to them. In this *Paper* he wrote,

> My opinion is, that the Son of God was eternally begotten by the eternal incomprehensible power and will of the Father; and that the Holy Spirit was likewise eternally derived from the Father, by or through the Son, according to the eternal incomprehensible power and will of the Father.[24]

In this *Paper* Clarke gave two assurances to the Bishops: He would not preach on the trinity again, nor would he write on the subject.

---

[21] Edward Welchman, *Dr. Clarke's Scripture-Doctrine of the Trinity Examined. To which are added some remarks on his sentiments, and a Brief Explanation of his Doctrine by way of Question and Answer* (Oxford, 1714).

[22] Ibid., 14.

[23] For the documents pertaining to the Convocation see John Lawrence, *An Apology for Dr. Clarke Containing an account of the late proceedings in Convocation upon his Writings concerning the Trinity. Being a Collection of several Original Papers,* in Clarke, *Works,* IV, 543–558.

[24] Clarke, *Works,* IV, 553. It is worthy of note here that Clarke does not affirm

While the Lower House was not satisfied with Clarke's letter, the Upper House was content with his acknowledgment of the eternal pre-existence of Christ. On July 5, 1714 the Upper House resolved not to proceed further against Clarke, making moot the dissenting Resolution of the Lower House two days later.

The difference between the vigorous defence of the earlier *Reply* and the brief, halcyon tone of the *Paper* has raised the question of why Clarke changed his approach. Ferguson suggests two reasons. First, "The Bishops themselves were anxious to avoid a dissension in this matter, with all the undesirable publicity it would bring," and second, "To the Bishop's anxiety to avoid scandal and the odium of persecution for heresy, we may add Clarke's own unwillingness to become a martyr."[25]

In light of the *Paper*, Clarke was strongly reproached by his supporters who believed he had given up the battle for "primitive Christianity." Most deeply hurt was William Whiston the heterodox latitudinarian mentioned in Chapter One. Whiston was a more radical subordinationist, a follower of Eusebius of Nicomedia, and an avowed Arian.[26] A Convocation had been held in 1711 concerning his trinitarian views for which he had already been removed from the Lucasian chair at Cambridge. Although Clarke is frequently mentioned together with him, the distinctions between them on the trinity were considerable. Clarke followed the thought of Eusebius of Caesarea and the Eastern theologians and explicitly denied being an Arian. Whiston, on the other hand identified himself with the Arian line of thought.

> I have fully, in more places than one, declqar'd how far I am an Arian. Nor can anyone doubt from all I have said that in my uncertain philosophick conjectures, I incline more to the followers of Arius himself than of Athanasius . . . I take Eunomius to have been a much more learned, judicious, wise and good man than Arius . . . altho' custom may call Eunomius a most compleat Arian, in a general acceptation, as distinguish'd from other parties then contending in the church.[27]

---

the *filioque* language of the West, but uses language more typical of the Eastern Church, viz., that the Spirit proceeded from the Father *by* or *through* the Son. This is in keeping with the influence of the Eastern Fathers noted in the previous chapter, especially Origen and the Cappadocians.

[25] Ferguson, *Heretic*, 86–87.

[26] William Whiston, *Animadversions on a Late Pamphlet Intituled, The New Arian Reprov'd* (London, 1712), 4.

[27] Ibid.

Whether in response to concern that he had given up his views, or not, Clarke clarified his position in a letter to the Bishop of London dated July 5, 1714. Here he reiterated his fundamental thesis that the Father alone was ἀναίτιος and παναίτιος.[28] He also reserved the right to respond in writing to criticism of his previous work and make any necessary alterations in forthcoming editions.

In 1715 the controversy continued with the publication of the *Explication of the Articles of Divine Unity, the Trinity and the Incarnation, commonly received in the Catholic Church, Asserted and Vindicated* by the Reverend Stephen Nye. Nye suggested that Clarke was teaching the existence of three gods because his concept of the word "person" necessitated three separate intelligent beings, each really divine. Because the Father possessed these divine powers underived, he alone was supreme and independent. Nye insisted that the term "person" in the trinitarian discussion referred to the *internal* nature of God. Nye received a response from John Jackson in his *An Examination of Mr. Nye's Explication*.[29] Jackson lauded Nye's perception that the meaning of "person" needed clarification, but claimed that Nye himself had misunderstood it, and had entered into a cloaked form of Sabellianism.

The next work to enter the debate was Richard Mayo's *A Plain Scripture Argument against Dr. Clarke's Doctrine Concerning the ever-blessed Trinity*. This tract grew out of, and was published with, some letters exchanged between Mayo and Clarke. In the third of these letters Mayo challenged Clarke's definition of "person" as an "intelligent agent." He asks rhetorically, "Can you possibly think that a supreme intelligent agent, which governs the world, is a definition of the essence of God?"[30] Mayo charged Clarke with being guilty of reducing the being of God to an attribute of that being, viz., intelligence, which created confusion in his understanding of the relationship of the persons of the trinity. Clarke argued in his correspondence that Mayo believed more was taught in scripture than he, and that the

---

[28] Clarke, *Works*, IV, 557.
[29] John Jackson, *An Examination of Mr. Nye's Explication of the Articles of the Divine Unity, The Trinity and Incarnation. Wherein is briefly shewn, The insufficiency of that Explication both from Scripture and Reason; with a Vindication of Dr. Clarke's Scripture Doctrine and Replies, from the charge of Tritheism* (London: 1715).
[30] Richard Mayo, *A Plain Scripture-Argument Against Dr. Clarke's Doctrine Concerning the Ever-Blessed Trinity; in a Letter to Dr. Clarke* (London: Printed for M. Lawrence and F. Downing, 1715), 9.

burden of proof was on Mayo. Mayo accepted the burden, and set
out to prove his point from scripture.[31]

Among the tracts produced in 1715 was James Knight's *The true
Scripture-Doctrine of the Most Holy and Undivided Trinity Continued and
Vindicated from the Misrepresentations of Dr. Clarke*. In Clarke's earlier *A
Reply to the Objections of Robert Nelson, Esq. and of an Anonymous Author*,
who was James Knight, he pointed out that Knight had addressed
only forty texts in his work, while he had ignored three-hundred
others, which demonstrated the dependency of the second person of
the trinity upon the first.[32] To this Knight responded in his new
work "that if the texts I have selected be represented to the reader
in their true meaning, there is sufficient ground, notwithstanding the
number which remain untouched for rejecting the notions advanced
by the Dr."[33] Knight proceeded to take issue with many of the citations of scripture used in Clarke's *Scripture-Doctrine* and widened his
selection of texts from the forty cited in his former work. In this
latter work Knight employed the same method of drawing heavily
upon the Church Fathers in their support of the Athanasian formula, and consequent rejection of Clarke's teaching.

In 1718 Dr. Thomas Bennet published *A Discourse of the Ever-Blessed
Trinity in Unity, with an Examination of Dr. Clarke's Scripture-Doctrine of the
Trinity*. Bennet criticized Clarke's inability to distinguish between
Christ's human and divine natures in the biblical references. Those
texts which referred to Christ's human nature Clarke used to support his subordinationism regarding Christ's divine nature. Like
Gastrell and Welchman before him, Bennet challenged Clarke's fifty-
five propositions. Like Edward Potter of Cambridge, Bennet believed
that Clarke had erred in making "person" synonymous with "intelligent being." In fact, Clarke was in keeping here with the classical
definition of Boethius, that a person was an "individual substance of
a rational nature" (*rationalis naturae individua substantia*).[34] Bennet recog-

---

[31] Ibid., 12.

[32] Clarke, *Works*, IV, 263.

[33] [James Knight], *The True Scripture Doctrine of the Trinity, Continued and Vindicated
from the Misrepresentations of Dr. Clarke. In Answer to his Reply* (London: Printed for Richard
Smith, 1715), 1.

[34] Boethius' definition was normative for centuries in medieval theology, although
it underwent modification in St. Thomas. See O'Carroll, *Trinitas*, 55, 180 and
Fortman, *The Triune God*, 161–64. The impact of Boethius' definition is still felt in
today's usage. The *Oxford English Dictionary* defines the philosophical use of "person"

nized the problematic of Boethius' definition of person when applied to the trinity, and believed that this error caused disruption in Clarke's trinitarian formulation.[35] Furthermore, for Bennet, this distinction was never proved from scripture itself. Bennet went on to say that the scripture was clear that the Word (the divine nature of Christ) was not derived from God, but had existed with and was God, from all time. Finally he asserted that the supremacy and independence, which Clarke had denied the Word, in their absolute sense, were never denied to the divine nature of Christ in scripture.

Although Clarke, in his Letter to the Bishop of London, had reserved the right to respond to questions concerning his previous writings, his cause was taken up by Arthur Ashley Sykes, Rector of Dry Drayton in the county of Cambridge, with his *A Modest Plea for the Baptismal and Scripture Notion of the Trinity Wherein the Schemes of the Reverend Dr. Bennet and Dr. Clarke are compared*. For Sykes, Bennet's notion of "person" was indistinct. Talk of three persons and one substance was a contradiction, not a mystery. In this, Sykes repeated the sentiments of his mentor.[36]

The most able participant in the trinitarian controversy entered late. Dr. Daniel Waterland was Regius Professor of Divinity at Cambridge when he publicly entered the debate seven years after Clarke published his *Scripture-Doctrine*. Waterland will be treated in detail in the next chapter because of the major role he played in the controversy. For now his position will be noted in the broad field of those participating in the controversy.

Waterland was brought into the debate by John Jackson's *A Collection of Queries*[37] published in 1716. Waterland was an unwilling participant in the debate, and was drawn in as a result of some private communication about the trinity with Jackson. He had written some "Queries" which he sent to Jackson, which in turn Jackson

---

as "a self-conscious or rational being." *Oxford English Dictionary*, 2d ed., eds. J.A. Simpson and E.S.C. Weiner (Oxford: Clarendon Press, 1989), Vol. XI, 597.

[35] Clarke here was relying on Boethius' classic statement on person which held that a person was an individual substance of a rational nature. The statement itself proved to be problematic in application to the trinity.

[36] See Clarke, *Works*, IV, xiii.

[37] John Jackson, *A Collection of Queries. Wherein the most material Objections from Scripture, Reason and Antiquity, which have as yet been alleged against Dr. Clarke's Scripture-Doctrine of the Trinity, and the defenses of it, are proposed and answered. With an Appendix: In which are offered to the consideration of the learned, some Queries from Scripture, Reason and Antiquity, concerning the vulgar Scholastic Explication of the Doctrine of the Trinity and Incarnation. By a Clergyman in the Country* (London: 1716).

published with his own responses.[38] In his *Vindication of Christ's Divinity, Being a Defense of Some Queries.* Waterland argued that although Clarke and Jackson talked of Christ's divinity, their talk was in vain because they had effectively stripped his divinity of full participation in the Godhead. For Waterland, Clarke was impaled on the horns of a dilemma; either he had to hold his subordinationism and repudiate scripture, or, if the Son really was God, but only in this inferior sense, then accept that his formula yielded two gods, not one.[39]

It should be noted at this point, that despite the tremendous opposition to Clarke's *Scripture-Doctrine*, there were those who befriended his cause. As early as 1714, sympathetic tracts appeared in support of Clarke's views. The first of these was written under the pseudonym of "A Clergyman in the Country" and was most likely by the Rev. Daniel Whitby.[40] Whitby's tract was written to substantiate Clarke's claim that the majority of the Ante-Nicene Fathers stood against the Athanasian formulation.

Also in 1714 a letter to Dr. Clarke was published entitled, *Reflections upon the Present Controversy concerning the Holy Trinity. Wherein are set forth the Inconveniences of some vulgar Explications.* The letter was signed "Philalethes." In his letter Philalethes suggested this hypothesis;

> Supposing that something of a Christian liberty or latitude were allow'd with respect to this article, namely that no more were exacted from Christians in general, than to believe ... that the second person of the adorable trinity is truly God of God, or the eternal Son of God, by a divine incomprehensible generation, consisting of all *communicable* divine perfections; ... that the Holy Ghost ... being himself also of all *communicable* divine perfections; ... supposing no stricter a profession of faith than this, with relation to the sacred trinity, were required of Christians in general ... I cannot see how the Church of Christ cou'd be any way a sufferer by it.[41]

---

[38] Daniel Waterland, *A Vindication of Christ's Divinity: Being a Defence of Some Queries, Relating to Dr. Clarke's Scheme of the Holy Trinity, in Answer to Clergyman in the Country* in *Works* (Oxford: At the Clarendon Press, MDCCCXXIII), I, 2, Preface, iii–iv. This work will be cited as *Defense* in this paper.

[39] Waterland, *Defense*, Query V, in *Works*, I, 2, 57.

[40] The author of this tract should not be confused with John Jackson, who used the same pseudonym extensively, nor with A.A. Sykes, who also used it. (See Ferguson, *Heretic*, 119).

[41] [Philalethes], *Reflections upon the Present Controversie Concerning the Holy Trinity. Wherein are set forth the Inconveniences of some vulgar Explications* (London: Printed for R. Burleigh, 1714), 9.

The problem with "Philalethes" solution was that it avoided the issue rather than settling it. Whether or not all of the divine nature was communicated to the Son and Spirit was precisely the issue under debate. Not to determine which of the perfections were communicable was to retreat from the question itself. The appeal for latitude was seen by Clarke's opponents as begging the question. Philalethes went on to justify Clarke's natural subordination and to deny the use of "mystery" as a shield from the investigation of the doctrine.[42]

One of the more unusual contributions to the debate was written anonymously by a divine named Thomas Burnet. The work was entitled, *The Scripture-trinity Intelligibly Explained.*[43] Burnet attempted to strike a middle ground between Clarke and Waterland. By outlining and defending seven propositions, Burnet tried to sustain the unity of the Godhead and the unique personhood of its members. For Burnet, the word "God" entailed three notions; self-existence, the proper object of worship, and the creator and governor of the world. He rejected the belief that the nature of God was communicable as suggested by Philalethes. God's nature was intrinsic. He affirmed Waterland's belief that if one held to the orthodox notion of God, then what was said concerning the essence of one person of the trinity must be true of all three.

However, Burnet contradicted himself in Proposition VII by saying that Christ and the Spirit were both creatures of God. Not only this, he insisted that the logos was the pre-existent *human* dimension of Christ. His formula was stated this way;

> And if these two Propositions be allowed, that Father, Son and Spirit are three distinct beings; and that tho' they are all one being in respect of their godhead, yet the Son and Spirit have an inferior created nature, distinct from their Godhead, both of which are abundantly proved; all difficulties in this controversy will soon give way.[44]

---

[42] Ibid., 59. This position is indicative of the age as we have seen in Chapter One. For the best example see Toland's *Christianity Not Mysterious.*

[43] Thomas Burnet, *The Scripture Trinity Intelligibly Explained: or an Essay Toward the Demonstration of a Trinity in Unity, From Reason and Scripture. In a Chain of Consequences from Certain Principles. Which will not only give the Reader a View into the whole Controversy; but may serve as an Answer to Dr. Waterland and Dr. Clarke and all Others who have wrote upon the Subject, whether Arians, Socinians, or whatever other Denomination they may be distinguish'd by. By a Divine of the Church of England.* (London: Printed and sold by J. Roberts in Warwick Lane, 1720).

[44] Ibid., 59.

This was Burnet's only contribution to the controversy, and one that did not help to clarify the matters under discussion.

The most devoted of Clarke's friends was a convert. The Reverend John Jackson, already mentioned, was the Rector of Rossington in Yorkshire, and had originally opposed Clarke's thesis. Jackson described in the first of his *Three Letters to Dr. Clarke, from a Clergyman of the Church of England; Concerning his Scripture-Doctrine of the Trinity. With the Doctor's Replies*, his conversion to Clarke's views. When he heard of Clarke's work and its reputation of being at least dangerous, and perhaps even heretical, although he had yet to read it, Jackson prayed for Clarke "beseeching His goodness and mercy to enlighten your understanding with the light of his gospel, and bring you back to the way of his reveal'd truth, from which I thought you had fallen."[45] Jackson came to believe that Clarke mediated the way between South's Sabellianism, and Sherlock's Tritheism, producing a scheme which was "the most agreeable to scripture and reason, and indeed no other than what I was persuaded Christ and his blessed apostles taught."[46] Jackson became the voice of the muted Clarke in the debate with Waterland.

A chronology of the literature of the Clarke/Jackson-Waterland debate is as follows:

> Jackson, *A Collection of Queries* (1716)
> Waterland, *A Vindication of Christ's Divinity* (1719)
> Clarke (Anon.) *The Modest Plea &C* (1720)[47]
> Waterland, *Lady Moyer Sermons* (1720)[48]
> Jackson, *A Reply to Dr. Waterland's Defense* (1722)[49]

---

[45] John Jackson, *Three Letters to Dr. Clarke from a Clergyman of the Church of England; Concerning his Scripture-Doctrine of the Trinity. With the Doctor's Replies*, (London: Printed for John Barker, 1714), 2. These letters are also available in Clarke, *Works*, Vol. IV, 563ff.

[46] Ibid., 3.

[47] Samuel Clarke, *The Modest Plea &c. continued, or a Brief and Distinct Answer to Dr. Waterland's Queries, Relating to the Doctrine of the Trinity* (1720) in *Works*, IV, 453–475. The reader should note the pagination errors in the text pp. 459–462.

[48] Daniel Waterland, *Eight Sermons, in Defence of the Divinity of our Lord Jesus Christ, Preached at the Lady Moyer's Lecture.* (1720) in *Works*, II. The Lady Moyer's Lectures were founded to provide for "an able minister of God's Word, to preach eight sermons every year on the trinity, and divinity of our ever blessed Saviour." It is likely that Waterland preached these sermons in 1719. William Van Mildert, *A Review of the Author's Life and Writings* in *Works*, I, 1, 65 n.d., 66. They were understood by Waterland himself as a continuation of his *Vindication of Christ's Divinity*, (*Works*, II, Preface, vii.).

[49] John Jackson, *A Reply to Dr. Waterland's Defense of his queries; Wherein is Contained a full State of the whole controversy; and every particular alleged by that learned writer is distinctly considered by a Clergyman in the Country* (London: for J. Knapton, 1722).

Waterland, *A Second Vindication of Christ's Divinity* (1723)[50]
Jackson, *Remarks on Dr. Waterland's Second Defense* (1724)[51]
Clarke (Anon.), *Observations on Dr. Waterland's Second Defense* (1724)[52]
Waterland, *A Farther Vindication of Christ's Divinity* (1724)[53]

After Jackson and Waterland had their first exchange, mentioned above, Clarke published anonymously *The Modest Plea &c. continued, or a Brief and Distinct Answer to Dr. Waterland's Queries, Relating to the Doctrine of the Trinity*. His title related his work to Sykes' earlier book by a similar title, in which two letters written by Clarke had been published.[54] Dr. Clarke had this pamphlet forwarded to Jackson, to help him prepare for his next exchange with Waterland. Clarke was aware that Jackson was already preparing such a work as the closing advertisement of his *Modest plea &c. cont'd* indicated, "There will in some time be published a large and particular answer to Dr. Waterland's defence of his questions."[55]

Waterland published the Lady Moyer Sermons in 1720. In the Preface he responded to the author of the *Modest plea &c. cont'd*. The "Modest Pleader" argued Waterland, must pick his position regarding the nature of the second person of the trinity. If Christ was only a man, the author was a Socinian. If Christ was more than a man, but dependent, the author was an Arian. If Christ was necessarily existing and a full member of the Godhead, then the author held the catholic doctrine.[56]

Jackson's response to Waterland's *Defence* appeared in 1722 as *A*

---

[50] Daniel Waterland, *A Second Vindication of Christ's Divinity: Or, a Second Defence of Some Queries relating to Dr. Clarke's Scheme of the Holy Trinity, In Answer to the Country Clergyman's Reply*. In *Works*, III.

[51] John Jackson, *Remarks on Dr. Waterland's Second Defence of Some Queries. Being a brief consideration of his notion of the Trinity, as stated by himself in Three Questions. With an Appendix, shewing the true sense of Creation, Eternity and Consubstantiality. In a Letter to the Doctor. By Philalethes Cantabrigiensis* (London: 1723).

[52] Samuel Clarke, *Observations on Dr. Waterland's Second Defense of his Queries* (1724) in *Works*, IV, 483–530.

[53] Daniel Waterland, *A Farther Vindication of Christ's Divinity* (1724) in *Works*, IV.

[54] A.A. Sykes, *A Modest Plea for the Baptismal and Scripture-Notion of the Trinity. Wherein the Schemes of the Reverend Dr. Bennet and Dr. Clarke are compared. To which are added Two Letters, One written to the late Reverend Mr. R.M. concerning his Plain Scripture-Argument, etc. The Other to the Author of a Book, intituled, The True Scripture-Doctrine of the Most Holy and undivided Trinity continued and vindicated: Recommended first by Robert Nelson Esq; and since by the Reverend Dr. Waterland. Wherein the Reader will find obviated the Principal Arguments urged by the Rev. Waterland, in his Defence of Some Queries. By a Clergyman in the Country* (London: 1719).

[55] Ferguson, *Heretic*, 133. See also the preface to the Lady Moyer lectures in Waterland, *Works*, II, xi.

[56] Waterland, Preface to the *Lady Moyer Lectures* in *Works*, II, xii.

Reply to Dr. Waterland's Defence of his Queries. The response was a lengthy
534 pages, and was virtually ghost written by Clarke.[57] The thrust of
Jackson's *Reply* was to return Waterland to the central issue of the
debate: the supremacy of the Father, which must be decided by
scripture alone. He reasserted that the Son was not only functionally
subordinate but necessarily so, otherwise he could not be referred to
as "begotten." The Father alone was the being to whom worship is
properly directed, albeit through the Son. Thus the unity of God
was preserved and exalted.

For his part, Waterland was prepared. Within two months, in 1723,
he produced his own mammoth work, *A Second Vindication of Christ's
Divinity, or a Second Defence of some Queries.*[58] Here Waterland challenged
several of Jackson's assertions in the *Reply*. All of the divine titles and
attributes belonged equally to the Son, including supremacy and
independence.[59] For Waterland there were three kinds of supremacy:
supremacy of nature, supremacy of order, and supremacy of office.
The first kind the Son shared with the Father, the second was the
Father's alone as he had his perfections "from none," the third belonged to the Father by "mutual agreement and voluntary economy."[60]
Waterland believed that Jackson and Clarke had failed to differen-
tiate among these types of supremacy and consequently had drawn
false conclusions. Waterland also challenged Jackson's reading of the
Nicene Council which, while affirming the procession of the Son from
the Father, insured that he was understood to be of the same essence.
Waterland held that Jackson's scheme made the Son a creature, which
was Arianism.[61]

Waterland's challenges did not go unmet. In 1723 Jackson responded in a pamphlet entitled, *Remarks on Dr. Waterland's Second Defense.*
This pamphlet was a response to Waterland's invitation to debate
the issue in the light of reason and natural philosophy.

---

[57] In a letter regarding the book Clarke wrote to Jackson, "I believe you need do
little more than transcribe all the places I have marked, with the remarks I have
made upon them: and then arrange them in some proper method, under distinct
heads, such as they will naturally fall under." (Ferguson, *Heretic*, 135, quoting from
the *Memoirs of the Life of the Rev. John Jackson* [1764], 80–81). For a fuller assessment
see Van Mildert's *Review* in Waterland, *Works*, I,1, 88–89, n. c.

[58] This work will be referred to as the *Second Defense*, in keeping with its attribu-
tion in the scholarship.

[59] Waterland, *Second Defense* in *Works*, III, 23, 51.

[60] Ibid., 23.

[61] Ibid., 26.

The year 1724 saw the publication of several more pamphlets. Clarke issued another anonymous work as a rejoinder to Waterland's *Second Defense*. The title was *Observations on Dr. Waterland's Second Defense of His Queries*, and here Clarke presented fourteen observations concerning Waterland's position. Clarke again asserted that Waterland's logic implied two Gods, and that it was Waterland who had misunderstood Nicaea.[62] He accused Waterland of denying a real generation of the Son,[63] and repeated his charge that to believe in three persons (intelligent agents) existing in one substance was a logical inconsistency.[64]

In the same year Waterland responded to Clarke's *Observations* with his *A Farther Vindication of Christ's Divinity. In Answer to a pamphlet entitled Observations on Dr. Waterland's Second Defense*. Waterland argued that it was the Arians (Jackson and Clarke) who had developed a plurality of gods. Their doctrine required a greater God (the Father) and lesser gods (the Son and Spirit) who were creatures of the greater God.[65] Here Waterland's response grew more caustic and his arguments took on an *ad hominem* tone. For example, he entitled Chapter III of his book, "Concerning the Author's Flouts, Abuses, declamatory Exclamations, Repartees &c. in lieu of Answers." The last two chapters were spent arguing the Patristic sources for his doctrine. Finally Waterland concluded that "the argument is in a manner brought to an end"[66] and retired from the controversy. Clarke did not respond to Waterland's *Farther Vindication* but Jackson did in his *Farther Remarks on Dr. Waterland's Farther Vindication of Christ's Divinity*. This work received no response.

One of the final contributors to the debate was Edward Hawarden, S.J., who wrote *An Answer to Dr. Clarke and Mr. Whiston, Concerning the Divinity of the Son and of the Holy Spirit. With a Summary Account of the Chief Writers of The Three First Ages*.[67] According to Van Mildert's preface to Waterland's *Works*, Hawarden was brought into the controversy as a result of a conference with Clarke in the presence of Queen

---

[62] Clarke, *Observations* in *Works*, 495.
[63] Ibid., Observation VI, 502ff.
[64] Ibid., Observation IX, 515.
[65] Waterland, *Farther Vindication*, in *Works*, IV, 5.
[66] Ibid., 112.
[67] Edward Hawarden, *An Answer to Dr. Clarke, and Mr. Whiston, Concerning the Divinity of the Son and of the Holy Spirit. With a Summary Account of the Chief Writers of the Three First Ages. By H.E.* (London: 1729).

Caroline. Hawarden listened to Clarke's exposition of his system and then asked him to answer "yes" or "no" to a single question: "Can the Father annihilate the Son and Holy Ghost?" Clarke responded that it was a question he had never considered.[68] Hawarden argued that Clarke's approach was anachronistic in seeking support in Ante-Nicene Fathers for a position which could not have occur to them. Prior to Arius' heresy, the language of the Fathers was naturally less guarded. This was what Edwards had earlier called the "unsafe language of some of the Fathers."[69] This language was not to be taken as an approbation of Clarke's views. On the contrary, Hawarden argued, it was only following the Council that one could legitimately seek the mind of the Church, after its determination on the Son's relationship to the Father had been made explicit. Hawarden also reflected the Catholic position respecting the authority of Church Councils in the determination of right doctrine, a position which both Clarke and Whiston had called into question. For Hawarden, even Dr. Waterland was found wanting on this point.

Samuel Clarke died in 1729, the same year Hawarden wrote, abruptly closing this chapter in the debate concerning the doctrine of God. Within this extensive field of literature generated by Clarke's *Scripture-Doctrine*, there emerged in the debate a certain theological center of gravity. This center of gravity is discovered in the core issues debated by Clarke and Waterland, to which we now turn.

---

[68] Charles Butler, *Historical Account of Confessions of Faith*, Chap. X, sect. 2 in Van Mildert's Preface to Waterland's *Works*, I, 1, 102–03, n. f.

[69] John Edwards, *A Supplement to the Animadversions on Dr. Clark's Scripture-Doctrine of the Trinity*, 3–4.

CHAPTER SIX

CLARKE AND WATERLAND

There is good reason to examine carefully the debate between Clarke and Waterland as the centerpiece of the trinitarian controversy. The crucial theological issues of the controversy were the focus of their debate. The biographers of both men tell us that from the time Waterland entered the debate he became the acknowledged leader of those opposing Clarke, and that the controversy took on a new character; Ferguson going so far as to call it "a dual between the two."[1]

Waterland's biographer, Van Mildert, understood Waterland's work as "a continuation of those of Bishop Bull."[2] In Chapter Three we noted Bull's contribution toward championing the position that the Ante-Nicene Fathers uniformly held what became the Nicene formulation. This was clearly Waterland's conviction as well, and anyone who doubted it he considered suspect.

Waterland argued that in trinitarian formulation there were only three possibilities: Catholic [Athanasian], Sabellian, and Arian.[3] He equated Socinianism with Sabellianism (as did Clarke) and believed that only the first of these three schemes was consistent with Scripture.[4] The question between them was precisely what the Catholic doctrine taught. In Waterland's mind there could be no middle ground between the Son's being God in the fullest sense, and his being a creature.

> There is certainly no medium betwixt orthodoxy and Arianism, (for Semi-Arianism, if so understood, is perfect nonsense and contradiction,) there being no medium between God and creature, between unmade and made . . . every man that disowns the consubstantiality, rightly understood, is as much an Arian as Eunomius or Aetius, or any of the ancient Arians were; or even as Arius himself.[5]

---

[1] Ferguson, *Heretic*, 129 cf. Van Mildert's *Review* in Waterland's *Works*, I, 1, 61.
[2] Van Mildert, *Review* in *Works*, I, 1, 44.
[3] Waterland, *Defence*, I, 2, 162.
[4] Waterland, "Preface to the Lady Moyer Lectures" in *Works*, II, viii. For Clarke's equation of Sabellianism and Socinianism see *SD*, 148.
[5] Waterland, *Defense*, I, 2, 159.

We find in Waterland no refinement of distinction between the Semi-Arian (better called Homoiousian) view and the Arian.[6] Although later scholarship, as we have seen in Chapter Three, has disagreed with Waterland, his view represented the reductionist and dogmatic reading of the Patristic sources by the disciples of Bull. Persons like Petavius in Patristics, Simon in biblical criticism, and others represented the emerging historical consciousness which was growing in its challenge to dogmatic theology. Clarke was representative of this emerging consciousness, while Bull and Waterland represent the older perspective.

Regarding method, Waterland asserted that what was held as a probability on the basis of scripture could attain the certainty of demonstration if it could be shown to have been the teaching of the primitive church.[7] On the other hand, Clarke accused Waterland of never laying down a scripture position at all, but "always some propositions of his own instead of it, as being the 'doctrine of the trinity' to be interpreted and explained."[8]

All throughout the debate, Clarke and Waterland used (and often denied using) metaphysical terms and presuppositions. In his *Second Defense* Waterland complained,

> You say farther that by the divinity of Christ, I mean my own particular metaphysical explication of it. A suggestion as false as it is mean. For neither is my sense any particular sense, but the common sense of all men, learned or unlearned, that know the difference between God and creature: . . . However, supposing my account of the Son's divinity to be metaphysical, is not your account of the Father's divinity metaphysical as the other? And if you, through your false metaphysics, exclude the Son from the one Godhead, I shall not be ashamed of making use of true metaphysics to correct your errors and to establish the son's divinity, upon the same foot whereon Scripture has fixed it.[9]

For his part, Waterland complained specifically of Clarke's use of metaphysical reasoning. Waterland asserted that Clarke had said that generation implied division, that necessary agents were no agents, that nothing individual could be communicated, and that three intelligent agents could not be one being, etc.[10] In fact, the metaphysical

---

[6] Ibid., 146.
[7] Waterland, "Preface to the Lady Moyer Lectures" in *Works*, II, viii.
[8] Clarke, *Observations* in *Works*, IV, 524.
[9] Waterland, *Second Defense* in *Works*, III, 4.
[10] Ibid., 4–5.

and highly philosophical structures of their thought, not to mention those of the Patristic sources upon which they drew, were unavoidable in any attempt to formulate a doctrine of the trinity.

If the Clarke-Waterland debate was permeated by accusations and questions regarding the role of metaphysics, it was also saturated with claims as to which of them could lay claim to the thesaurus of the Patristic sources. We have already seen in Chapter Three Clarke's extensive use of Patristic materials. Waterland's usage was even more extensive. In most of his publications during the debate with Clarke, his documentation from Patristic sources was copious.[11] Waterland believed that Clarke had drawn conclusions from the premises of the Ante-Nicene Fathers which they themselves would have denied, since they held to the eternity and consubstantiality of the Son.[12] His statement was based on the assumption that since the Fathers at Nicaea were anti-Arian, they necessarily disagreed with the position articulated by Clarke, which Waterland insisted was Arianism.

According to Waterland, Clarke laid claim to the Fathers for three reasons: they spoke of a certain subordinationism, they spoke of a temporal generation by the will of the Father, and when they spoke of God absolutely, they ordinarily meant the Father, distinguishing his person by some eminent titles and appellations.[13] Waterland believed all of these could be accounted for by the orthodox understanding. Moreover, he argued, Clarke's use of the Patristic sources was misleading. Clarke made certain "concessions" in the Fathers' theology appear to be their general opinion[14] and then failed to relate these concessions to his own conclusions, instead repeating them over and over until they eventually become conclusive in and of themselves, without ever having been properly demonstrated.[15]

Waterland believed that Clarke (and Jackson) had little to boast of in the Ante-Nicene Fathers, and drew up a list of eleven positions which he believed they held which were untenable according to the teaching of the Fathers.

1. That the Son is not consubstantial with the Father.
2. That the Son is not coeternal with the Father.

---

[11] For example see *Defense*, Queries XXV, XXVI, XXVII, and XXVIII; *Second Defense*, et passim, *Farther Vindication*, et passim, but especially chapters IV and V.
[12] Waterland, *Defense*, I, 2, 282–84.
[13] Ibid., 280.
[14] Ibid., 314–15.
[15] Ibid., 317.

3. That "God" is a relative word, θεός and θεότης signifying not substance, but dominion and authority.
4. That God the Father only was God of Abraham, Isaac and Jacob.
5. That the titles of one, only, etc. are exclusive of the Son.
6. That the Son had not distinct worship paid to him till after his resurrection.
7. That the Father and Son (or any two persons) ought not to be called one God.
8. That the title of "God" in Scripture, in an absolute construction, always signifies the Father.
9. That an inferior God may be admitted besides the Supreme, and worship paid to both.
10. That the Son is not efficient cause [sic] of the universe, and of all created beings.
11. That the Son himself is made, not created.[16]

Waterland argued that the first two points were the most important when he wrote, "These two main points being determined against you, the rest are of less moment."[17] In fact the others tended to flow by way of logical consequence in his reasoning. It was the first two points to which he returned again and again in his challenge to Clarke, and it is therefore these points upon which this chapter will focus. The first issue was whether the Father and the Son were consubstantial, and what that term meant. The second issue, while mentioned here as coeternity, was really at a deeper level the issue of aseity. Waterland believed that Clarke had departed from orthodoxy on these two crucial issues in formulating his doctrine of God. Clarke insisted that he had not, that his position in fact represented the true understanding of the mind of the Fathers, and that his formulation made better sense of scripture, the Fathers, and reason as a whole.

The Consubstantiality of the Father and the Son

Waterland, in Query XIV of his *Defense* stated that Clarke denied the consubstantiality of the Son.[18] Two issues were involved here.

---

[16] Waterland, *Defense*, I, 2, 279–80.
[17] Ibid., 279.
[18] Waterland, *Defense*, in *Works*, I, 2, 151.

The first was the definition of "consubstantial"; the second was the relation between the terms "person" and "being" and their relationship to substance. Clarke, in his *Modest Plea* challenged Waterland to define his terms. Clarke argued that Waterland knew the word "consubstantial" had several meanings. It could mean *specific* consubstantiality, which Waterland denied because that would introduce two self-existent substances, or it could mean *individual* (το ταυτούσιαν) which Clarke denied, because it was Sabellianism. Finally it could mean "being derived in some ineffable manner from the substance (ἐκ τῆς οὐσίας) of the Father."[19] This was the position which Clarke held. Therefore, Clarke responded, Waterland's accusation that he denied the consubstantiality of the Father and Son was a "palpable and direct calumny."[20]

Waterland had stated in his *Defense* in response to Jackson, that the word ὁμοόυσιος did imply specific consubstantiality, but more than that. Here he drew upon the general language of the Nicene Creed. In Waterland's reading of the Fathers, the term ὁμοόυσιος expressed an "equality of nature" between the Father and Son.[21]

> ὁμοόυσιος the Son must be, or he could not be God at all, in the strict sense; and yet if he was barely ὁμοόυσιος, like as one human person is to another, the two would be *two Gods*. And therefore the Nicene Fathers, not content to say only that the Son is ὁμοόυσιος, insert "God of God, Light of Light, begotten, &c." and, "of the substance of the Father;" and this they are known to have declared over and over, to be "without division:" all which taken together express a great deal more than ὁμοόυσιος would do alone.[22]

Here it is clear that Waterland had moved beyond the words of the creed to interpretation. Jackson and Clarke reminded Waterland that

---

[19] Clarke, *Modest Plea* in *Works*, IV, 462–463 (N.B. pagination error on 462).

[20] Ibid., 463. The Reformed scholastics had made the distinction between an ingenerate essence in all three persons, and a generation of persons, yielding the Son and Spirit. This was the point of debate between the Leiden Reformed Professors and Arminius in 1606. The Reformed held that the Son possessed aseity in terms of his essence, and begottenness according to his person. Arminius rejected their distinction, and believed the Son possessed aseity neither according to his divinity nor his filiation. See Richard Muller, "The Christological Problem in the Thought of Jacobus Arminius" *Nederlans Archief voor Kerkgeschiedenis* 68 (1988): 152–53. Given the connection between the Arminians and the Platonists outlined in Colie's *Light and Enlightenment*, it is possible that this Arminian perspective came into English theology through the Platonists and their Latitudinarian descendants.

[21] Waterland, *Defense*, in *Works*, I, 2, 326–27.

[22] Ibid.

the words of the Creed were not that the Son was "of the substance of the Father" i.e. the same identical substance, but "from the substance of the Father" (ἐκ τῆς οὐσιάς). In the Preface to his *Second Defense* Waterland denied ever having said that he understood consubstantiality as "same identical substance." But immediately afterwards he wrote,

> But the Council supposes the Son to be both *from* the substance of the Father, and *of* the substance of the Father, and but one substance in both, because of the inseparable union and connection of both. The doctrine is plainly this, God of God, and both one God; light of light, and both one light; substance of substance, and both one substance.[23]

The second issue involved was the relationship between the terms "person" and "being" and their relation to "substance." Waterland defined God as,

> one necessarily existing, all perfect, all sufficient substance, or Being: which substance, &c. consists (according to scripture account) of three persons, Father, Son, and Holy Ghost, one Jehovah. This is one God.[24]

In Waterland's understanding, it was conceivable that there could exist one Being which consisted of three persons. Waterland accused Clarke of holding that person and being were the same, thereby obliterating the intra-trinitarian distinctions.[25] Clarke responded that he had not insisted that being and person were the same, but that intelligent being (or intelligent agent) and person are the same.[26] Here it becomes clear that the problem in Clarke's mind was not so much the use of the terms, as what was implied by Waterland's construction.

> If two or more intelligent agents can be the same being, or subsist in the same individual substance, provided the Agents be not all of them self-existent as well as the substance; (which is manifest polytheism;) this will no way affect the truth of any of Dr. Clarke's propositions.[27]

---

[23] Waterland, *Second Defense*, in *Works*, III, Preface, 11–12. For a contemporary appraisal of Nicaea which resonates Clarke's position, see Kelly, 234–37, who writes that although later theology understood that the *homoousios* must mean that the persons were one identical substance because God is immaterial and indivisible, that this interpretation was not that of the Nicene Fathers, who understood the term in the generic sense.

[24] Waterland, *Farther Vindication*, in *Works*, IV, 29.

[25] Waterland, *Defense*, in *Works*, I, 2, 230.

[26] Clarke, *Modest Plea*, in *Works*, IV, 468.

[27] Clarke, *Modest Plea*, in *Works*, IV, 468.

The reason why Clarke could not accept Waterland's construction was that it demanded aseity among the intelligent agents, which Clarke believed was contrary to the scripture doctrine.

For Waterland, the notion of "being" signified either what simply existed, or what existed separately. In the later sense he relied on the scholastic vocabulary of *tres res, tres entes*. In the former sense of "being" however, they could all be one.[28] The catholic doctrine relied upon the twin foundations of "homogenous substance" which made each ὑπόστασις a *res divina* and "inseparability" which made all to be *una substantia, una summa res* "one undivided, or individual, or numerical substance; one God."[29]

Waterland commenced his definition of God (above), in the typically Western manner of exploring the idea of substance. Clarke, on the other hand, began with the idea of person. This is a further evidence of the Eastern influence upon Clarke's thought. For Clarke,

> The word "God" being expressive, not of bare substance or being, but of a living agent; does therefore necessarily, in the nature of language, and in fact through the whole scripture, always "signify one person." Yet neither does it "irresistibly" or at all follow, "that the Father, and none else, is the one person" always signified by that word; (because in some few places, the same word signifies also the one person of the Son.) Nor yet does it follow, that "the three persons are three Gods;" because there is no text of scripture, wherein the word, "God," denotes the person of the Holy Ghost. Nor does the Son's being stiled by St. John and St. Paul the "God" (and the Lord) *by* whom are all things; in any wise exclude the Father from being still alone the one God, (or first cause,) *of* whom are all things.[30]

Clarke was concerned to work from the language of scripture itself in which he found that the term "God" was always used of a person, (never referring to substance, essence, or being) and that both the Father and Son were so named. For him the problem was not "how three persons can be one God" (Waterland), but rather how the infallible teaching of scripture that there is only one God can be maintained in the face of scripture's ascription of the term "God" to the Son.[31]

The crucial verse for Clarke was "To us there is but one God, the

---

[28] Waterland, *Defense*, in *Works*, I, 2, 119.
[29] Ibid., 277.
[30] Clarke, *Modest Plea*, in *Works*, IV, 469.
[31] Ibid.

Father, of whom are all things; and one Lord, Jesus Christ, by whom are all things (1 Cor. 8:6).[32] Clarke understood this verse in such a way as to make explicit the distinction between Father and Son by making the Father the efficient cause ("*of* whom are all things"), while the Son was the instrumental cause ("*by* whom are all things"). This protected the unity of the Godhead by making the Father the source of the other persons, while allowing for the biblical ascription of "God" to the Son. Clarke rejected Waterland's formulation of "one substance or being in three persons" because it meant that two (or more) supreme intelligent agents, and therefore real persons, who were equally supreme in every respect, even if they were undivided in metaphysical substance, must necessarily still be two Gods.[33]

Waterland took issue with Clarke's view that the word "God" denoted person and not substance.

> Jehovah, you observe, does not signify *substance*, but the "person whose the substance is." I beseech you, what is Person but substance? Is it intelligent, agent nothing? "Person" as I take it, is intelligent, acting *substance*; (though that is not a full definition;) and so that sense of what you have said amounts to this; that Jehovah does not signify substance, but the intelligent acting substance, whose that substance is . . . The truth may be said at once, in a very few words, that the name Jehovah denotes the necessary existence of as many Persons as it is applied to; and being applied to Christ, it is the proof that he is necessarily existing as well as the Father, and one Jehovah with him, since Jehovah is one.[34]

Clarke responded to Waterland's challenge by replying that the term "person" was not merely the name of an abstract intelligence, but necessarily supposed substance, as Waterland suggests. But it was the life and intelligence of that substance which made it a person. Consequently, the word "God" pointed to a very specific substance (a person) who consisted in supreme and independent dominion. It was this supremacy and dominion which made this particular substance (person) to be God, and not some other substance. Therefore, any other person who shared these qualities, even if they inhered in the same substance, if they were really a person, would be a second God.[35]

---

[32] Ibid.
[33] Clarke, *Modest Plea* in *Works*, IV, 457; cf., *Observations* in *Works*, IV, 499–500 for an almost identical assessment.
[34] Waterland, *Second Defense* in *Works*, III, 167.
[35] Clarke, *Observations* in *Works*, IV, 500.

In fact, there does seem to be confusion in Waterland's use of the term "person." At one point in his *Second Defense* he wrote to Clarke and Jackson, "You tell me, I acknowledge *person* and *intelligent agent* to be the same. I never acknowledged any such thing; but always denied their being reciprocal."[36] Yet on the next page in explaining his usage of the term "person" he writes,

> We must therefore be more particular; and at length we may bring it to this: a single person is an intelligent agent, having the distinctive characters of I, Thou, he; and not divided nor distinguished into more intelligent agents capable of the same characters.[37]

Two pages later he wrote, "You will also perceive that intelligent acting substance (that is, intelligent agent as you call it) is not equivalent to person, neither are the phrases reciprocal."[38]

Clarke's argument with Waterland was that the latter defined "person" as having distinctive characteristics, being indivisible into other persons with the same characteristics. If the Father was such a person, then how was it that the Son shared all his characteristics completely, leaving nothing unique to him? If this was the case, then, Clarke argued, the Father and the Son must be the same person, which was heresy. Either the uniqueness of the persons of the Father and of the Son must be maintained, which was Clarke's position, or the Son was not really a person in the true sense, and Waterland had fallen into Sabellianism.

Part of the difficulty with Waterland's position was that the meaning of the term "person" underwent a metamorphosis when it shifted in application from human beings to being applied to God. For Waterland, in common understanding, all persons were divided and separate from each other in nature, substance and existence. They did not mutually include or imply each other. However, when the term was applied to God, the persons were undivided and had no separate existence, instead existing as *supposita* (independent subsistences) of one substance.[39] This raised the question of consistency in Waterland, who changed the definition of terms to mean something quite

---

[36] Waterland, *Second Defense*, in *Works*, III, 338.
[37] Ibid., 339.
[38] Ibid., 341.
[39] Ibid., 339–40. Waterland's attempt here echoes the medieval attempt (Thomas and Bonaventure) to adjust Boethius' definition in a trinitarian direction. This attempt was picked up in the seventeenth century by the Protestant Edward Leigh, *A Treatise of Divinity*, II (London: 1646), xvi (p. 150).

different in applying them to the Godhead. This inconsistency was apparent when Waterland wrote,

> I suppose not any of the divine persons a person in a sense different from the common meaning of the word person: they are persons in the same common sense of person; but persons of a different kind, and differently circumstantiated from what human, or angelical, or any other kinds of persons are.[40]

Clarke summarized his objections to Waterland's whole understanding of the relation of the terms "person" "substance" and "being" when he wrote,

> When therefore Dr. Waterland says, that many supreme Gods in one undivided substance, "are not many Gods, for that very reason, because their substance is undivided;" he might exactly with the same sense and truth have affirmed that many supreme persons in one undivided substance, are not many persons, for that very reason, because their substance is undivided. I say, these two assertions are exactly the same, both in sense and truth; because the word, "person", does just as much and as necessarily denote substance, as the word "God" does. And when the Doctor affirms that the one supreme God is not one (supreme God) in person, but in substance; what is this, but affirming that the one supreme God is two (supreme Gods) in person, though but one (supreme God) in substance?[41]

The Aseity of the Son

The second major point of contention in the debate between Clarke and Waterland was the issue of aseity. Their views can be discussed under three aspects: The first is whether the Son was self-existent or necessarily existent, and the applicability of the Arian formulae to these positions. The second is whether the Son was generated by the will or from the nature of the Father. The third is whether the Son's subordination (or, conversely, the Father's priority) were determined by nature or office.

Clarke had maintained in Propositions V, XII, XIV, XIX, and XXIII of his *Scripture-Doctrine* that the Son and Holy Spirit were not self-existent. Likewise, Waterland did not hold that the Son was self-

---

[40] Waterland, *Second Defense* in *Works*, III, 341. On the same point see *Farther Vindication* in *Works*, IV, 72–73.

[41] Clarke, *Observations* in *Works*, IV, 500.

existent, but he did hold him to be *necessarily* existent. The distinction was a crucial one for him, and one which he believed was grounded in both classical and early Christian teaching.

> It is very manifest that the ideas of necessary existence and self-existence (however they may be imagined with or without reason to imply each other) are not the same ideas. Aristotle and the later Platonists [Cudworth's *Intellectual System* pp. 250ff. is cited here] supposed the world and all the inferior Gods (as Plato and the Pythagoreans, some supramundane deities) to proceed by way of emanation without any temporary production, from a superior cause: that is, they believed them to be necessary, but not self-existent. Something like this has been constantly believed by the Christian Church in respect of the λόγος.[42]

Waterland argued that at the time of Ignatius the word ἀγέννητος was not yet in use, and that to express their sense of God's being unmade, underived, or eternal, the early Christians used ἀγένητος.[43] Subsequently they equated this term with necessary existence.[44] Thus Waterland held that when the early Fathers said that the Son was "not made," this was tantamount to their asserting his necessary existence.[45] Waterland then cited a variety of sources in support of his notion of the Son's necessary existence.[46] From this Waterland derived his contention that there could be no middle state between necessary existence and being a creature.[47] When the Son is said to be "begotten, not made" this implied necessary existence. Waterland, having read the *Modest Plea &c. Continued*, was unsure at first whether Clarke had in fact denied necessary existence to the Son.[48] After reading Jackson's *A Reply to Dr. Waterland's Defense*, (which, as we have seen was largely a collaborative effort with Clarke) Waterland felt assured that Clarke has denied necessary existence.

---

[42] Waterland, *Defense*, Vol. I, 2, 86.
[43] Waterland, *Second Defense* in *Works*, III, 240. Brown has recently argued that the issue of whether the Word was begotten or created may be something of a false problem. It results from the misapplication of reading the generation language of Sonship back into the language of the pre-existence of the Word. Colin Brown, "Trinity and Incarnation: In Search of Contemporary Orthodoxy," *Ex Auditu* 7 (1991): 87–90. For the Patristic contribution to the dilemma see Maurice Wiles, "Eternal Generation," in *Working Papers in Doctrine* (London: S.C.M. Press, 1976), 18–27.
[44] Ibid., 241.
[45] Ibid., 239.
[46] Ignatius (239), Justin (246), Athenagoras (250), Clement of Alexandria (254) and Origen (257).
[47] Ibid., 330–31.
[48] Ibid., 334–35.

While Clarke never clearly denied necessary existence, as such, to the Son, it seems clear that he equated it with self-existence, and attributed this to the Father alone. Responding to Waterland he wrote,

> Acknowledge Jesus Christ to be the same yesterday and to day and for ever, before all ages, and to all ages, permanently and immutably: Still, if he is not so by a *necessity* altogether independent of the Father himself, that is, if he is not really as self-existent as the Father; his existence is (in Dr. Waterland's account) as mutable and precarious, as that of the meanest being in the universe.[49]

It is clear from this passage that Clarke saw no real distinction between self-existence and necessary existence. Perhaps if he had, he may have been able to respond more effectively to the question of Hawarden as to whether the Father could annihilate the Son.

For Waterland, the great consequence of Clarke's denying necessary existence to the Son (which in Clarke's understanding was aseity) was that this reduced the status of the Son to a creature. Hence, although Clarke had openly repudiated the two tenets of Arianism; that the Son was "created out of nothing" and "that there was a time when he was not,"[50] for Waterland, these were the logical consequences of Clarke's doctrine, which restricted aseity to the Father alone. For this reason Waterland throughout his work constantly referred to Clarke's views as Arian, thereby popularizing the idea that Clarke himself was an Arian, a view which, as we have seen, made its way into the mainstream of the history of the doctrine.[51]

Whereas Waterland argued that there was no *via media* between the Son's necessary existence and his being a creature, Clarke believed there was. The key term was the creedal formulation of "begotten not made." We have already seen Waterland's interpretation that "not made" meant that the Son was necessarily existent. For Clarke, the emphasis was on his begottenness. Where Waterland believed the Son must either exist necessarily or be a creature, that is, "created out of nothing," Clarke asserted that there was a third option,

---

[49] Clarke, *Observations* in *Works*, IV, 509.

[50] Propositions XIV and XVI in the *SD*.

[51] An early example is found in Edward Calamy, *Sermons concerning the Doctrine of the Trinity, preached at Salter's Hall* (1722) in which Clarke's opinions are said to have been the foundation of many schisms which occured among the dissenters. Clarke is also said to be indirectly responsible for the growth of Arian, Unitarian and Socinian congregations. Waterland's role, and views, in the debate were widely publicized through this tract. For other tracts see Van Mildert's *Review* in Waterland's *Works*, I, 1, 130ff., n. 1.

which was the correct one. The Son neither possessed self-existence, nor was he a creature: created out of nothing, but he was "true God of true God." Waterland had argued that all beings other than God were creatures. Clarke responded,

> But if the word "creature", be understood to mean that only which is made out of nothing; then the answer [to Query X] depends on another Query, viz: whether any thing or person can be derived (ἐκ τῆς οὐσίας τῶ πατρὸς) from the self-existent substance. If it can; as Dr. Waterland makes no doubt but it can, and who dares affirm it cannot? (for, to be from nothing, and from the self-existent substance, are both of them equally beyond our conception, and neither of them expressly mentioned in scripture;) then, 'tis evident, a person who is not a creature, may yet not be the one supreme being.[52]

The Son therefore was not a creature, but was "from the substance of the Father," an altogether different category of existence.

If the Son were "from the Father," then the next question pertained to the temporality of his generation. Waterland held that another consequence of Clarke's denial of the necessary existence of the Son was that it meant that he must embrace the second of the Arian formulae, "there was a time when he was not." This argument was predicated on Waterland's previous assertion that, according to Clarke's scheme, the Son was a creature. Since he did not exist necessarily, and was therefore a creature, then it must be true that there was a time when he did not exist.[53] Here Waterland coordinated necessary existence with eternal existence, and the question arose as to the precise temporality of the Son's generation.

Both authors admitted that the church Fathers understood the generation of the Son in a variety of ways. Clarke wrote that some understood the Son as originally the λόγος ἐνδιάθετος which made him nothing more than an attribute, eternally existing only mentally or ideally in the Father. Others believed him really to have existed in the Father from eternity, but not to have been emitted as a person, or distinct agent until the creation of the material world. Others believed that he was part of the substance of the Father as a branch from a tree. Some believed that he was co-immense with the Father's substance.[54]

---

[52] Clarke, *Modest Plea* in *Works*, IV, 460.
[53] Waterland, *Defense* in *Works*, I, 2, 152.
[54] Clarke, *Modest Plea* in *Works*, IV, 472.

Waterland postulated three generations of the Son when he wrote, "Every body that has seen my books knows that I assert, maintain and inculcate three generations; the first eternal, the other two temporal."[55] By this Waterland meant that the Son was generated eternally with the Father, generated forth from the Father to be his agent in creation, and finally generated again as a human being.[56] Clarke had already taken Waterland to task on this point in his *Observations*.

> But then because these writers [Ante-Nicene] supposed the Son of God not to be but generated immediately from the Father himself; (in consequence whereof, their philosophy taught them that he was in the Father ἀγεένητος *before* he was generated from him;) hence the Doctor infers, that this his being in the Father before he was generated from him, is a *prior* generation, and the most proper filiation or generation. And yet no one writer either before or at the time of the Council of Nice, ever once mentions two generations of the Son before the beginning of the world, ever once mentions any prior generation.[57]

Waterland affirmed an eternal generation of the Son, which he referred to as "coexistence" with the Father.[58] For him, this was the only way it could be called "eternal." He accused Clarke of opposing derivation to coexistence,

> which showed what kind of derivation he intended; a derivation from a state of non-existence, a derivation commencing *after* the existence of the Father, and because later than the Father's existence infinitely later, as it must be if at all later. In short then, it is a derivation of a creature from his Creator: this is the eternal generation he is contending for, in opposition to mine; while he is endeavouring to show that mine is not generation; as his, most certainly, is not eternal, nor generation, but creation.[59]

Clarke had indeed said that Waterland's view of generation was not real. He referred to it as "no generation at all"[60] and wrote that it amounted to the Son's merely being sent out economically to make and govern the creation. In this sense it differed not at all from every action of the Son as sent out by the Father. He went on to say that Waterland's scheme described no true generation of the Son

---

[55] Waterland, *Farther Vindication*, 23. See Brown, "Trinity and Incarnation," 89.
[56] See Clarke, *Observations* in *Works*, IV, 507, citing Waterland's *Second Defense*.
[57] Clarke, *Observations* in *Works*, IV, 503.
[58] Waterland, *Farther Vindication* in *Works*, IV, 28.
[59] Ibid., 28–29.
[60] Clarke, *Observations* in *Works*, IV, 506.

because the Son could (if the Father were so pleased) have generated the Father. For Clarke, the Son was no more generated after Waterland's kind of generation than before.[61] He quoted Waterland saying that all any writer meant by the eternal filiation of the Son was the eternal *existence* of the Son. For Clarke, this made a mockery of the language of filiation, and allowed for the existence of a Son who was no Son, because he was never genuinely generated. The upshot of all this was that for Clarke, Waterland's view of generation implied "no real derivation either of being, power, authority, or any other perfection; made the Father to be indeed, in any real sense, neither head, nor fountain, nor Father."[62]

For his part, Waterland accused Clarke of being insincere in asserting the eternity of the Son.[63] He mentioned Clarke's letter of July 2, 1714 which was laid before the Bishops in Convocation, in which Clarke professed the Son to be "eternally begotten by the eternal will and power of the Father."[64] Waterland stated that Clarke subsequently denied this and asserted that "he was begotten eternally, that is, without any limitation of time . . . in the incomprehensible duration of the Father's eternity"[65] Waterland added the comment that "this is too plain to need any comment." Rather than a denial of the Son's eternity, however, this seems to be a simple affirmation of it, in keeping with Clarke's position as stated in the *Scripture-Doctrine*, his paper laid before the Bishops on July 2, and iterated in his letter of July 5 to the Bishop of London.[66]

The second point of debate between Clarke and Waterland under the heading of aseity concerned the question of how the generation of the Son occurred; whether it was from the nature of the Father, or by his will. This issue was related to the previous point as to whether or not the Son existed necessarily. Both Waterland and Clarke were consistent in their formulations on this point. For Clarke, since the Son did not exist necessarily (or, in his terms, contain self-existence), he could not properly have been generated from the nature of the Father. In Clarke's mind, natural generation meant necessary generation.

---

[61] Ibid., 506–07.
[62] Clarke, *Observations* in *Works*, IV, 508, cf., Waterland's *Second Defense* in *Works*, III, 284, 280, 283, 526.
[63] Waterland, *Defense* in *Works*, I, 2, 152.
[64] See Clarke, *Works*, IV, 553–54.
[65] Ibid., 555–56.
[66] Letters of July 2nd and 5th in Clarke, *Works*, IV, 553–54 and 557.

Conversely, Clarke held that the generation of the Son was strictly a product of the divine will. This relieved its formal necessity, and protected the supremacy of the Father. Clarke's position was summarized in his statement that "A necessary emanation from the Father, by the will and power of the Father; is an express contradiction."[67]

Waterland maintained that the "generation of the Son may be by necessity of nature, without excluding the concurrence or approbation of the will."[68] Whereas Clarke's positioning of nature and will on the issue of the Son's generation was antithetic, Waterland's was synthetic. According to Waterland, Clarke had argued in his *Demonstration of the Being and Attributes of God* that according to Plato's followers, the world was viewed as "as an eternal voluntary emanation from the all-wise and supreme cause."[69] Waterland cited Plotinus in making God's will to be one with God's essence, deriving the very being of God from his will, which is to say, from himself. In other words, Waterland held that the view of the Platonists, like his own, was synthetic, and could not be used to support Clarke's opposing of the terms.[70] Moreover, according to Waterland, none of the Fathers ever believed that the generation of the Son was by the will of the Father, in opposition to his nature.[71]

For Waterland, the opposition of God's nature and will was a false dichotomy.[72] The attributes of God were grounded in the *natural* perfections of the Deity, which he can no more cease to have than he can cease to exist. Even the "rectitude of his will is natural, necessary, and unalterable: and the reason why he never wills amiss is because he cannot."[73] It was true, said Waterland, that the Son was dependent on the Father in the sense that he was from him, but he was not dependent on the will of the Father. While the members of the trinity were independent of all things *ad extra* they had a necessity of relation toward one another.

Clarke responded to Waterland in his *Observations* by making two points. The first was that Waterland himself, although holding to a

---

[67] Clarke, *Modest Plea* in *Works*, IV, 459.
[68] Waterland, *Defense* in *Works*, I, 2, 91.
[69] Clarke, *Demonstration*, in the 4th ed., 31.
[70] Waterland, *Second Defense*, in *Works*, III, 242.
[71] Waterland, *Farther Vindication* in *Works*, IV, 25.
[72] This idea is traditional and in older dogmatics was related to the doctrine of God's simplicity.
[73] Ibid., 81.

necessary generation of the Son by nature, had consistently shown that in the minds of the Fathers, generation was a voluntary act of the Father.[74] The second point was that Waterland resisted holding that the Son was generated by the will of the Father because he believed this will made the Son's existence precarious. Waterland had in fact defined precarious existence as that which was not necessary.[75] Clarke chided Waterland for assuming that whatever arises out of the power and will of the Father, no matter how immutable that will may be, can be considered precarious. He invited Waterland to apply the same reasoning to the following problem.

> "God", says the Apostle, "cannot lie." The only reason why he cannot is because he will not. Is therefore the veracity of God, a thing as mutable and precarious, because it entirely depends upon his will; as is the existence of any creature whatsoever?[76]

Waterland responded that God's moral attributes were founded in his *natural* perfections as Deity. "Even the rectitude of his will is natural, necessary and unalterable."[77] For Clarke this was unacceptable because it introduced a prior principle (rectitude) to which the will of God must conform, thus denying the absolute ground of God's being, i.e. that he is the *principium* of all things.

The final element of the aseity debate, and interwoven with the other two, was the question of precisely how the Son was subordinated to the Father. Clarke's position throughout the debate had been that the Son was really subordinate to the Father, as the one generated from the one ingenerate.

> The "subordination" of the Son, "allowed" (as Dr. Waterland confesses) by the primitive writers, is not a subordination merely nominal, consisting (according to Dr. Waterland) in mere position or order of words, which in the truth of things is a co-ordination; but that it is a real subordination of the Son to the Father in point of authority and dominion over the universe. This is the main, the true, and only point.[78]

Clarke affirmed that the Son "by that nature which the Son derived from the Father, has true divine power and dominion."[79] It was not

---

[74] Clarke, *Observations* in *Works*, 505–06. Here Clarke cites numerous texts from Waterland's *Second Defense*.

[75] Waterland, *Farther Vindication* in *Works*, IV, 81.

[76] Clarke, *Observations* in *Works*, IV, 509.

[77] Waterland, *Farther Vindication* in *Works*, IV, 81.

[78] Clarke, *Modest Plea* in *Works*, IV, 472–73.

[79] Ibid., 471.

some inferior or other nature than the Father's. "That is to say, he is truly and really (as the Evangelist and the Apostle stiles him) that God or that Lord (John 1.i, 3 and 1 Cor. viii. 6) *by* or *through* whom are all things."[80] Nevertheless, since he was not self-existent, and did not contain the perfections of God absolutely, he was not the one God *of* whom are all things.

Waterland responded to Clarke by stating that although they used similar terms, they meant different things by them.

> We say, the Son is subordinate, meaning it of a subordination of order, as is just and proper: you also lay hold of the word subordinate, and seem wonderfully pleased with it; but understand by it an inferiority of nature. We say, that the Son is not absolutely supreme nor independent; intimating thereby that he is second in order as a Son, and has no separate or independent existence from the Father, being coessentially and coeternally one with him: you also take up the same words, interpret them to a low sense, and make the Son an inferior dependent being; depending at first on the will of the Father for his existence, and afterwards for the continuance of it.[81]

It should be clear from Clarke's statement above, that whatever kind of subordination he meant, it was not, as Waterland suggested, "an inferiority of nature." On the other hand, Waterland insisted that his own notion of subordination was not merely "nominal." Waterland defined subordination as implying "a difference of order only, while the nature is supposed equal."[82] When Waterland was probed as to *why* the ordering is the way it is, he retorted,

> If you ask, why the person called the Son might not have been the Father; I have nothing to say but that is fact he is not: so it is written, and so we believe. The Father is Father, and the Son is Son, there is a natural priority of order, (I say, natural, not economical,) by which the Son is referred up to the Father as his head and not vice versa.[83]

For Waterland the economical subordination was a logical outworking of the natural subordination. It was theoretically possible for the Father to have carried out the tasks of the Son, "but it was more congruous that he who is first in order should be first in office too."[84]

Clarke seized upon this passage in his *Observations* to show that

---

[80] Ibid.
[81] Waterland, *Defense* in *Works*, I, 2, 147–48.
[82] Waterland, *Lady Moyer Lectures* in *Works*, II, Preface, xvi.
[83] Waterland, *Second Defense* in *Works*, III, 169.
[84] Ibid., 169.

what Waterland in fact meant by "natural subordination" was really
no subordination at all. He accused Waterland of making the terms
"subordination" and "coordination" meaningless by applying them
only to the terms involved (Father and Son) with no outside referent
such as time, place, situation, power, authority etc. Since the only
way in which subordination is commonly understood, is by the use
of such referents, Waterland's employment of the term "subordination of nature" was meaningless.[85]

For Clarke, the fruit of Waterland's line of thought was borne in
his inability to give a reason why the Father was the Father and the
Son was the Son. He pressed the point home when he wrote,

> By the Doctor's hypothesis therefore, there was no impossibility in
> the nature of things, but unoriginate might have been originate, and
> originate unoriginate; underived might have been derived, and de-
> rived underived; the Father might have been begotten, and the Son
> unbegotten.[86]

In his *Farther Vindication*, Waterland responded that he had asserted
the priority of order (unoriginateness and originateness) to be *natural*
which he now defined as "necessary or unalterable, and eternally so:
so that one could never have been the other."[87] He justified his statement about the possibility of the inversion of the priority (or subordination) by arguing that the "why" question is "asking a reason
a priori in a case which admits of none" and that he was "unwilling to
pretend to it." He was content to demonstrate the fact *a posteriori.*[88]

In conclusion we see that the trinitarian controversy in England,
although starting prior to Clarke's *Scripture-Doctrine of the Trinity* in
1712, developed along the contours of the questions he raised there
and was imprinted by the mind of its author. Many writers made
contributions to the debate. Most noteworthy were Jackson, Edwards,
Wells, Knight, Gastrell, Welchman, Nye and Mayo. At the center of
the contest, however, were Clarke and Waterland. They differed on
two essential foci of the trinitarian formulation: the nature of the
consubstantiality of the Father and Son, and the notion of aseity.

Both claimed to hold to the consubstantiality of the Father and
Son, but each understood it differently. Clarke held that the Son

---

[85] Clarke *Observations* in *Works*, IV, 494.
[86] Ibid., 494.
[87] Waterland, *Farther Vindication* in *Works*, IV, 36.
[88] Ibid., 36.

was "from the essence of the Father" and like him in every way with
the exception of self-existence and absolute supremacy. Waterland
believed that since scripture referred to the Son as "God," that he
must be God in a manner identical with the Father, therefore possessing both necessary existence (which Clarke did not distinguish
from self-existence, although Waterland did), and absolute supremacy.

They also disagreed on the aseity of the Son. Waterland's position
on the existence of the Son can be summarized in his own words.

> Derived or underived; we say derived: being or not being; we say being;
> necessary or not necessary in existence; we say necessary: self-existent
> or not self-existent; we say not self-existent: Supreme God or not su-
> preme God; we say supreme God.[89]

Clarke's perception was different. He believed Waterland's derivation to be nominal. He preferred the language of "person" over that
of "essence." He did not believe the Son to exist necessarily, which
he equated with aseity. Finally, the Son was emphatically not the
Supreme God, but was certainly God in every way excluding self-
existence and supremacy, which belonged to the Father alone.

---

[89] Waterland, *Second Defense* in *Works*, III, 329.

CONCLUSION

In the taxonomy of Christian doctrine historians have classified the trinitarian theology of Samuel Clarke under the heading of Arianism. This monograph has called that classification into question, and offered an alternative thesis: that Clarke's theology was a reassertion of the early Origenistic-Eusebian-Cappadocian trajectory of thought as it pointed toward both the Homoiousian and later Cappadocian positions on the doctrine of God.

This reassertion was intrinsically linked to the intellectual milieu in which Clarke thought and wrote. The advent of modern science, with its epistemological demands for verification inaugurated by Bacon's thought, coupled with the methodological skepticism of Descartes, formed one of the foundations of the rational approach to theology to which Clarke was so committed. The second foundation of this rational religion was the legacy of the Protestant reformation. The England in which Clarke lived had suffered civil war, regicide, restoration and revolution all in an attempt to come to grips with its emerging religious pluralism and the resultant social implications. The outcome of these events proved unsatisfactory, and produced the promulgation of the Latitudinarian agenda of toleration. Coupled with the Reformation return *ad fontes*, this desire for toleration resulted in a return to a minimalist "biblical religion" based upon scripture, baptism and the Apostles' Creed. Along with this return to primary sources, was the rising historical consciousness which shifted the locus of argumentation from dogmatic to historical footings. These twin foundations of the rise of modern science and the legacy of the Reformation, became the platform upon which the cathedral of rational religion was erected.

Clarke stood with those whom we have identified as heterodox Latitudinarians. He was deeply indebted to the Cambridge Platonists, particularly Cudworth and More, for his thought. Likewise he was influenced by the circle at Great Tew, and the rationalism of its greatest spokesman, Wm. Chillingworth. Clarke opposed the Deists' denial of the role of revelation, but was more restrictive in his affirmation of mystery and tradition than the orthodox Latitudinarians. It was this restriction which caused Clarke to examine the traditional

(Athanasian) formulation of the doctrine of the trinity and reject it. He believed that that formulation could not be sustained on the basis of either reason or antiquity. Nor could it be shielded behind the cloak of mystery.

Clarke's understanding of early Church history, and his reading of the Ante-Nicene and Post-Nicene Fathers in particular, were the greatest cause of his departure from the "three persons in one substance" formulation. Whereas the necessity of reasonable explanation, which was so typical of his age, compelled Clarke to examine the doctrine, it was his conclusions regarding the opinions of the Fathers which caused him to challenge it. For Clarke, the Nicene Fathers had never intended to produce such a formula. Their intention had been to unmask the twin tenets of Arianism: "that there was a time when he was not," and that he was "created out of nothing." For Clarke, the Fathers had recognized that the ὁμοούσιος had been condemned as heretical in the theology of Paul of Samosata, and they were hesitant to use it. They adopted it, with the caveat that it was to be understood in a non-material sense, as the only sure bulwark against Arianism. Clarke believed that the Fathers *understood* the term to mean the Son was the "same kind of substance" as the Father. He held that the "generic" interpretation was their intention. In other words, he affirmed the interpretation that Eusebius had given, which became articulated as the ὁμοιούσιον position at the Second Council of Sirmium in 357, and which scholars like Harnack have argued, was the interpretation of the Cappadocians as well. In his *Scripture-Doctrine of the Trinity*, Clarke selected Patristic sources which he believed demonstrated that the Fathers in general held this position and interpreted the words of the Creed accordingly. He drew heavily upon Irenaeus, Origen, Eusebius and the Cappadocians, particularly Basil, in arguing his position on the supremacy of the Father and subordination of the Son. Contemporary scholarship, particularly the works of Hanson, Prestige, Kopecek and Kelly have confirmed Clarke's reading of the period over and against Bull's thesis that the Ante-Nicene Fathers held what later became the "orthodox" position. These scholars have rejected the reductionistic interpretation of the period which outlines the options for the doctrine of God as orthodox [Athanasian], Arian, and Sabellian. We have seen that those scholars, like Hagenbach, Fisher, Shedd, Sheldon and Hodgson, who viewed Clarke as an Arian, have operated with this reductionistic framework in mind. In this framework the ὁμοιούσιον (later, unfortunately, called Semi-Arian) position was absorbed into the Arian position, resulting in the misunderstanding of Clarke's position.

Clarke's understanding of the trinity was further bolstered by his relationship with Isaac Newton. He shared Newton's emphasis on "dominion" as the determining description of God's relationship to the creation. This emphasis was carried over into their understandings of the relationship of the Father to the Son. We have seen that Newton and Clarke shared a similar interpretation of the early history of the church, and that Newton himself held the ὁμοιόυσιον position, which explains why neither Clarke nor Newton could support their friend William Whiston, the avowed Arian. Newton was Clarke's senior by more than thirty years, and we know that he reached his trinitarian conclusions by at least the 1690's, when Clarke was still a young man. Clarke was clearly Newton's lieutenant in natural philosophy, and although it is unlikely that he had quite the same student-mentor relationship in his own field of expertise, it is probable that Newton exercised considerable influence upon Clarke's thinking on the trinity. He may well have encouraged Clarke's questioning of the orthodox formulation, and directed him to sources with which he himself was already well acquainted. It seems impossible, given the depth and breadth of their relationship, that they did not discuss the trinity often, and at length. While Clarke never mentioned Newton in his work on the trinity, the evidence is too strong to avoid the conclusion that Newton must be seen as a source for Clarke's thought.

Due to Clarke's outstanding reputation in the Church of England as a result of his Boyle Lectures, his *Scripture-Doctrine of the Trinity* received close scrutiny. It served as a watershed in the trinitarian disputes which were inaugurated by Bull's *Defensio*. While a host of opposition arose against Clarke's work, his main adversary was Waterland. At the center of the debate between Clarke and Waterland were the two issues of consubstantiality and aseity. Waterland, like later historians of doctrine, assumed the framework mentioned above. He held that there were only three possible options in the doctrine of God, and was thus forced to conclude, based on this preconceived framework, that Clarke was an Arian, and therefore a heretic.

Clarke worked in an intellectual climate which insisted that religious doctrine be reasonable. The question must be raised as to whether Clarke was reading his rationalism back into the Fathers' doctrine of God. While it is clear that it was the rational impulse of

his age, with its demand for reasonable doctrine, which prompted
the questions Clarke raised and the direction he took in his search
for solutions, contemporary scholarship has confirmed Clarke's reading of the history of the early church. A non-confessional reading of
the Fathers reveals nuances of thought which Clarke perceived, but
were lost upon both his contemporaries and later historians of doctrine. As a result it is my conclusion that, *pace* Ferguson, Samuel
Clarke was not a heretic. His line of thought on the doctrine of God
was in keeping with that of Origen, Eusebius, the Cappadocians,
and the Eastern tradition in general, and was within the broad scope
of what has been acceptable as orthodox in the history of the church.
One hopes that this realization should be determinative in any evaluation of Clarke in future histories of doctrine.

BIBLIOGRAPHY

Primary Sources

Anonymous. *An Enquiry into the Ill Designs, Errors, etc. of Dr. Clarke's (pretended) Scripture-Doctrine of the Trinity; Wherein also the Wrong Acceptation of some Scripture Terms, relating to that doctrine, is attempted to be rectified, and also the Orthodox Doctrine of Three Persons in the One Individual Substance of God, is made manifest. With a Preface, Wherein a late Pamphlet concerning The Difficulties attending the Study of the Scriptures in the way of private Judgment, is fully considered.* London, 1714.

Anonymous. *An Essay towards an Impartial Account of the Holy Trinity, and the Deity of our Saviour, as contained in the Old Testament. In which are some Remarks on the Scripture Account lately published by Dr. Clarke.* London, 1712.

Anonymous. *Observations on Mr. Whiston's Historical Memoirs of the Life and Writings of Dr. Samuel Clarke; containing a Vindication of Dr. Clarke's conduct and behaviour at the time the Convocation fell upon him, from the unjust aspersions cast upon him by Mr. Whiston and others; and from the weak objection made to his conduct by some of his friends.* London, 1748.

Anonymous. *Remarks upon a late Pamphlet, Intituled, The innocency of Error Asserted and Vindicated. By a member of the Church of England.* London, 1715.

Anonymous. *Speculum Clarkianum: or Cl__k against Cl__k. Being a Confutation of His Scripture-Doctrine of the Trinity, out of his own previous writing.* London, 1714.

Aristotle, *The Complete Works.* 2 Vols. Edited by Jonathan Barnes. The Revised Oxford translation. *The Bollingen Series LXXI, 2.* Princeton: Princeton University Press, 1984.

Bacon, Francis. *New Organon* and *Of the Advancement of Learning* in *The Philosophical Works of Francis Bacon.* Edited by John M. Robertson. Reprinted from the texts and translations, with the notes and prefaces of Ellis and Spedding. London: George Rutleage and Sons, 1905.

Bennet, Thomas. *A Discourse of the Ever-Blessed Trinity in Unity, with an Examination of Dr. Clarke's Scripture-Doctrine of the Holy and Ever-blessed Trinity.* London, 1725.

Berriman, William. *An Historical Account of the Controversies that have been in the Church, concerning the Doctrine of the Holy and Ever-blessed Trinity.* London, 1725. *Biographia Britannica.* 6 Vols. London, 1748.

Blount, Charles. *The Two First Books of Philostratus Concerning the Life of Apollonius of Tyaneus: Written Originally in Greek, and now published in English: Together with Philological Notes Upon Each Chapter.* London: Printed for Nathaniel Thompson, 1680.

——. *Religio Laici.* London: Printed for R. Bentley and S. Magnes, 1683.

——. *The Oracles of Reason.* London: 1693.

Boyle, Robert. *The Works.* 5 Vols. London: Printed for A. Millar, MDCCXLIV.

Browne, John. *Brief Animadversions on Two Pieces: The one entitled, Remarks on Dr. Waterland's Second Defence of some Queries. The other, Farther Remarks on his Farther Vindication of Christ's Divinity. Bearing the ingenious name of Philalethes Cantabrigiensis for their Author.* London, 1725.

Bull, George. *Opera Omnia.* London: Samuel Bridge, 1703.

——. *The Works.* Collected and Revised by Edward Burton. Oxford: At the University Press, MDCCCXLVI.

Burnet, Thomas. *The Scripture-trinity intelligibly explained: or, an Essay toward the demonstration of a trinity in unity . . . which . . . may serve as an answer to Dr. Waterland, as also to Dr. Clarke . . . By a divine of the Church of England.* London, Printed by J. Roberts, 1720.

Calvin, John. *Institutes of the Christian Religion.* 2 Vols. Edited by John T. McNeil.

Translated by Ford Lewis Battles. Philadelphia: Westminster Press, 1960.
Chillingworth, William. *The Religion of the Protestants, A Safe Way to Salvation* in *Works*. Philadelphia: Pub. Rev. R. Davis, sold by Hooker and Agnew, MDCCCXLI.
Clarke, Samuel. *The Works*. 3d ed., Edited by John Clarke. 4 Vols. London: John and Paul Knapton, 1738; reprint, N.Y.: Garland Press, 1978.
Collins, Anthony. *A Discourse of Free Thinking, Occasion'd by the Rise and Growth of a Sect Call'd Free Thinkers*. London: MDCCXIII.
Cudworth, Ralph. *The True Intellectual System of the Universe: Wherein all the Reason and Philosophy of Atheism is Confuted and Its Impossibility Demonstrated*. 2 Vols. Andover: Published by Gould and Newman, New York, 1838. First pub., London: 1678.

Descartes, Rene. *The Philosophical Writings of Descartes*. 2 Vols. Translated by John Cottingham, Robert Stoothoff and Dugald Murdoch. Cambridge: Cambridge Univ. Press, 1985.

Edward, Herbert, Lord of Cherbury. *De Veritate*. Translated by Meyrick H. Carre. Bristol: Published for Univ. of Bristol by J.W. Arrowsmith Ltd., 1937. Originally published in Paris, 1624 and London, 1633.
——. *De Religione Laici*. Edited and translated by Harold R. Hutcheson. New Haven: Yale U. Press, 1944, originally pub. 1645.
Edwards, John. *Some Animadversions on Dr. Clarke's Scripture-Doctrine, (as he styles it) of the Trinity, briefly shewing that his quotations out of the Fathers are forced; his texts produced from Scripture are wrested; his arguments and inferences are weak and illogical: His whole performance falls short of his design*. London, 1712.
——. *A Supplement to the Animadversions on Dr. Clarke's Scripture-Doctrine of the Trinity. Wherein It is probably gathered from Scripture and Reason, and the Testimony of some of the Fathers, That there is no subordination in the Holy Trinity, and that the Son of God is Self-existent as well as the Father. Humbly offered to the Consideration of the Learned and Judicious. With a Defence of the Liturgy of our Church against Dr. Clarke's gross misinterpretations of several passages in it*. London, 1713.
——. *Some brief Critical Remarks on Dr. Clarke's last Papers; which are his Reply to Mr. Nelson, and an Anonymous Writer, and the Author of Some Considerations, etc. Shewing that the Doctor is as deficient in the Critic Art, as he is in Theology*. London, 1714.

Gastrell, Francis. "Considerations on the Trinity." in John Randolph's *Enchiridion Theologicum or A Manuel for the Use of Students in Divinity*. 2 Vols. Oxford: Clarendon Press, MDCCCXII.
——. *Remarks upon Dr. Clarke's Scripture-Doctrine of the Trinity. By the Author of, Some Considerations concerning the Trinity and the Ways of managing that Controversy*. London, 1714.

Hawarden, Edward. *An Answer to Dr. Clarke, and Mr. Whiston, Concerning the Divinity of the Son and of the Holy Spirit. With a Summary Account of the Chief Writer of the Three First Ages. By H.E.* London, 1729.
Hearne, Thomas. *An Account of all the considerable Books and Pamphlets, that have been wrote on either side, in the Controversy concerning the Trinity, since the year 1712: In which is also contained an account of the pamphlets writ this last year on each side by the Dissenters, to the end of the year 1719*. London, 1720.
Hoadly, Benjamin. *Works*. 4 Vols. London: W. Bowyer and J. Nichols, MDCCLXXIII.
Hobbes, Thomas. *Leviathan or the Matter Form and Power of a Commonwealth Ecclesiastical and Civil*. London: Printed for Andrew Crooke, 1651.
——. *Leviathan*. Introduction by Herbert Schneider. Indianapolis: Bobbs-Merrill, 1958.
Hooker, Richard. *Of the Laws of Ecclesiastical Politie*. London: Will. Stansby, 1611.

Jackson, John. *Three Letters to Dr. Clarke from a Clergyman, concerning his Scripture-Doctrine of the Trinity, with the Doctor's Replies*. London, 1714.

——. *An Examination of Mr. Nye's Explication of the Articles of the Divine unity, the Trinity and Incarnation. Wherein is briefly shown, The insufficiency of that Explication both from Scripture and Reason: with a Vindication of Dr. Clarke's Scripture-Doctrine and Replies, from the charge of Tritheism.* London, 1715.

——. *A Collection of Queries. Wherein the most material Objections from Scripture, Reason, and Antiquity, which have as yet been alleged against Dr. Clarke's Scripture-Doctrine of the Trinity, and the Defences of it, are proposed and answered. With an Appendix: In which are offered to the consideration of the learned, some Queries from Scripture, Reason and Antiquity, concerning the vulgar Scholastic Explication of the Doctrine of the Trinity and Incarnation. By a Clergyman in the country.* London, 1716.

——. *A Reply to Dr. Waterland's Defence of his Queries. Wherein is contained, A Full State of the Whole Controversy: And every Particular, alleged by that learned Writer, is distinctly considered. By a Clergyman in the Country.* London, 1722.

——. [Philalethes Cantabrigiensis]. *Remarks on Dr. Waterland's Second Defence of Some Queries. Being a brief consideration of his notion of the Trinity, as stated by himself in Three Questions. With an Appendix, shewing the true sense of Creation, Eternity and Consubstantiality. In a Letter to the Doctor.* London, 1723.

——. [Philalethes Cantabrigiensis]. *Farther Remarks on Dr. Waterland's Farther Vindication of Christ's Divinity.* London, 1724.

——. *Christian Liberty Asserted, and the Scripture-Doctrine of the Trinity Vindicated; Against a book written by Dr. Waterland, and entitled, The Importance of the Doctrine of the Holy trinity asserted, etc. By a Clergyman in the Country.* London, 1734.

——. *Memoirs of the Life and Writings of Dr. Waterland. Being a summary view of the Trinitarian Controversy for twenty years, between the Doctor and a Clergyman in the Country; Wherein, (In defence of a book, entitled, Christian Liberty asserted etc. in answer to some Animadversions upon it, and to a Defence of Dr. Waterland) is shewn the Pravity of the Doctor's Book, called, The Importance, etc. and the Tendency of it, to introduce heresy, schism, and persecution into the Church. By a Clergyman.* London, 1736.

Knight, James. *The True Scripture-Doctrine of the Holy Trinity, the Eucharist, and the Satisfaction Made for us by our Lord Jesus Christ. In Three Books. Wherein all the texts in the Old and New Testaments relating thereunto, and the principal passages in the liturgy and Articles of the Church of England are collected, and compared, explained and vindicated from the errors of Dr. Clarke.* London, 1713.

——. *A Letter to the Reverend Dr. Clarke, Rector of St. James's Westminster; from the author of the Scripture-Doctrine of the Holy Trinity, the Eucharist, etc. Occasion'd by some passages in a Letter from Dr. Clarke to Dr. Wells.* London, 1714.

——. *The true Scripture-Doctrine of the most holy and undivided Trinity vindicated from the misrepresentations of Dr. Clarke. To which is prefixed a Letter to the Reverend Doctor, by Robert Nelson.* London, 1714.

——. *The true Scripture-Doctrine of the most holy and undivided Trinity continued and vindicated from the misrepresentations of Dr. Clarke. In answer to Reply. By the author of the Scripture-Doctrine published and recommended by Robert Nelson, Esq.* London, 1715.

Leibniz, Gottfried Wilhelm. *Philosophical Papers and Letters.* 2d edition. Edited and with an introduction by Leroy E. Loemker. Dordrecht, Holland: D. Reidel Publishing, 1969. First edition, 1956, Univ. of Chicago Press.

Locke, John. *Works.* 3d ed. London: Printed for Arthur Bettesworth etc., Paternoster Row, MDCCXXVII.

——. *The Correspondence of John Locke.* Edited by E.S. De Beer. Oxford: Clarendon Press, 1976–89.

——. *An Essay Concerning Human Understanding and A Treatise on the Conduct of the Understanding.* Philadelphia: James Kay, Jun. and Brother, Pittsburgh: C.H. Kay & Co., 1853.

——. *An Essay Concerning Human Understanding.* Abridged and edited with an introduction by A.C. Woozley. London: Fontana/Collins, 1964. First published, 1689.

——. *Two Treatises on Government.* A critical edition with an introduction and apparatus criticus by Peter Laslett. N.Y.: New American Library, 1963. First published, 1690.
——. *The Reasonableness of Christianity As Delivered in the Scriptures.* Edited and introduced by George Ewing. Washington, D.C.: Regnery Gateway, 1965. First published, 1695.

Mayo, Richard. *A Plain Scripture-Argument against Dr. Clarke's Doctrine concerning the Everblessed Trinity; in a Letter to Dr. Clarke; With some previous Letters, relating to our Creeds, and Forms of Worship: By the Collector of the Texts, in a Book intituled. Several Hundred Texts of Holy Scripture, plainly proving, that our Lord Jesus Christ is the most High God.* London, 1715.

Newton, Isaac. *Certain Philosophical Questions: Newton's Trinity Notebook.* Cambridge: Cambridge U. Press, 1983.
——. *The Correspondence of Isaac Newton,* Vol. VI 1713–1718. Edited by Alfred R. Hall and Laura Tilling. Cambridge: Cambridge University Press for the Royal Society of London, 1976.
——. *The Mathematical Principles of Natural Philosophy.* Translated by Andrew Motte. 3 Vols. London: Printed for H.D. Symonds by Knight and Compton, 1803.
——. *Theological Manuscripts.* Selected and edited with an introduction by H. McLachlan. Liverpool: Univ. Press, 1980.
——. *Papers and Letters on Natural Philosophy and Related Documents.* Cambridge: Harvard University Press, 1958.
——. *Two Letters of Isaac Newton to Mr. LeClerc.* London: Printed for J. Payne, MDCCLIV.
Nye, Stephen. *The Explication of the Articles of the Divine Unity, the Trinity and Incarnation, commonly received in the Catholick Church, Asserted and Vindicated. By occasion of the late books of the Reverend Dr. Samuel Clarke, and his Opposers; and of another Book, by a learned Socinian. With two Dissertations; One concerning the Meaning and Obligation of Assent and Consent, or Subscription to Public Forms, imposed by the Government in Church or State: And the other concerning the pretended Authority and Rights of private conscience or the Judgment of Discretion so called.* London, 1715.

Payne, William. *The Mystery of the Christian Faith and of the Blessed Trinity Vindicated, and the Divinity of Christ Proved. In Three Sermons preached at Westminster Abbey upon Trinity—Sunday, June the 7th, and September 21, 1696.* London: Printed for Richard Cumberland at the Angel in St. Paul's Church-Yard, 1697.
Pearson, John. *An Exposition of the Creed.* 3d ed. Oxford: Printed by J.F. for Joh. Williams, 1669.
Petavius, Dionysius [Petau, Denis]. *Opus De Theologicus Dogmatibus.* 8 Vols. Edited by Ludovicus Guerin. Paris-Brussels: Barri-Ducis, MDCCCLXIV.
[Philalethes]. *Reflections upon the Present Controversie concerning the Holy Trinity. Wherein are set forth the inconveniences of some vulgar Explications. In a letter from a Clergyman to the Reverend Clarke.* London, 1714.
[Philotriados]. *The Equality of the Son and the Holy Ghost with the Father, in the Everblessed Trinity; Demonstrated from the Name, attributes, Operations, etc. of the Father, As they are revealed to us in the Holy Scriptures. In a short plan and easy Method. With a letter to Mr. Whiston. To which is subjoined, A Confutation of Dr. Clarke's Scripture-Doctrine of the Trinity, out of his own previous writings. By a Divine of the Church of England.* London, 1714.
[Pseudo] Plato, *Alcibiades 2.* Translated by W.R.M. Lamb in *Loeb Classical Library* Vol. 8. Cambridge: Harvard Univ. Press, MCMLV.
Potter, Edward. *A Vindication of our Blessed Saviour's Divinity; chiefly against Dr. Clarke.*

Wherein is shewn from Scripture, (after a foundation is laid, by proving that this doctrine is not inconsistent with reason,) that He is of the same essence and perfections with the Father: And that this was the opinion of the Ante-Nicene Fathers; and of the Compilers of our Liturgy. And the chief Objections are answered. Cambridge, 1714.

Randolph, John. *Enchiridion Theologicum, or A Manuel for the Use of Students in Divinity.* 2 Vols. Oxford: Clarendon Press, MDCCCXII.
Ray, John. *The Wisdom of God Manifested in the Works of the Creation.* 2d ed. London: Printed for Samuel Smith at Princes Arms in St. Paul's Church-yard, 1692.
Rohault, Jacques. *Rohault's System of Natural Philosophy Illustrated with Samuel Clarke's Notes taken mostly out of Isaac Newton's philosophy.* Edited by John Clarke. London: Printed for J. Knapton, 1723.

Sherlock, Thomas. *Works.* Vols. I–IV. London: A.J. Valpy, 1830.
Spratt, Thomas. *The History of the Royal Society of London for the Improving of Natural Knowledge.* London: 1687.
Stillingfleet, Edward. "Discourse of Scripture Mysteries" in John Randolph's *Enchiridion Theologicum, or A Manuel for the Use of Students in Divinity.* 2 Vols. Oxford: Clarendon Press, MDCCCXII.
———. "Second Dialogue on the Doctrine of the Trinity and Transubstantiation Compared." in John Randolph's *Enchiridion Theologicum, or a Manuel for the Use of Students in Divinity.* 2 Vols. Oxford: Clarendon Press, MDCCCXII.
Sykes, Arthur Ashley. *The Innocency of Error asserted and vindicated. In a letter to . . . By Eugenius Philalethes.* London, 1715.
———. *The Innocency of Error asserted and vindicated. In a letter to . . . The Third Edition, very much corrected and improved by the Author.* London, 1729.
———. *A Modest Plea for the Baptismal and Scripture-Notion of the Trinity. Wherein the Schemes of the Reverend Dr. Bennet and Dr. Clarke are compared. To which are added Two Letters, One written to the late Reverend Mr. R.M. concerning his Plain Scripture-Argument, etc. The Other to the Author of a Book, intituled, The True Scripture-Doctrine of the Most Holy and undivided Trinity continued and vindicated: Recommended first by Robert Nelson Esq.; and since by the Reverend Dr. Waterland. Wherein the Reader will find obviated the Principal Arguments urged by the Rev. Dr. Waterland, in his Defence of Some Queries. By a Clergyman in the Country.* London, 1719.

Tindal, Matthew. *Christianity as Old as the Creation: or, the Gospel as a Republication of the Religion of Nature.* 2d ed. in octavo. London: MDCCXXXII.
Toland, John. *Christianity Not Mysterious or, a Treatise Shewing, That there is nothing in the Gospel Contrary to Reason, Nor Above it: And that no Christian Doctrine can be properly call'd a Mystery.* London: 1696. Edited by Rene Wellek, reprint; N.Y.: Garland Publishing, Inc., 1978.

Waterland, Daniel. *The Works.* 10 Vols. Oxford: At the Clarendon Press, MDCCCXXIII. Containing:
Vindication of Christ's Divinity, being a Defence of some Queries relating to Dr. Clarke's Scheme of the Holy Trinity. Vol. I,2.
Eight Sermons, in Defence of the Divinity of our Lord Jesus Christ, preached at the Lady Moyer's Lecture. Vol. II.
A Second Vindication of Christ's Divinity, or a Second Defence of some Queries relating to Dr. Clarke's Scheme of the Holy Trinity. Vol. III.
A Farther Vindication of Christ's Divinity. Vol. IV.
Welchman, Edward. *Dr. Clarke's Scripture-Doctrine of the Trinity Examined. To which are added some remarks on his sentiments, and a brief explanation of his doctrine by way of question and answer.* Oxford, 1714.

Wells, Edward. *Remarks on Dr. Clarke's Introduction to his Scripture-Doctrine of the Trinity.* Oxford, 1713.

——. *A Letter to the Reverend Dr. Clarke, Rector of St. James's Westminster, In Answer to his Letter to Dr. Wells.* Oxford, 1713.

Whichcote, Benjamin. *Works.* Vols. I–IV. Aberdeen: Printed by J. Chalmers for Alexander, MDCCLI; reprint N.Y.: Garland Publishing, 1977.

Whiston, William. *Animadversions on a late Pamphlet Intituled, The New Arian Reprov'd.* London, 1712.

——. *Historical Memoirs of the Life of Dr. Samuel Clarke.* London: Fletcher Gyles, J. Roberts, 1730.

——. *Memoirs of the Life and Writings of W.W.* London: 1749.

——. *Mr. Whiston's Defense of Himself, from the Articles Objected to him by Dr. Pelling before the Court of Delegates, in a Cause of Heresy. To which is Prefix'd the Articles Themselves.* London: Printed for J. Roberts, 1715.

——. *Primitive Christianity Revived. Volume V. Containing the Recognitions of Clement: or the Travels of Peter. In Ten Books. Done into English by William Whiston, M.A. With a Preface, or Preliminary Discourse: As also Two Appendices; the one containing some observations on Dr. Clarke's Scripture-Doctrine of the Trinity; and the other a farther account of the Convocation; and other proceedings with relation to Mr. Whiston.* London, 1712.

Whitby, Daniel. *A Discourse shewing that the Expositions which the Ante-Nicene Fathers have given of the Texts alleged against the Reverend Dr. Clarke by learned Layman, are more agreeable to the Interpretations of Dr. Clarke, than to the Interpretations of that learned Layman. By a Clergyman in the Country.* London, 1714.

Woolston, Thomas. *Six Discourses on the Miracles of our Saviour and Defences of his Discourses.* 5th ed. London: Printed for the author, 1728, reprint; N.Y: Garland Publishing, N.Y. and London, 1979.

Secondary Sources

Aaron, Richard, *John Locke.* 2d ed. Oxford: At the Clarendon Press, 1965.

Abbey, C.J. and Overton, J.H. *The English Church in the Eighteenth Century.* Revised and abridged edition. London: Longmans, Green, and Co., 1887.

Acton, Henry. *Religious Opinions and Examples of Milton, Locke, and Newton.* Boston: Printed for the American Unitarian Assoc. by C. Bowen, 1833; repr., New York: AMS Press, 1973.

Alexander, H.G., ed. *The Leibniz-Clarke Correspondence.* Manchester: Manchester Univ. Press., 1956.

Allen, Phyllis. "Scientific Studies in the English Universities of the Seventeenth Century." in *Journal of the History of Ideas,* 10 (April, 1949).

Asch, E. Dorothy. "Samuel Clarke's *Scripture-Doctrine of the Trinity* and the Controversy It Aroused." Ph.D. diss., Univ. of Edinburgh, 1951.

Bechler, Zev, ed. *Contemporary Newtonian Research.* Dordrecht, Holland; Boston: D. Reidel Pub. Co.; Hingham, MA, 1982.

Berman, David. "Deism, Immortality, and the Art of Theological Lying." in *Deism, Masonry, and the Enlightenment.* ed. by J.A. Leo Lemay. Cranbury, N.J.: Associated University Presses, 1987. 61–78.

Borck, James S., ed., *The Eighteenth Century: A Current Bibliography.* N.Y.: AMS Press, 1977, 1979, 1980, 1981.

Brewster, David. *Memoirs of the Life, Writings and Discoveries of Sir Isaac Newton.* 2 Vols. Edinburgh: Thomas Constable and Co., MDCCCLV.

——. *The Life of Sir Isaac Newton.* New York: Printed and published by J & J Harper, 1831.

Briggs, Charles A. *Theological Symbolics.* International Theological Library Series. N.Y.: Charles Scribner's Sons, 1914.

Broad, C.D. "Leibniz' Last Controversy with the Newtonians." *Theoria* 13 (1946): 143–168.

Brown, Colin, *Christianity and Western Thought: A History of Philosophers, Ideas and Movements.* Vol. 1 *From the Ancient World to the Age of Enlightenment.* Downer's Grove: Intervarsity Press, 1990.

———. *Miracles and the Critical Mind.* Grand Rapids: Wm. Eerdmans, 1984.

———. "Trinity and Incarnation: In Search of Contemporary Orthodoxy." *Ex Auditu* 7 (1991): 83–100.

Burns, Robert M. *The Great Debate on Miracles: From Joseph Glanvill to David Hume.* Lewisburg: Bucknell Univ. Press, 1981.

Burtt, Edwin Arthur. *The Metaphysical Foundations of Modern Science.* Atlantic Highlands, N.J.: Humanities Press, 1952; repr., 1980.

Butterfield, Herbert. *The Origins of Modern Science.* New York: Macmillan, 1951.

Christianson, Gale E. *In the Presence of the Creator: Isaac Newton and His Times.* New York: Free Press, 1984.

Cohen, I.B. "The Case of the Missing *Tanquam*; Leibniz, Newton and Clarke." *Isis* 52 (1961): 555–66.

———. "Newton in the Light of Recent Scholarship." *Isis* 51 (1960): 489–514.

Colie, Rosalie. *Light and Enlightenment: A Study of the Cambridge Platonists and the Dutch Arminians.* Cambridge: Cambridge University Press, 1957.

Copleston, Fredrick, S.J. *A History of Philosophy.* Bellarmine Series. Westminster, Maryland: The Newman Press, 1964.

Costello, William T. *The Scholastic Curriculum at Early Seventeenth-Century Cambridge.* Cambridge, MA: Harvard Univ. Press, 1958.

Cragg, G.R., *The Church and the Age of Reason.* Grand Rapids: Eerdmans, 1962.

———. ed., *The Cambridge Platonists.* New York: Oxford U. Press, 1968.

Curley, E.M. *Descartes Against the Skeptics.* Cambridge, MA: Harvard Univ. Press, 1980.

Daniel, Stephen H. *John Toland: His Methods, Manners, and Mind.* Kingston and Montreal: McGill-Queen's Univ. Press, 1984.

Davis, Edward. "Newton's Rejection of the 'Newtonian World View': The Role of Divine Will in Newton's Natural Philosophy." *Fides et Historia* XXII, 2 (Summer 1990): 6–20.

Deason, Gary. "The Protestant Reformation and the Rise of Modern Science." *The Scottish Journal of Theology* 38 No. 2 (1985): 221–240.

———. "Reformation Theology and the Mechanistic Conception of Nature." in *God and Nature: Historical Essays on the Encounter Between Christianity and Science* Edited by D. Lindberg and R. Numbers. Berkeley: Univ. of California Press, 1986. 167–191.

Dillenberger, John. *Protestant Thought and Natural Sciences.* Notre Dame: U.N.D. Press, 1960.

Ferguson, James P. *Dr. Samuel Clarke: An Eighteenth Century Heretic.* Kineton: The Roundwood Press, 1976.

———. *The Philosophy of Dr. Samuel Clarke and Its Critics.* New York: Vantage Press, 1974.

Fisher, George Park. *History of Christian Doctrine.* 2d ed. International Theological Library Series. Edinburgh: T&T Clark, 1896.

Force, James E. *Essays on the Context, Nature and Influence of Isaac Newton's Theology.* Dordrecht; Boston: Kluwer Academic Publishers, 1990.

——. "Hume and the Relation of Science to Religion Among Certain Members of the Royal Society." *Journal of the History of Ideas* 45 No. 4 (1984): 517–536.

——. "The Newtonians and Deism." in *Essays on the Context, Nature, and Influence of Isaac Newton's Theology.* Dordrecht: Kluwer Academic Publishers, 1990, 43–76.

——. *William Whiston, Honest Newtonian.* Cambridge: Cambridge University Press, 1985.

Fortman, Edmund J. *The Triune God: A Historical Study of the Doctrine of the Trinity.* Philadelphia: Westminster, 1972.

Franks, R.S. *The Doctrine of the Trinity.* London: Gerald Duckworth and Co. Ltd., 1953.

Funkenstein, Amos. *Theology and the Scientific Imagination from the Middle Ages to the Seventeenth Century.* Princeton: Princeton University Press, 1986.

Gay, John. "The Idea of Freedom as the Basis of the Thought of Samuel Clarke." Ph.D. diss., Columbia University, 1958.

Gjertsen, Derek. *The Newton Handbook.* London: Routledge & Kegan Paul, 1986.

Gray, George. *A Bibliography of the Works of Sir Isaac Newton.* Cambridge: Bowes and Bowes, 1907.

Greene, Donald. "Latitudinarianism and Sensibility: The Genealogy of the 'Man of Feeling' Reconsidered." *Modern Philology* Vol. 75, No. 2, (November, 1977): 159–183.

Greene, Marjorie. *Descartes Among the Scholastics.* Milwaukee: Marquette Univ. Press, 1991.

Gregg, Robert, ed., *Arianism: Historical and Theological Reassessments.* Patristic Monograph Series, No. 11. Philadelphia: The Philadelphia Patristic Foundation, Ltd., 1985.

Griffin, Martin Jr. *Latitudinarianism in the Seventeenth-Century Church of England.* Annotated by Richard H. Popkin. Edited by Lila Freedman. Brill Studies in Intellectual History Series. Leiden: E.J. Brill, 1992.

Gueroult, Martial. *Descartes' Philosophy Interpreted According to the Order of Reasons.* Translated by Ariew. Minneapolis: University of Minnesota Press, 1984–5.

Hagenbach, K.R. *A Textbook of the History of Doctrines.* New York: Sheldon & Co., 1862.

Hall, Alfred Rupert. *From Galileo to Newton.* Repr., New York: Dover, 1982. The Rise of Modern Science Series, Vol. 3, ed., A.R. Hall.

——. *Philosophers at War: The Quarrel Between Newton and Leibniz.* Cambridge: Cambridge Univ. Press, 1980.

——. *The Revolution in Science Fifteen Hundred to Seventeen Fifty.* London: Longmans, 1983.

——. *The Scientific Revolution, 1500–1800; the Formation of the Modern Scientific Attitude.* London and New York: Longmans, 1954.

Hall, A.R. and M.B. "Clarke and Newton." *Isis* 52 (1961): 583–85.

Hanson, R.P.C. *The Search for the Christian Doctrine of God: The Arian Controversy 318–381.* Edinburgh: T&T Clark, 1988.

Harnack, Adolph. *History of Dogma.* 7 Vols. Translated from the third German edition by E.B. Speirs and James Miller. London, Edinburgh, Oxford: Williams & Norgate, 1898.

Harrison, John. *The Library of Isaac Newton.* Cambridge: Cambridge U. Press, 1978.

Hefelbower, Samuel G. *The Relation of John Locke to English Deism.* Chicago: University of Chicago Press, 1918.

Hefele, Charles Joseph. *A History of the Christian Councils, from the Original Documents, to the Close of the Council of Nicaea, A.D. 325.* Translated and edited by William R. Clark. 2d ed. Edinburgh: T&T Clark, 1894.

Herrmann, R.-D. "The Religious and Metaphysical Thought of Isaac Newton." *Journal of Religion* 56 (1976): 204–219.
Hodgson, Leonard. *The Doctrine of the Trinity: The Croall Lectures 1942–43*. London: Nisbet and Co. Ltd., 1943.
Hill, Christopher. "Science, Religion and Society in the Sixteenth and Seventeenth Centuries." *Past and Present* 31 (July 1965): 97–103.
Hyman, J.D. *William Chillingworth and the Theory of Religious Toleration*. Cambridge, MA: Harvard University Press, 1931.

Jacob, Margaret. "Christianity and the Newtonian Worldview." in *God and Nature: Essays on the Encounter Between Christianity and Science*. Edited by D. Lindberg and R. Numbers. Berkeley: Univ. of California Press, 1986. 238–255.
Jones, Richard Foster. *Ancients and Moderns: A Study of the Background of the Battle of the Books*. Washington Univ. Studies—New Series, Language and Literature—No. 6 St. Louis: Washington Univ., 1936.

Kannengiesser, Charles. *Arius and Athanasius: Two Alexandrian Theologians*. Aldershot, Hampshire, Great Britain: Variorum; Brookfield, Vermont, USA: Gower, 1991.
Kelly, J.N.D. *Early Christian Doctrines*. Revised edition. San Francisco: Harper and Row, 1978.
Kennedy, Thomas. "God and the Grounds of Morality: The Eighteenth-Century British Debate." Ph.D. diss., Univ. of Virginia, 1986.
Keynes, J.M. "Newton the Man." in *The Royal Society Newton Tercentenary Celebrations 15–19 July 1946*. Cambridge: At the University Press, 1947.
Kocher, P.H. *Science and Religion in Elizabethan England*. New York: Octagon Books, 1969.
Kockelmans, Joseph J. "Reflections on the Interaction between Science and Religion." in *Challenge of Religion*; Edited by F. Ferre, J. Kockelmans & J. Smith. New York: Seabury Press, 1982. 296–316.
Kopecek, Thomas A. *A History of Neo-Arianism*. 2 Vols. Patristic Monograph Series, No. 8. Philadelphia: The Philadelphia Patristic Foundation Ltd., 1979.

Lee, Sidney, ed. *Dictionary of National Biography*. London: Smith, Elder & Co., 1899. Vol. LIX. S.v. "Waterland, Daniel," by J.M. Rigg.
Loemker, Leroy E. *Struggle for Synthesis: The Seventeenth Century Background of Leibniz's Synthesis of Order and Freedom*. Cambridge, MA: Harvard Univ. Press, 1972.
Longsworth, William. "Religious Beliefs and Moral Judgments: Some Patterns of Relations Derived from an Analysis of Samuel Clarke." Ph.D. diss., Yale Univ., 1977.
Luibheid, Colm. *The Council of Nicaea*. Galway: Galway Press, 1982.
——. *Eusebius of Caesarea and the Arian Crisis*. Dublin: Irish Academic Press, 1981.

McAdoo, Henry R. *The Structure of Caroline Moral Theology*. London and New York: Longmans, Green, 1949.
McLachlan, H. *The Religious Opinions of Milton, Locke, and Newton*. Manchester: Manchester University Press, 1941.
McMullin, Ernan. "The Significance of Newton's *Principia* for Empiricism." in *Religion, Science, and Worldview: Essays in Honor of Richard S. Westfall*; Edited by M. Osler and P. Farber. Cambridge, U.K.; New York: Cambridge Univ. Press, 1985. 33–59.
Manuel, Frank. *The Changing of the Gods*. Hanover: Published for Brown Univ. Press by Univ. Press of New England, 1983.
——. *The Eighteenth Century Confronts the Gods*. Cambridge: Harvard Univ. Press, 1959.
——. *A Portrait of Isaac Newton*. Cambridge: Belknap Press for Harvard Univ. Press, 1968.

——. *The Religion of Isaac Newton*. Oxford: Clarendon Press, 1974.

Mason, S.F. "Science and Religion in Seventeenth Century England." *Past & Present* 3 (February 1953).

——. "The Scientific Revolution and the Protestant Reformation." *Annals of Science* 9 (1953).

Merton, Robert K. "Puritanism, Pietism and Science." in eds. A.B. Arons and A.M. Bork *Science and Ideas*. Englewood Cliffs, N.J.: Prentice Hall, 1964.

——. "Science, Technology and Society in Seventeenth Century." *Osiris* IV (1938): 360–624.

More, Louis Trenchard. *Isaac Newton: A Biography 1642–1727*. New York and London: Charles Scribner's Sons, 1934.

Morgen, William Thomas. *Bibliography of British History 1700–1715, with Special Reference to the Reign of Queen Anne*. Indiana University Studies. Bloomington: Indiana University Press, 1934. Vols. 1, 2 and 3.

Muller, Richard A. "The Christological Problem in the Thought of Jacobus Arminius." *Nederlands Archief voor Kerkgeschiendenis* 68 (1988): 145–163.

——. *God, Creation and Providence in the Thought of Jacob Arminius: Sources and Directions of Scholastic Protestantism in the Era of Early Orthodoxy*. Grand Rapids: Baker Book House, 1991.

——. *Post-Reformation Reformed Dogmatics: Vol. 1. Prologomena to Theology*. Grand Rapids: Baker Book House, 1987.

Mulligan, L. "Anglicanism, Latitudinarianism and Science in Seventeenth-Century England," in Annals of Science XXX, No. 2, June, 1973.

——. *The New Catholic Encyclopedia*. Edited by J. McDonald, et al. 15 Vols. Washington D.C.; N.Y.: McGraw Hill, 1967.

North, John. *Isaac Newton*. In The Clarendon Biography Series, 12. London: Oxford U. Press, 1967.

Oberman, Heiko, *The Dawn of the Refomation: Essays in Late Medieval and Early Reformation Thought*. Edinburgh: T&T Clark Ltd., 1986.

O'Carroll, Michael. *Trinitas: A Theological Encyclopedia of the Holy Trinity*. Wilmington, Delaware: Michael Glazier, Inc., 1987.

Oakley, Francis. *Omnipotence, Covenant, & Order: An Excursion in the History of Ideas from Abelard to Leibniz*. Ithaca and London: Cornell University Press, 1984.

Orr, J. *English Deism: Its Roots and Fruits*. Grand Rapids: Eerdmans, 1934.

Orr, Robert R. *Reason and Authority: The Thought of William Chillingworth*. Oxford: Clarendon Press, 1967.

Osler, Margaret J. and Paul Lawrence Farber. *Religion, Science, and Worldview: Essays in Honor of Richard S. Westfall*. Cambridge: Cambridge U. Press, 1985.

Payne, Levi. *A Critical History of the Evolution of Trinitarianism and Its Outcome in the New Christology*. Boston: Houghton, Mifflin and Co. Cambridge: The Riverside Press, 1900.

Popkin, Richard A. *The History of Scepticism from Erasmus to Descartes*. N.V. Assen, Netherlands: Van Gorcum & Comp., MCMLX.

——. "Newton as a Bible Scholar." in *Essays on the Context, Nature and Influence of Isaac Newton's Theology*. Edited by James E. Force and Richard H. Popkin. Dordrecht: Kluwer Academic Publishers, 1990, 103–118.

Powicke, F.J. *The Cambridge Platonists: A Study*. Reprin., Westport Conn.: Greenwood Press, 1970. Orig. publ. London: J.M. Dent and Sons, 1926.

Prestige, George. *God in Patristic Thought*. London: S.P.C.K., 1952.

Pünjer, Bernhard. *History of the Christian Philosophy of Religion from the Reformation to Kant*. Trans. W. Hastie. Edinburgh: T&T Clarke, 1887.

Quasten, Johannnes. *Patrology*. 4 Vols. Westminster Maryland: Christian Classics Inc., 1990. First Published 1950.

Rabb, Theodore K. "Puritanism and the Rise of Experimental Science in England." *Cahiers d'Histoire Mondiale* 7 (1962).
———. "Religion and the Rise of Modern Science." *Past & Present* 31 (July 1965).
Randall, John Herman, Jr. *The Making of the Modern Mind: A Survey of the Intellectual Background of the Present Age*. Revised edition. Cambridge, MA: Houghton Mifflin, 1940.
Raven, Charles E. *English Naturalists from Neckham to Ray: A Study of the Making of the Modern World*. Cambridge: Cambridge Univ. Press, 1947.
Redwood, J.A. "Charles Blount (1654–93), Deism, and English Free Thought," *Journal of the History of Ideas* 35 (1974): 490–495.
Rescher, Nicholas. *The Philosophy of Leibniz*. Englewood Cliffs, NJ: Prentice-Hall, 1967.
Reventlow, Henning Graf. *The Authority of the Bible and the Rise of the Modern World*. Translated by John C. Bowden. London: SCM Press, 1984.
Rusch, William G. *The Trinitarian Controversy*. Sources in Early Christian Thought Series, Edited by Wm. Rusch. Philadelphia: Fortress Press, 1983.
Russell, Bertrand. *A Critical Exposition of the Philosophy of Leibniz*. 2d ed. London: George Allen & Unwin, 1937.

Schlatter, Richard. "The Higher Learning in Puritan England." *Historical Magazine of the Protestant Episcopal Church* 23 (June 1954).
Seeberg, Reinhold. *Text-Book of the History of Doctrines*. Translated by Charles E. Hay. 2 Vols. Grand Rapids: Baker Book House, 1954.
Shedd, Wm. *A History of Christian Doctrine*. 2 Vols. 9th ed. New York: Charles Scribner's Sons, 1887.
Sheldon, Henry, C. *History of Christian Doctrine*. 2d ed. 2 Vols. New York: Harper and Brothers Publishers, 1895.
Singer, Charles. *A Short History of Scientific Ideas to 1900*. Oxford: At the Clarendon Press, 1959.
Spellman, W.M. *The Latitudinarians and the Church of England, 1160–1700*. Athens, Georgia and London: The Univ. of Georgia Press, 1993.
Stein, Ronald. "A Critical Examination of the Ethical Thought of Samuel Clarke." Ph.D. diss., at S.U.N.Y., Buffalo, 1972.
Stephen, Leslie, Sir. *History of English Thought in the Eighteenth Century*. 2 Vols. N.Y.: Harcourt, Brace and World, Inc., 1962. First published 1876.
———, ed. *Dictionary of National Biography*. London: Smith, Elder & Co., 1886. Vol. VIII. S.v. "Bull, George," by J.H. Overton.
———, ed. *Dictionary of National Biography*. London: Smith, Elder & Co., 1887. Vol. X. S.v. "Chillingworth, William," by M. Creighton.
Stewart, Larry. "Samuel Clarke, Newtonianism, and the Factions of Post-Revolutionary England (1689–1720)." *Journal of the History of Ideas* 42 (1981): 53–72.
Stimson, Dorothy. *The Gradual Acceptance of the Copernican Theory of the Universe*. New York, 1917.
———. "Puritanism and the New Philosophy in Seventeenth Century England." *Bulletin of the Institute of the History of Medicine*, III (May 1935).
———. *Scientists and Amateurs: A History of the Royal Society*. New York, 1948.
Stukeley, William, *Memoirs of Sir Isaac Newton's life, by William Stukeley*. Edited by A. Hastings White. London: Taylor and Francis, 1936.
Stumpf, Samuel. *Socrates to Satre: A History of Philosophy*. 4th ed. New York: McGraw-Hill Book Company, 1988.
Sullivan, Robert E. *John Toland and the Deist Controversy: A Study in Adaptations*. Cambridge MA: Harvard Univ. Press, 1982.

Tulloch, John. *Rational Theology and Christian Philosophy in England in the Seventeenth Century.* 2 Vols. Hildesheim: Georg Olms Verlagsbuchhandlung, 1966.

Veitch, John. *The Method, Meditations and Philosophy of Descartes.* New York: Tudor Publishing Co., 1901.

Von Leyden, W. *Seventeenth-Century Metaphysics: An Examination of Some Main Concepts and Theories.* London: Gerald Duckworth and Co., 1968.

Wallis, Peter John. *Newton and Newtoniana, 1672–1975: A Bibliography.* Folkstone, England: Dawson, 1977.

Watson, George, ed., *The New Cambridge Bibliography of English Literature.* Cambridge: Cambridge Univ. Press, 1974.

Westfall, Richard. "The Career of Isaac Newton: A Scientific Life in the Seventeenth Century." *American Scholar* 50 (Summer 1981): 341–353.

———. "Isaac Newton's *Theologiae Gentilis Origines Philosophicae.*" in *The Secular Mind: Transformations of Faith in Modern Europe.* Edited by W. Wagar. New York: Holmes and Meier, 1982. 15–34.

———. *Never at Rest: A Biography of Isaac Newton.* Cambridge: Cambridge U. Press, 1980.

———. "Newton and Christianity." in *Religion, Science and Public Policy.* Edited by F. Birtel. New York: Crossroad, 1987. 79–95.

———. "Newton's Theological Manuscripts." in *Contemporary Newtonian Research.* Edited by Zev Bechler. Dordrecht: D. Reidel Publishing Company, Hingham, MA, 1982.

———. "The Rise of Science and Decline of Orthodox Christianity: A Study of Kepler, Descartes, and Newton." in *God and Nature.* Edited by D. Lindberg and R. Numbers. Berkeley: Univ. of California Press, 1986. 218–237.

———. *Science and Religion in Seventeenth Century England.* New Haven: Yale Univ. Press, 1958.

Westman, Robert S. *Hermeticism and the Scientific Revolution: Papers Read at a Clark Library Seminar March 9, 1974.* Los Angeles: William Andrews Clark Memorial Library, Univ. of Cal., 1977. Series title *William Andrews Clark Memorial Library Seminar Papers.*

Wiles, Maurice. "Eternal Generation." in *Working Papers in Doctrine.* London: SCM Press, 1976.

Willey, Basil. *The Eighteenth Century Background: Studies on the Idea of Nature in the Thought of the Period.* New York: Columbia University Press, 1940.

———. *The Seventeenth Century Background: Studies in the Thought of the Age in Relation to Poetry and Religion.* New York: Columbia Univ. Press, 1958.

INDEX OF NAMES AND PLACES

INDEX OF SUBJECTS

Studies in the History of Christian Thought

EDITED BY HEIKO A. OBERMAN

50. HOENEN, M. J. F. M. *Marsilius of Inghen*. Divine Knowledge in Late Medieval Thought. 1993
51. O'MALLEY, J. W., IZBICKI, T. M. and CHRISTIANSON, G. (eds.). *Humanity and Divinity in Renaissance and Reformation*. Essays in Honor of Charles Trinkaus. 1993
52. REEVE, A. (ed.) and SCREECH, M. A. (introd.). *Erasmus' Annotations on the New Testament*. Galatians to the Apocalypse. 1993
53. STUMP, Ph. H. *The Reforms of the Council of Constance (1414-1418)*. 1994
54. GIAKALIS, A. *Images of the Divine*. The Theology of Icons at the Seventh Ecumenical Council. With a Foreword by Henry Chadwick. 1994
55. NELLEN, H. J. M. and RABBIE, E. (eds.). *Hugo Grotius – Theologian*. Essays in Honour of G. H. M. Posthumus Meyjes. 1994
56. TRIGG, J. D. *Baptism in the Theology of Martin Luther*. 1994
57. JANSE, W. *Albert Hardenberg als Theologe*. Profil eines Bucer-Schülers. 1994
59. SCHOOR, R.J.M. VAN DE. *The Irenical Theology of Théophile Brachet de La Milletière (1588-1665)*. 1995
60. STREHLE, S. *The Catholic Roots of the Protestant Gospel*. Encounter between the Middle Ages and the Reformation. 1995
61. BROWN, M.L. *Donne and the Politics of Conscience in Early Modern England*. 1995
62. SCREECH, M.A. (ed.). *Richard Mocket, Warden of All Souls College, Oxford, Doctrina et Politia Ecclesiae Anglicanae*. An Anglican Summa. Facsimile with Variants of the Text of 1617. Edited with an Introduction. 1995
63. SNOEK, G.J.C. *Medieval Piety from Relics to the Eucharist*. A Process of Mutual Interaction. 1995
64. PIXTON, P.B. *The German Episcopacy and the Implementation of the Decrees of the Fourth Lateran Council, 1216-1245*. Watchmen on the Tower. 1995
65. DOLNIKOWSKI, E.W. *Thomas Bradwardine: A View of Time and a Vision of Eternity in Fourteenth-Century Thought*. 1995
66. RABBIE, E. (ed.). *Hugo Grotius, Ordinum Hollandiae ac Westfrisiae Pietas (1613)*. Critical Edition with Translation and Commentary. 1995
67. HIRSH, J.C. *The Boundaries of Faith*. The Development and Transmission of Medieval Spirituality. 1996
68. BURNETT, S.G. *From Christian Hebraism to Jewish Studies*. Johannes Buxtorf (1564-1629) and Hebrew Learning in the Seventeenth Century. 1996
69. BOLAND O.P., V. *Ideas in God according to Saint Thomas Aquinas*. Sources and Synthesis. 1996
70. LANGE, M.E. *Telling Tears in the English Renaissance*. 1996
71. CHRISTIANSON, G. and T.M. IZBICKI (eds.). *Nicholas of Cusa on Christ and the Church*. Essays in Memory of Chandler McCuskey Brooks for the American Cusanus Society. 1996
72. MALI, A. *Mystic in the New World*. Marie de l'Incarnation (1599-1672). 1996
73. VISSER, D. *Apocalypse as Utopian Expectation (800-1500)*. The Apocalypse Commentary of Berengaudus of Ferrières and the Relationship between Exegesis, Liturgy and Iconography. 1996
74. O'ROURKE BOYLE, M. *Divine Domesticity*. Augustine of Thagaste to Teresa of Avila. 1997
75. PFIZENMAIER, T.C. *The Trinitarian Theology of Dr. Samuel Clarke (1675-1729)*. Context, Sources, and Controversy. 1997

Prospectus available on request

E. J. BRILL — P.O.B. 9000 — 2300 PA LEIDEN — THE NETHERLANDS